AF543070

Padmini *of* Malwa

THE AUTOBIOGRAPHY OF
RANI RUUPMATI

AS TOLD TO
PRIYADARSHI THAKUR 'KHAYAL'

SPEAKING
TIGER

SPEAKING TIGER BOOKS LLP
4381/4, Ansari Road, Daryaganj
New Delhi 110002

First published in English by Speaking Tiger 2021

Copyright © Priyadarshi Thakur

ISBN: 978-93-90477-96-8
eISBN: 978-93-90477-99-9

10 9 8 7 6 5 4 3 2 1

Typeset in Minion Pro by SÜRYA, New Delhi
Printed at Chaman Enterprises, New Delhi

All rights reserved.
No part of this publication may be reproduced, transmitted, or stored in a retrieval system, in any form or by any means, electronic, mechanical, photocopying, recording or otherwise, without the prior permission of the publisher.

This book is sold subject to the condition that it shall not, by way of trade or otherwise, be lent, resold, hired out, or otherwise circulated, without the publisher's prior consent, in any form of binding or cover other than that in which it is published.

Born in Motihari, Bihar in 1946, Priyadarshi Thakur 'Khayal' studied history at Patna University and later at Delhi University in the 1960s. He taught history for three years at Delhi University before joining the Indian Administrative Service (IAS) in 1970. He retired as a secretary to the Government of India in 2006 and later worked as the director general of the International Center for Promotion of Enterprises at Ljubljana in Slovenia. He now lives in Gurugram.

Priyadarshi Thakur 'Khayal' has eight volumes of poetry in Hindi and Urdu to his name, and is included in the list of poets on the noted website *Rekhta.org*. His ghazals have been sung by Jagjit Singh, the Hussain brothers, Dr Suman Yadav and others. He has also translated Orhan Pamuk's novel *Snow* into Hindi.

The Rani wanted this autobiography of hers
to be dedicated to Rekha, my wife;
I, her scribe, am merely complying
with her command.

The Scribe's Note

Despite dabbling in verse and literary translations for over half a century, I haven't a decent story to my name, far less a novel. And suddenly a novel of nearly three hundred pages in three months! No, this is not my work, and I need not be writing this preface.

Believe it or not, this is truly Rani Ruupmati's autobiography. I merely put on paper what she told me. However, I am aware that there will be few takers for what is bound to be declared my 'spiel', and to most readers, this will be just another historical novel. Hence, a few things do need to be clarified at the outset.

The sole aim of this work is to bring to those interested, a new account of Rani Ruupmati's brief life and her psyche. While recording the visions neither of us had the slightest intention of hurting the sentiments of the followers of any faith. It is hoped that readers will not take offence at the use of the term 'mlechchha' at several places in the book. As can be seen from several books mentioned in the bibliography, like *Charu Chandralekh* and *Age of Wrath*, this derogatory epithet was frequently used for Islamic invaders in medieval times. Also, the Rani herself has a rather rational take on the true meaning of this term, and concludes that the creature called 'mlechchha' can be found on either side of any man-made boundary! We must also ask readers to remember that words like 'habshin', too, were not necessarily derogatory terms back then.

Readers need not be too sceptical of characters like Nayla or Pandijju and let this come in the way of the Rani's story. It may be noted that Nasir Shah, a Khilji sultan of Malwa some eighty years before Ruupmati's time, is known to have had a regiment of five hundred Abyssinian women in his employ and there are hundreds of Maithil Brahmin families in Madhya Pradesh whose present generation cannot tell when their forbears came to the region.

The masterworks of Amir Khusro, Vallabhacharya, etc. the Rani quotes in her narrative had spread far and wide by mid-sixteenth century.

The crushing defeat that the Chandela queen Rani Durgawati inflicted on Baz Bahadur is a matter of historical record, but what led to the conflict is lost to us. Rani Ruupmati could well be telling us how it really happened. As regards Rani Ruupmati's reference to her correspondence with Adham Khan Koka, it may be noted that the same is also mentioned in the first account of Rani Ruupmati's life with Baz Bahadur written by Ahmad ul-Umari only a few decades later.

For readers who might wish to know more about the historical and cultural backdrop of the time, I have added a list of historical characters relevant to the story, a few endnotes and a bibliography at the end of the book.

Love and marriage between individuals from different faiths and communities not entirely at peace with each other was an extremely sensitive subject in the Rani's time, and continues to be so, to this day. On behalf of Rani Ruupmati, this scribe, therefore, asks his readers for the humanity and understanding that this story deserves.

—Priyadarshi Thakur 'Khayal'

List of Characters

Rani Ruupmati, (c.1540-1561): The beloved queen of Baz Bahadur, the last independent sultan of Malwa before it was annexed by the Mughals. A well-known poetess,[1] musician[2] and singer of her time, she is known as the composer of raga Bhoop Kalyan. Rani Ruupmati was about twenty-one years of age when she committed suicide.

Baz Bahadur, (c.1532-1582): Formal name Bayzeed Khan, the last sultan of independent Malwa sultanate (1555-61) and a renowned poet and musician of his time. A few years after the annexation of Malwa, Emperor Akbar sent his special envoy, Hasan Khan Khazanchi, to Mewar to invite and escort Baz Bahadur to join the imperial court as a musician. Baz Bahadur is believed to be the composer of Baz-Khani Khayal.

Shujat Khan, (c.1485-1555): Father of Baz Bahadur and a trusted army commander close to Sher Shah Suri, who made him the governor of Malwa after he became the emperor of Delhi. Sometime after the death of Sher Shah, Shujat declared himself as the independent sultan of Malwa.

Sher Shah Suri, (c.1584-1545): Governor of Bihar, and later, wrested the region from the Mughals. In 1540 he defeated Humayun, the second Mughal emperor and ruled as emperor from Delhi. Sher Shah earned himself great fame as an able administrator. He died in an accident during the siege of Kalinjar Fort in 1545.

Humayun, (c.1508-1556): The second of the major Mughal emperors. Succeeded Babur in 1530, but was ousted by Sher

Shah Suri in 1540 and fled to Iran. He recaptured Delhi in 1555.

Mohammad Jalaluddin Akbar, (c.1542-1605): Akbar the Great, recognized as the greatest of the Mughal emperors. He ruled for nearly half a century, and is known for his liberal policies and reforms.

Adham Khan Koka, (c.1531-1562): The son of Maham Angaa, the childhood nurse of Akbar. Having breast-fed Akbar as an infant and later protected him from his uncles' murderous designs, Maham Angaa was very close to Akbar, and Adham Khan being his koka or milk-brother enjoyed his special favour alongside his mother. Adham Khan was entrusted the command of the Mughal campaign of Malwa in 1561. Within a year of the Malwa expedition, Adham Khan murdered the emperor's chief advisor Shamsuddin Mohammad Atghaa Khan, and then behaved insolently with the emperor, who sentenced him to death on the spot. Adham Khan was thrown down to his death from the royal apartments on an upper storey. It is believed that he had to be thrown down a second time before he died. Maham Angaa also died mourning her son shortly after his death.

Bairam Khan or **Khan-e-Khanaan**, (c.1501-1561): A loyal army commander of the Mughals from the days of Babur and Humayun, who protected the thirteen-year-old Akbar when he succeeded Humayun in 1556. He remained his regent and the de facto ruler from 1556 to 1560.

Maham Angaa: The childhood nurse of Akbar, who was very close to him. Always a powerful presence at court, she became the main power centre behind the throne during 1560-62, after the removal of Bairam Khan.

Rani Durgawati, (c.1524-1564): The daughter of Keerat Rai, the Chandela king. Was married to Dalpat Rai, the ruler of Gondwana in 1542, and after his untimely death, became the ruler of Chandela-Gond kingdom (south-eastern parts of modern-day Uttar Pradesh, and Chhattisgarh) as the regent of her three-year-old son, and ruled until 1564 with her trusted ministers, notably Aadhar Singh and Man Thakur. She was a brave warrior who personally led her forces. She actually inflicted a crushing defeat on Baz Bahadur.

Aadhar Singh: The dewan or principal minister of Rani Durgawati.

Malik Mustafa Khan: Baz Bahadur's younger brother, and rival for the throne of the Malwa sultanate after Shujat Khan. For some time he remained in occupation of Raisen Fort, but was eventually driven out by Baz Bahadur and sought refuge at the Mughal court.

Hoshang Shah: An important Ghuri dynasty sultan. Ruled from 1406 to 1435, and is credited with the construction of a number of important buildings in Mandavgarh, including his own mausoleum.

Qadir Shah: The Sultan of Malwa immediately preceding Shujat Khan.

Daulat Khan Ajiyala: The adopted son of Shujat Khan. Ajiyala was killed by Baz Bahadur during the succession struggle.

Adam Khan: The maternal uncle of Baz Bahadur and one of his army commanders.

Taj Khan Khasakhel: An army general of Baz Bahadur.

Salim Khan Khasakhel: An army general of Baz Bahadur.

Sufi: An army general of Baz Bahadur.

Mullah Peer Mohammad Khan: The deputy commander of Mughal forces under Adham Khan Koka on the Malwa campaign of 1561. He is believed to have subjected Mandavgarh to a brutal massacre. He was subsequently driven out of Mandav by Baz Bahadur, chased and routed on the banks of river Reva (Narmada) so badly that he died by drowning in the river.

Abdullah Khan, Qiya Khan, Qiya Khan Kang, Shah Mohammad Khan Kandhari, Adil Khan, Sadiq Khan, Mohammad Quli Khan, Haidar Ali Khan, Mohammad Quli Toqbai, Meerak Bahadur, Habib Quli Khan, Samanji Khan, Payanda Mohammad Khan Moghal, Mohammad Khan Kushtigir, Mehr Ali Silduz, Meeran Arghun, Shah Fani: All Mughal warriors of repute who fought in the Malwa campaign of 1561.

Abul Fazl: One of the nine important courtiers at Akbar's court known as the 'Navratna' or the nine gems. The author of *Akbarnama*, which is one of the principal sources for Akbar's reign.

Miyaan Tansen: Also one of Akbar's Navratnas. The most renowned singer and musician at the imperial court during his reign.

Ahmad ul-Umari Turkoman: An employee of a Mughal nobleman in the sixteenth century. Wrote the first account of the tragic tale of Rani Ruupmati and Baz Bahadur, based on eyewitness accounts and legends gathered during his travels in Malwa.

Rai Chand: Mentioned in Umari's book as the most renowned singer and musician at Baz Bahadur's court.

Suleman Khan: Mentioned in Umari's book as an eyewitness to the last years of Baz Bahadur as sultan and Rani Ruupmati as his favourite consort. Perhaps a supervisor of guards in the royal household.

Prologue

I had only vaguely heard of the ruins of medieval forts and palaces in Mandu in the Malwa region of Madhya Pradesh, surrounded by legends of the romance of Rani Ruupmati and Sultan Baz Bahadur. I had no idea even of the exact century they lived in, or what their story really was. I only knew that Mandu is a popular tourist destination that abounds in romantic folklore about the music-loving couple. Many a time I thought of visiting Mandu but it never happened.

Then, one day, a huge wave of impulse swept me off my feet. 'I shall write the story of Ruupmati's life very soon, really soon… I shall begin today…no, right now!' It was as though I was in the grip of a delirium.

I snapped open my laptop immediately, and looked up all the websites and blogs containing an unbelievable variety of information on Rani Ruupmati and Baz Bahadur's romance. While reading late into the night, I learnt that in the sixteenth century a man called Ahmad ul-Umari had written a book on Rani Ruupmati's life in Persian within a few decades of her tragic end. Umari's book was translated into English by an Englishman named L.M. Crump under the title *The Lady of the Lotus, Rup Mati, Queen of Mandu: A Strange Tale of Faithfulness* which was published close to a hundred years ago, in 1926 to be precise. I wondered where a copy of such an old book could be found.

I could hardly comprehend the intensity of my urge, but there it was, like a spoilt brat demanding a desired toy with a loud 'Now!' I wanted to have Crump's book right then. Pondering long over it, I concluded that the library of the National Archives might possibly have it. Brushing aside the lateness of the hour, I rang Ankit, a relative, who is a member there. Wrong number! Inexplicably saddened, I wondered when I would be able to lay my hands on the book and start my work. God alone knows when my impulse had turned into an obsession.

Little did I know then that I would soon become a mere scribe, a clerk of sorts, taking down a spoken autobiography!

Be that as it may, surfing the net until the small hours of the morning, I actually found the full text of Crump's book on the Internet, and went through it from cover to cover, besides soaking up just about anything I could find about Malwa's medieval history and culture, as though I had to sit for an examination the next morning.

But when all that was done, my bubbling enthusiasm subsided at twice the speed at which it had risen, as though someone had sprinkled water on a pot of milk about to boil over. Clearly, all I could write about Rani Ruupmati had been already been done in several books and novellas, on countless websites and what have you. The story had gone stale. Any number of conjectures had been made as to who she was and how she came to be with Baz Bahadur. Conflicting streams of folklore lay so inextricably tangled before me that anything was possible, and nothing was clear.

Suddenly I had lost my appetite for the story and decided that there was no point in losing sleep over it.

But then, equally suddenly, she appeared in person—Rani Ruupmati herself! All the legends and history books were shoved aside, and the biography that I had planned turned into an autobiography.

So, dear reader, you could legitimately ask: is this autobiography a series of dreams I had? Well, I'll make a clean breast of it and say, it's possible, but truly, the Rani did ask me whether I was prepared to take down her autobiography for her, and I responded in the affirmative with a silent nod. As far as I know, this is her autobiography.

I listened to what she had to say night after night and spent my days putting it all down on paper. That is all I did…

Vision 1

Am I asleep? Is this a dream? Or, is she really here in person—a solid reality? I am unable to say anything with certainty, but she is in front of me, and I'm struck dumb. I have words but no speech. I have a sense of being familiar with exquisite beauty, but beauty such as this, I've never before seen: skin so translucent that blue veins shine through the skin at her neck; fair complexion washed in the faintest pink; large limpid eyes; her countenance glows as though bathed in moonlight, with the ghost of a smile adorning her lips. Her slender frame clad in flowing Chanderi raiment seems to be the very definition of grace. Her head is draped in her pallu, but the face is unveiled. Indeed, everyone had it right—she is a Padmini... She is Ruupmati, Beauty itself.

I only gaze at her, without blinking, for one can either look at her or talk, and I would rather look.

She is the one who speaks:

So, you want to write my story? The same old tale that countless others have told already. A too-familiar story punctuated endlessly with ifs and buts! Isn't it pointless to repeat a tale so stale? Well, if you must write, why don't you take down my autobiography? I'll tell you everything I know, though I have to tell you that there are many things even I don't know. But I have a condition: *never* call my Baz a coward. He was a brave man, and you must acknowledge him as one. He wasn't my kidnapper. He was like a god who rescued me from mortal harm, he saved my life. And he never made an unmanly escape, never left me in the lurch. It's quite another matter that fate didn't favour him. I'll tell you all that, but let me not run so far ahead of the story.

Perhaps the first thing you'll want to know is who I really was. I mean, what was my caste, community, lineage; whether I was the daughter of a Rajput nobleman or a learned brahmin, or of a shepherd, or the illegitimate child of a courtesan; whether Hindu or Mussalman? It's difficult for me to say which of these I was, maybe a bit of each! Truth be told, I'm the daughter of Reva Maiyaa. If she hadn't saved me, I wouldn't have lived to be seven, let alone twenty-one.

The memories of childhood come back to me like broken lightning in the night sky. I imagine this is how it is with everyone: a scene from the past flashes briefly and then the screen goes blank, then a fragment of a different memory appears in bright, white light and then vanishes. No continuum. No idea where the head or tail is, yet a tantalizing certainty lingers that a long-forgotten face will suddenly come back to one, or a long-forgotten name… But the whole remains forever elusive! Beginnings have no end and ends, no beginnings. Everything is sort of topsy-turvy.

Like that scene in which the terrified scream of a little girl struggling to call out to a saviour is thwarted by the iron fist of a horseman, and the clatter of galloping hooves reverberates like a demon's guffaw in the black night… A vague sense of a scuffle, and then an angry male grunt followed by *chhappaak*—a huge splash, a hair-raising sting of icy waters and then everything goes blank. Who kidnapped the little girl, where was he headed with her in his clutches? Nothing is clear.

But there is one picture indelibly etched in my memory, almost in its entirety—a series of images that appear to have been carved by someone with great love and care.

Vision 2

I do not know the name of the town. I can only recall that deep inside its maze of narrow lanes there is an apartment on the first floor of an old haveli with a high-arched entrance that has wooden shutters a dozen fingers thick, with metal studs and medallions cast in the shape of a lotus. They open into a square courtyard, in the middle of which stands a lone maulshri tree with a luxuriant round canopy. On the left is a cavernous staircase with walls and terracotta tile roofing leading up to the apartment on the first floor.

I cannot remember what the ground floor is used for. The stairs lead into a long corridor with scores of windows that overlook the courtyard with the maulshri tree. As you open the windows, the delicate fragrance of maulshri wafts in. In the far distance across its round green top, there are domes surrounded by little pavilions, perhaps the entrance to some palace or temple. On the other side of the gallery, doors open into rooms of which I can only recall three. After all, how much can a little girl of five remember!

Her question comprises its answer as well. She chuckles. Teeth like a row of pearls are briefly revealed in a radiant smile, like the first rays of the sun caressing the petals of a white lotus.

What can I, a mere scribe, say?

The seedy little fortress, Garh Dharmapuri, where I lived with Jaddu Baba in my later years was not as desolate as the nameless maulshri mansion where I passed my early childhood.

There were only three doors that opened, and only two women there. One of them was obviously a maid who cooked, cleaned and silently braided my hair; when she was done with one side of it, she would say, 'Kunwarani, please turn your head a little to this side...' I cannot remember her saying anything else to me. I have forgotten what she looked like, but I do remember how reverently she seemed to utter the word 'kunwarani'.

The other woman must have been my mother, for only a mother can speak with such deep affection, though I cannot remember calling her mother. She would, however, often say, fondling my hair, 'Come sonchiraiyaa, my golden bird, it's getting late...time for your evening meal.' Indeed, she must have been my mother: a tall, statuesque woman (or maybe I found her so big because I myself was so little), a broad forehead, fair complexion, eyes black as kohl, hair cascading down to her shoulders in ringlets. She was a handsome woman in her prime, yet there were dark half-moons of some inexplicable melancholy under her eyes. I can never forget the love those eyes seemed to pour over me, never mind that she never addressed me as Kunwarani as the other woman did. By what name other than sonchiraiyaa she called me, I can no longer remember. What I do remember, though, is that she never fed her golden bird before her evening pooja.

The first of the doors to the left of the corridor opened into a large rectangular hall, its high ceiling with wooden beams and rafters held up by six fluted stone columns. On the walls, there were niches with pointed arches on which earthen lamps would be lighted in the evenings. One short side of the rectangle was a plain wall and the other had a large niche, in which stood her idols of Radha and Krishna. I have never in my life seen such idols anywhere else: Krishna sculpted from perfectly black touchstone and Radha from pure white marble, both without any adornments but for the jewels set to be their eyes that shone like the eyes of animals in the dark.

An elaborate pooja for the deity was a daily ritual of the woman who was most likely my mother. Every day a basketful of yellow marigolds would materialize, in all probability brought by that other woman who did all the chores. My mother would sit on a well-worn mattress spread on the floor in front of her idols, painstakingly stringing the flowers into two garlands, one each for the lord and his lady, to place around their necks. And yes, while doing so, she invariably made sure that I held one end of the garland. After offering an aarti of earthen lamps, lighted and placed on a round metal platter, she would sit back on the mat, and closing her eyes fervently, sing to the deity a bhajan that seemed to go on for the longest time:

O Kanhaiya, the beloved of Radha
You who guide everyone across
The ocean of worldly life,

I'll acknowledge your omnipotence too
If you help my boat cross over as well,
O beloved of the gopis
I'd sacrifice my all for you
Pray, help my boat cross over too
O Kanhaiya, the beloved of Radha...

When I myself took to learning vocal music during my days at Garh Dharmapuri, I realized what a maestro's voice she had. Despite its huskiness—as though something rough was stuck in her larynx—it never for an instant wavered even at the highest pitch.

Most evenings that I can recall, she sang the same bhajan, praying for the blessing of deliverance, as though she needed no other. I never saw her laugh or smile much. At any event, there was hardly anyone to give her company in small talk or mirth. But I never thought that she was in torment, for the simple reason that I did not know the meaning of torment then.

The way she squatted on the mat praying to Krishna for deliverance did not, however, match the usual pooja posture of Pandijju. She did not sit cross-legged, preferring to sit on the balls of her heels in vajrasana, her palms not joined in pranaam-mudraa but a little apart and raised skyward, as though she were calling out not only to the deity in front of her but also to some unknown Power above.

In later years, Pandijju, my guru, would often say to me, 'Ruup, listen to me carefully and internalize what I'm saying. One's previous birth and the life to come are not quite the way people generally imagine them to be. In this life itself one is reborn time after time. Yesterday was another life, and today is a new one.'

I didn't know the name of my mother in my previous life.

Neither do I remember what we ate or wore in that life, nor how we managed the household without any apparent means of livelihood. Ah yes, I do remember that of the three doors that used to be opened, the second was a kitchen and the third, a bath and toilet. Across the corridor from the three doors was the row of windows overlooking the courtyard with the flourishing but lonely maulshri, and beyond it, the entrance-top of an unknown structure.

Inside and out, these are the only images that are left of that childhood habitat, like the fading memory of a lover's embrace lost forever.

Vision 3

I have no memory of how that previous life of mine ended. After the images of the maulshri mansion, the only scene that still flashes through my mind occasionally is that of an unknown rider on horseback stifling the scream of a little girl and the dark night reverberating with the sounds of galloping hooves. Later, an angry male voice crying out in pain and someone swearing out loud. Did the struggling little creature bite into his fist? Then, that impenetrable darkness of ice-cold water, stamping out consciousness follows. Was I playing the role of that little girl on the last night of my previous life?

No one ever gave me the details of exactly what took place that night; neither Jaddu Baba nor Ketki or anyone else. Pandijju did drop a hint once, in a roundabout manner: 'Ruup, you're truly the daughter of Reva Maiyaa, she's the one who gave you a new life.' Then his gaze suddenly turned inward, as though whatever he had intended to add was best left unsaid.

It wasn't that I did not try to find out about the cataclysmic change in my circumstances. I did, but no one seemed willing to discuss it.

Eight years have passed since I was discovered floating unconscious at the riverside near Garh Dharmapuri. The Garh and the little hamlet around it are located on a small island between two streams of the river Reva, with the massive ramparts of Mandavgarh Fort rising up to merge with the steep hillside in the distance across the shallower of the two streams.

I had no better way of keeping a count of the passing years than the Navraatras, because the festival days were unforgettable. Pandijju would be on a fast without any food or water for all the nine days. He would only take a frugal repast of fruits and water after sundown, just enough to keep body and soul together. His eyes would sink deep into their sockets and lips crack of dehydration. Even then, he would keep chanting the Durga Saptashati from memory through the nine days. I would be scared: is the old man going to die! O Krishna, is the lone star of my solitary existence about to fade out? I would shut my eyes and pray for his life. He's the only support for my intellectual growth, for my literacy even. If he were to disappear, what would become of me, my Lord?

But I needn't have worried. Pandijju's ageing frame still had a lot going for it. On the Maha-ashtami day he would himself offer an animal sacrifice to Goddess Durga. The heavy sword in his seemingly frail hands would come down with a whistle and sever the goat-kid's head in a single stroke. The floor of the Devi temple in the rocky basement of the Garh would be spattered with blood. Even his large wooden chest of books, grey with age, would be sprayed with tiny red droplets.

The first time it happened, I shut my eyes in anticipated horror but Pandijju remained unaffected. After all, what did an animal's life matter to him? He had seen his own father's severed head rolling on the ground! Pandijju himself never mentioned the incident. I only learnt of his father's tragic end from someone else but more on that later.

On the last day of Navraatra, Pandijju would wipe the floor of the underground temple with his own hands, and serve me a sumptuous meal as reverently as though he were feeding the Devi herself. After I had finished eating, he would put a silver coin on my palm as dakshina, and even touch my feet in a symbolic obeisance to the Devi. I could never forget the day, and no sooner was it over than I began to count days until the next Navraatra.

The lean frame of Pandijju must have borne the rigour of at least fifty odd Navraatras. He never wore anything more than a dhoti and anga-vastra, a muslin wraparound for the upper body, and the sacred thread with pavitri, a silver ring to keep it from impurities. His head was always shaved, a thick Chanakya-like choti, a tuft of hair dangling behind from the back of his head. His eyebrows were stitched together in a perpetual frown on his fair-skinned forehead as though he was forever immersed in deep thought. But the sandal-paste tilak in the middle of the frown seemed to reflect an inner calm and the deeply humane streak of his persona that was dearer to him than any social understanding of dharma, regardless of the fact that he religiously observed all the brahmin rituals. Had it not been so, he might well have readily given a nod of assent to Rao's execution orders, and I might not have lived to be even fifteen!

Whatever education I had was a gift from Pandijju, ranging from history, geography, arithmetic to mythology and the epics—the Ramayana and the Mahabharata. His dusty wooden chest of books was an inexhaustible treasure trove of hand-written books and calligraphies, some on taal-patra so ancient that they seemed on the verge of crumbling to pieces. The chest had books to do with not only mythology and religion but also poetry, aesthetics and musicology. Anthologies and epics and the classics, such as the works of Kalidasa, Kalhana, Banabhatta, Chand Bardai to the verse of Amir Khusro and Vallabhacharya, were all in there. But to begin with, Pandijju was rather miserly in letting me look at the poetry volumes. He would gently try to reason with me, 'Ruup, you have to first learn to comprehend the serious realities of life, you can indulge yourself in aesthetics later.'

Look at me, going on and on about Pandijju! But he is so dear to me that once I start talking of him, there's no end to it. And then again, I don't have any previous experience of storytelling. I have to tell you my story in whatever order I can recall events and people, as if I were taking dips in a pool of memories and coming up with whatever I can find at a given moment.

As she smiled, apologizing obliquely, a halo of light seemed to envelop her face. I wanted to say to her: Rani Ruupmati, don't stop, I'm all ears. But my voice failed me.

Vision 4

At times life seems like an elaborate play; a play full of heroes, villains and countless other characters of various shades. As soon as a new act begins, the characters, the backdrop and the dialogues all change, and it is likely that someone who started out as a hero might end up as the villain, and the one who had the makings of a villain turns out to be Narsimha, the lion-man.

My life in Garh Dharmapuri, located on a river-isle of the Reva, a thousand arm's lengths below the Mandav plateau, was the very opposite of what it had been in the deserted maulshri mansion. This new act of the play was peopled by a large number of characters instead of just the two women, and the solitary maulshri was replaced by an ocean of greenery swaying on the steep slopes climbing up to the plateau. At the top of the precipitous slope one could make out the battlements of Mandav Fort, often covered in a veil of mist.

The kidnapping and the fall into the Reva that turned my life upside down, left me stunned and I remained mute for a long time. When my eyes opened, I neither cried out nor wept. Terrified to the core, I merely looked upwards, my bewildered eyes vacantly taking in the scores of faces peering down at me. Garh Dharmapuri lacked the bustle of a big village with a bazaar, but the community around it was so numerous that it took me weeks, perhaps months, to get to know them all. I uttered not a word for several weeks, just kept looking at the faces around me.

Jaddu Baba was a tall, well-muscled, fair-complexioned man with a barrel-chested frame, aquiline nose, piercing eyes, a salt-and-pepper beard combed upwards on either side to meet up with bushy sideburns and moustache twirled like those of a warrior chieftain. He was always clad in plain peasant clothes—an angrakhaa, the frock-like upper-body garment, made of coarse cloth, a dhoti tightly tied up above the knees and pointy, grimy rustic shoes that hadn't been cleaned in a while. But he did have a dandy cummerbund over his angrakhaa, with a dagger dangling from it. All others bowed to him, respectfully greeting him with folded hands, and addressed him as Rao. When I came to my senses, after being rescued from the river, he was the one who had silently gestured to Ketki to take me inside the Garh.

Like my mother in my previous life, Ketki was a woman in her prime, well short of being middle-aged, with a marked preference for black dresses. She had round, shifty eyes and a flattish nose with a finely filigreed silver nose-stud, almost black with grime. It must have surely been an inauspicious moment when she first set eyes on me. I sensed instantly that I was a thorn in her side. I could never tell why.

Little children might indeed be wanting in life experience, but not necessarily in instinctive retaliation: if Ketki didn't like me, I didn't like her either. I was put on alert instantly. As far as she was concerned, I'd have to keep looking over my shoulder all the time. I was leaving my childhood behind very fast!

Ketki was not the only one I took a dislike to at first sight. She had a younger brother, Bhanwar, whom we girls later called Bhaunra to his face, and Bhaunda behind his back. He must have been five or six years older to me. At first I thought he was a bit mentally slow, but in reality he was a sly one, his mouth perpetually hanging open, and his lowered eyes kind of appraising the girls. He had a peculiar habit of not looking anyone in their eyes while talking to them. He would follow us at a distance, wherever we went, and sit and stare stealthily. He tended to pick me out in particular, but that really began a few years after my coming to the Garh. I have to tell you, though, that years later I came to see Bhanwar in a totally different light.

Pandijju was not in Garh Dharmapuri the day I started my new life there. I heard someone say that he was away in Ujjayini for a darshan of Mahakaaleshwar.

Before a year had passed, the faces of my new habitat began to wear a familiar look. Kaluram Rebari, the right-hand man of Rao, was roughly the same size and age but with a much leaner and more sinewy frame, as though his body was made by twisting together the muscles and the veins and the bones and what have you. The stories of his physical strength and daredevilry was the stuff of legend: people recalled that he had, in his youth, killed a panther with bare hands. He wore clothes similar to Rao except that his hand weapon was concealed beneath the angrakhaa and he carried a metal-tipped bamboo staff that could double as a spear, if needed. It wasn't unlikely that it would, considering that the dense forest around the Garh teemed with predators and outlaws. Kaluram was like the commander-in-chief of Rao's forces; his army.

There were about fifty shepherd families in the community around the Garh. All the men were close kin of Kaluram, clad in similar turbans, angrakhaas and dhotis, metal-tipped staff in their hands. They all looked alike to a child's eye.

Other than Jaddu Baba alias Rao, Ketki, Bhanwar alias Bhaunda and myself, all the others of the community lived in the outhouses along the sides of the all-weather cobbled path that ran down to the water's edge, and then turned towards Mandav across the shallower stream of the river. The ruined tenements had been made habitable with long-grass thatched roofs.

Each household had women, but they were all so busy with their household chores and tending the cows and sheep in the barns, they hardly ever came to the Garh. Sheep in Dharmapuri must have numbered in thousands. Early every morning, the men-folk would leave to graze their flocks in all directions except the nearby slopes of the plateau. Often they would go so far out, they looked like an army of ants from the high walls surrounding the Garh. I sometimes wondered why they needed to go that far when there was so much grass on the slopes closer to home, and ended up thinking that perhaps some royal edict forbade grazing on the slopes below the Sultan's fort.

As I said, the women rarely visited the Garh. As for the boys, as soon as they were able to walk, they would begin to tag along with their fathers and brothers to learn shepherding. The girls did come to the Garh though, after they were done helping out their mothers, and we had a great time playing together in the ruins of uninhabited little rooms around its courtyard walls. Once I had regained my speech, three of them who were about my age became friends with me—Tara, a real star, was the apple of my eye, the other two being Savita and Kishori.

I was gradually settling down into my new life and really loved playing with them. I noticed, however, that they tended to keep gazing at me, particularly Tara, whose face had been among the first ones I saw after I was brought out of the river. I suspected they kind of pitied me for being an orphan. No wonder they tiptoed around me, even avoided applying the rules of games rigorously on me.

Though I was settling down, the memory of the haveli with the lone maulshri tree, the deeply-loving gaze of my mother, as she caressed my hair, her mellifluous bhajan, all came at me every once in a while like a howling squall and pierced my heart! Ah, where did the sonchiraiyaa days go? Why am I here among strangers, suspecting even my friends of pitying me? I don't know why tears never came to my eyes in front of people. I would slip away to some deserted corner of the ruins, or to my little room on the first floor, and weep my heart out. After a while, I'd feel lighter, more composed. Even though I was so little, I instinctively knew that it was impossible to go back in time. There was nothing that I could do other than playing out my part in act two, at Garh Dharmapuri. In any case, I had but a puny little past. The fragments of the dream that I had brought with me were fading away by the day.

Two more years went by in a trice, as it were, and the Garh became my home. But my heart was not entirely at peace.

Vision 5

The two pillars of my lonely existence were Pandijju and Tara. There was no one else that I could relate to, or talk with freely. Jaddu Baba frequently disappeared for unspecified periods of time. No one could tell when he left, or when he would return. In any case, his piercing eyes and his gravitas disconcerted me.

At times I thought of running away from the Garh, but where would I go in the fearsome forest that surrounded it! Either I'd fall prey to some predator, or worse, another horseman like the one in my previous life.

Sometimes I would wonder whether my mother missed me too, and wept inconsolably as I did. Had she somehow escaped the hands of my kidnappers, and was she still alive? Would I ever see her again? Was she looking for me? There was no one who could tell me anything, and then again, someone would answer my questions only if I asked them! Whenever I was tormented by such questions, an inexplicable reluctance seemed to seal my lips. Ah! I was absolutely on my own in a world that belonged to the rest.

Ketki didn't like me one bit. She was always grumbling, kind of muttering curses under her breath. With the greatest reluctance, she only spoke to me if it was absolutely necessary. At mealtimes she would serve food, and shoving the plate toward me, say tartly: 'Take, eat.' I'd always been a small eater, and her searing stare made me feel as though the very first morsel was stuck in the gullet. Every time I failed to finish a part of the quantity served—drawing her acid sarcasm 'Arree! Did you bring along sacks full of grain that you're wasting so much?'—I would get up silently, thinking to myself: what did I ever do to deserve her unceasing ire?

There was no question of talking to Bhaunda. The moment I set my eyes upon him, I'd boil over with disgust, exactly as Ketki would on seeing me. At times I even laughed at myself: what did he ever do to you that you cannot bear the sight of him!

I had no idea then how soon he was to be at the root of so much trouble for me. At the time, his perpetually open mouth and creepy stare were fodder for endless ridicule from the girls. At times, tired of our whispers and giggles, he would openly plead to play hide-and-seek with us, but Tara, the sternest of us all, would shatter his hopes with an earful, 'What business do you have among girls? Go shepherding!' and mumble under her breath, 'Always buzzing around like an accursed fly!' Bhaunda's face would redden as he'd quietly slunk away. Occasionally, I'd feel a tiny bit of pity well up inside me, 'Poor guy! He too, like me, has no one at all in the world he can truly call his friend... Ketki's hardly likely to play hide-and-seek with him!' I would think.

When Tara and I became particularly friendly, I once asked her, 'Tara, you were right there when they brought me here. Do you know where I came from?'

'Only that they found you floating unconscious in Reva Maiyaa. You got stuck in a jagged outcrop of rocks on the river bank. I have no idea of the details, but why worry over such things! We're all here for you. What's more, Rao loves you like a daughter.' Then taking me in her arms, she began to console me, patting me on the back like I was a baby. I felt a huge wave of warmth wash over me. My throat felt constricted and tears streamed down the sides of my nostrils. Between sobs, I said in a choked voice, 'But Tara...who am I?'

'You're my darling, that's all I know,' Tara tittered as if speaking to a baby, 'Don't cry, dear, you'll only hurt more, what's the point...'

She couldn't complete the sentence.

'What silly drama is going on here, girls?' Ketki had come into the room, like a snake slithering silently; she was good at such things. Tara and I parted with a start, and stood, heads bowed, as though accused of some serious crime.

'What happened to her? Why is she crying?' Ketki's questions sounded like a whiplash.

A terrified Tara blurted out, 'She was asking who she is, where she came from...' Ketki burst out laughing raucously. I saw her guffaw for the first time ever. It was not mirth, just a vicious variant of it.

'Hah... Hah... Hah...she's a fairy from the moon, who else! Stop being dramatic, come and eat.' She commanded when she was done with her sarcasm.

I felt like jumping up and scratching her face. Honestly, if I were a grown-up I would have taken her on, but alas, she was a big-boned woman, and I so little that I barely came up to her hips. I turned and ran to my room, and fell on the bed, swearing silently between sobs, 'You go and eat the cowdung that you cook. I would rather die than eat that muck!'

For three days I didn't have a drop of water, far less eat. By the second evening, I was half-dead. My tongue felt like firewood left to dry in the sun, and multi-coloured spots danced behind my closed eyelids. By the third afternoon, I was in delirium, mumbling nonsense. Ketki did come to my room a few times for the sake of it: 'Hey! Stop this drama...come and eat now, or are you bent on killing yourself and turning into an evil spirit to haunt me?'

When I made no response, she finally left in a huff, 'All right, die if you will! I'm not going to beggar myself, let Rao come and feed you!'

But Ketki never touched me, never tried to feed me forcibly. Maybe she wants me dead, I thought. Good riddance for her!

Whenever Ketki came, Bhaunda tagged along too and stood peeping at me from behind her. My bile would rise. I could scratch his face if not Ketki's! Tara and my other two playmates did not come even once. Maybe their entry into the Garh had been banned.

By the evening of the third day, I was surely dying, but apparently my time wasn't up yet. Rao returned from wherever he'd gone. As he entered my room, I saw his eyes were filled with deep compassion. I couldn't help breaking into a fresh bout of sobbing. 'Come, get up, and break your fast now. Everything's going to be all right. I'll tell you all you want to know,' he said.

Not denying Rao was perhaps just an excuse. At the end of the third day, I'd have broken my fast if even Ketki had asked me one more time!

The next day, Rao came to my room again and sat on the edge of my bed. I had slept fitfully after the meal following the three days of fasting. My muscles ached and I felt light-headed. My pulse quickened with faintly recalled patches of nightmares and the intimidating presence of Rao. As I tried to sit up my head reeled so terribly, I sank back on the bed. Rao lifted me by the armpits and sat me gingerly on his lap. Stroking my hair gently, he said 'Don't be afraid, Ruup, you can call me Baba if you like.'

'Is m…my n…name Ruup, Ba…ba?' I said, stammering.

That's when he told me that my name was Ruupmati, and addressed me as 'kunwarani' for the first time. I was about to ask him what it meant, but the sudden appearance of Ketki put an end to that conversation.

Vision 6

Tara's small cowrie-like eyes rounded in disbelief.

'No way,' she said. 'I've lived here all my life. If I hadn't seen, I'd have heard of it at least!'

'You think I'd lie to you? Why? To what end?' My look of hurt silenced her, but I could still see disbelief writ large on her face. I said no more, but she chuckled and added, 'You must have dreamt of it!'

I felt as though she'd slapped me. I said hotly, 'You pretend to be my best friend, aren't you ashamed of calling me a liar?' Her face fell, and eyes clouded with some misgiving, but she said nothing and left quietly. In any case, what proof could I give her? I couldn't have taken her there and said, 'See, there it is!'

Pandijju had instructed me to walk with my eyes shut. I'd no idea how many steps I'd walked straight, and then how many after turning left and then to the right, before descending the steps to that underground chamber. He'd kept telling me: one more step, yes, another one, then one more. Finally, he said, 'Yes, now you can open your eyes.' As I did so, I found myself standing in front of a huge idol of goddess Durga, exquisitely carved in stone, her eight arms carrying the celestial weapons gifted by gods, and her ferocious lion frozen in a roar with its mouth open and its front paw resting triumphantly on the remains of the slain demon, Mahishaasura.

The subterranean shrine seemed to have been hewn out of an enormous rock somewhere deep underneath the Garh. But the cavernous chamber was neither dark nor airless. Indeed, there were a number of brass and earthen lamps lit on the ledge below the Devi's idol, but those didn't appear to be the sole source of light, for the statue was gleaming far more brightly. Nor could the Devi's jasmine garland be the only thing that filled the shrine with such soulful fragrance. It seemed as though a fresh breeze, passing through flowering branches, was blowing in through some invisible apertures, but much as I craned my small neck around, I couldn't spot any.

I stood spellbound for a long moment, gazing up at the Devi's idol. Then, as I looked down, I gasped. Jaddu Baba was sitting cross-legged on the floor with his back resting on the wall beside a large wooden chest.

'Pandijju, Jai Ganesha. You may begin the Vidyaarambha rites,' he said.

Pandijju set two small mats down in front of the idol and said, 'Sit, Ruupmati.' So, he too knows my name, I thought.

For some time, he stood facing the deity, chanting mantras with holy water, durbaa grass-twigs and wet rice grains cupped in his right palm. Then turning to me, he sprinkled the mix, and sat down beside me on the other aasana, and taking my right fingers between his thumb and forefinger, made me write a few words that I could not read at the time, and said, 'Sri Ganeshaay Namah.' Later, when I had learnt to read and write, I knew that those were the words he had had me write for the initiation ceremony on the rectangular piece of wooden slate that had been dyed black, using a piece of white soft-stone for chalk.

'Now get up and touch your guru's feet, Ruup,' said Baba. As far as I could estimate later, I was perhaps seven years of age at the time.

This is what I had described to Tara, but she turned it into a lie, saying I had to have been dreaming, that there was no temple underneath the Garh!

My first Navraatra came only a few weeks later and Pandijju took me down to the Devi's temple, blindfolded as before. As I opened my eyes, I was filled with a terrible sense of humiliation.

Vision 7

Tara was not the only one present there! The entire community, including Kaluram, lined the side-walls with their hands folded in front, all repeating after Pandijju the mantras he was reciting, as though instead of shepherds they were brahmins or kshatriyas who had been chanting these mantras for generations. They stood reverently with their sons and daughters in front of them.

Even as I was being led to the underground shrine that day, I had absolutely no idea that I would find such a large congregation when I opened my eyes. Frankly, I was quite stupefied to see so many people there. From the conversation between Pandijju and Rao on the day of my initiation, I had gathered the impression that no one other than the three of us was privy to the Devi's temple. What was going on here?

There were aasanas for important people in front of the idol and only two in the first row. Rao sat on one and the other lay empty. In the row behind it, sat Ketki and Bhanwar.

Tara stood in front of Kaluram. Until then I did not know that she was his daughter. As our eyes met, she lowered her head with a quick smile, as though silently hinting that I didn't know how to keep a secret. My eyes were welling up from humiliation, and I dropped my gaze as well. My instinct told me that I was excluded from some deep mystery which everyone shared except me.

'Sit down here,' said Baba, patting the empty aasana beside him. I looked at him in dismay. Why me? Why not Ketki? I thought. I was consumed by unanswered questions that arose all the time, but I had to bury them silently in my bosom.

Pandijju sat down facing the idol with a heap of flowers and other items for the rituals, and began to recite shlokas from Durga Saptashati. He recited the hymns from memory for nearly an hour, his eyes half-closed and hands folded in front. By then, Revadiya had come in, dragging the sacrificial goat-kid by a short cord wrapped around his palm. Revadiya, a powerfully-built, handsome man in his thirties, seemed to always hang around with Kaluram. Presently, he tied the goat-kid by the cord to a heavy block of wood and held the poor thing prone on the ground. Pandijju rose to his feet and drew a short sword out of its scabbard, kept on the wooden chest. I cringed and shut my eyes instinctively. I wasn't an eyewitness to animal-sacrifice that first Navraatra at the Garh. I did hear the sword come down with a hiss, though. The gathering roared: 'Victory to Mother Goddess!' When I opened my eyes, the floor was splattered with blood, flowing in little rivulets in every direction. When the gathering dispersed, people left crimson footmarks in their wake, which no one except me seemed to notice. The sight left me queasy and perturbed.

After that day, Pandijju never asked me to shut my eyes while taking me down to the underground temple for my daily lessons which had started soon after my initiation. At the very least, I'd been let into the secret of the Devi's temple.

Vision 8

'Yes, it was a test of sorts for you, and also a warning to be more careful in future,' said Pandijju, explaining gently. 'You needn't be ashamed, but you do need to bear in mind that absolutely no one except the close-knit community around the Garh is aware of the existence of the Devi's shrine. This secret has remained intact for nearly two hundred and fifty years, and we need to keep it that way in future as well. There is no telling what calamity might befall under mlechchha-rule.' He was watching me closely all the while, perhaps expecting an assurance that I would never again mention the temple to anyone.

But all I could manage to mumble, my eyes widening in surprise, was, 'Two hundred and fifty years!' By that time Pandijju had already taught me how to count, and I knew how much time that was.

'Yes, more or less. It's a heart-rending story how Rao's forebears, four or five generations ago, brought this idol from a holy shrine endangered by iconoclast invaders.' The study-hour was almost over, but Pandijju never tired of telling historical anecdotes and began to narrate the story of the rescue of the Devi's idol, gazing at some point in the distance as though he were seeing it all happen. 'Those were days of decline for the kingdoms and principalities of the Malwa Parbhars. Vanquished by Muslim conquerors, they were fading into history. Ambitious military commanders and adventurers from the Delhi sultanate had already established near-independent realms of their own all around Malwa, except to its east. How long could the fertile and prosperous Malwa escape greedy eyes! Eventually, the glorious legacy of Vikramaditya and Raja Bhoj proved too heavy a burden for their descendants to carry forward, and Ujjayini fell to the mlechchha invaders. The great city was plundered, raped, pillaged and destroyed. Parbhar soldiers had been either put to the sword or were chased away. Tens of thousands of innocent civilians were massacred, even women and children were not spared. Indeed, so many were killed that the gutters of the city ran red with blood. The severed heads of defending commanders killed in action hung from the city walls as a warning against future resistance. The few thousand of the inhabitants who survived were the ones who traded their faith for their lives at the instance of the military mullahs.

'While plundering cities, temples were the first target of invaders after the royal treasury. Even more than iconoclastic fervour, for the reason that they housed precious jewels and wealth accumulated over centuries from affluent devotees. The Devi's original shrine on the outskirts of Ujjayini was also one such temple, marked to be razed to the ground.

'The city had been brought to its knees, the hue and cry of the massacre and plunder had ceased. Columns of smoke rising from arson sites lined the cityscape, and the air was heavy with the smell of congealing blood. As evening fell, the victors itched to get away and begin celebrating; the demolition was postponed to the next day.

'It was not uncommon those days for devout bands of defeated Hindu warriors to stake their lives and make a last effort to whisk away idols to a haven,[3] where they could be kept out of harm's way. This is what happened in Ujjayini that night.

'A daredevil contingent of survivors sneaked back, under the cover of darkness and the smoke billowing all around, and brought the Devi's idol to Dharmapuri. The then Rao of Garh Dharmapuri, perhaps the great-great-grandfather of Rao, was the commander of these men, and an ancestor of Kaluram, his chief aide. It wasn't child's play, though, to transport the idol weighing eight hundred maunds from such great distance.

Legend has it that in the last lap of the journey one of the bullocks dropped dead of sheer exhaustion, and Kaluram's ancestor took that end of the yoke on his shoulders for the last three kos. They all took an oath that day, in the name of Reva Maiyaa and their children, to keep the Devi's idol an inviolable secret, and never mention it to anyone whosoever. To this day, if such a thing happens, they get to know immediately. Now you understand what happened when you spoke to Tara, but let's forget that now, don't brood over it. Now that I look back on it, perhaps it was my mistake that I didn't expressly forbid you, instead of just asking you to keep your eyes shut when bringing you down here. All right then, that's all for today. We'll learn more of history tomorrow.'

I got up and left quietly. As I sat alone, a thousand questions peppered my mind. Quite a few days had passed since the Navraatra pooja and Tara had not come to see me, far less Savita and Kishori. Perhaps the feeling of guilt and embarrassment that plagued my mind was also tormenting Tara in another way. I had tried to confide in her simply as one friend to another, not quite knowing that it was forbidden to talk of the temple. Did I really need to feel so guilty about it? But did she have to go snitching against me, as she no doubt had?

My grouse against her kept roiling inside me for a long time.

My dear scribe, are you by any chance getting an impression that, for an eight-year-old, I'm boasting of emotions far more complex than I could have experienced at the time? Speaking with hindsight, I might be mixing up perspectives gained later, when Pandijju's lessons had broadened my mental faculties.

Anyway, for heaven's sake, stop staring at me like they all did when I grew a little older!

As she chided me, I realized I had indeed been gawking at her for a while, and she'd seen through me. Abashed, I lowered my eyes quickly...

Vision 9

Pandijju's wooden chest was an enormous treasure trove of information and knowledge, and his head an even larger one. Over the next two years, he poured a good deal of it into mine. From simple literacy and rudimentary arithmetic to history, geography and mythological stories from Treta, Dwaapar and Kaliyug, literature from Kalidasa right down to Amir Khusro and Vallabhacharya, he taught me all. Had it not been for Pandijju's tutoring, I would not even be literate, far less be capable of writing verse. He was also the inspiration behind the honing of my musical talent.

Pandijju often taught in a freewheeling style, mixing history and philosophy together, 'Ruup, the scope of information in the universe is so vast, that it is impossible to master it all, even if one kept at it for seven lifetimes, but the paradigms of real learning are rather modest, simple and eternal. Should one apply himself single-mindedly, they can be easily grasped. The most important thing is to be sthitpragya: quietly aware and alive to one's circumstances and accept one's limitation with equanimity. For example, we must all recognize the fact that Maalav-des is now ruled by Mussalman rulers.'

Then he would sometimes add, 'Sultanates and kingdoms are all maya, totally ephemeral. Shadows of countless swords continually hang over the head of the ruler of the day, and there is no telling when one of these threats might materialize to reality. Be that as it may, the days of Parbhar hegemony are as good as gone forever. The few sparks that remain are fireflies roaming a long night without end.' His comment about 'remaining sparks' was perhaps just a general hint at sporadic resistance that the sultans faced from Purabiya Rajputs, but there were times when I wondered whether he had something more specific in mind.

Pandijju didn't like to be interrupted with searching

questions, but one day I did ask him pointing to the Devi's idol, 'Guruji, you had said that this idol was brought by the Parbhar ancestors of Rao, hadn't you?'

'Indeed, I had,' he replied a bit warily, as though admitting to a mistake.

'So, is Rao a descendant of the Parbhars?' I asked.

'Well, logically it would seem so. If the ancestor was a Parbhar, so would his descendant.' He sounded evasive.

'Then why does he dress like shepherds, and how come he has only them for companions?' I ploughed on.

'Ruupmati, we're already done with the history of Maalav-des, why go on and on! Shujat Khan is the sultan here and we are his subjects. The vanquished have to start over and somehow go on living, haven't they? From tomorrow we'll study the poetry of Amir Khusro.' I could tell that he wanted to change track, and was bribing me with something I loved. I fell quiet, but he carried on, 'And yes, Ruup, I'd like you to familiarize yourself with the flora and fauna of Maalav-des, its cultural heritage and musical traditions as well. Frankly, I've no ear for music, but Revadiya is well-versed in raga-raginis. I'll tell him to teach you some.'

I tried to engage with him in a similar conversation once again. He was teaching me the various traditions of keeping count of passing years and centuries. Suddenly my mind wandered away to who my real parents might be.

'Guruji, do you know anything about my parents?' I asked innocently. Quickly looking up, he replied, 'Ruupmati, it would be good if you accept Rao and Ketki as your parents. You've already gone through a lot. Why would you want to take on the burden of unnecessary information?'

'But Baba said that he would tell me everything,' I said in a voice close to tears.

'Then, you will have to ask him, won't you? Now, shall we return to the different traditions of keeping count of time?' said Pandijju, putting a stop to the digression. 'So, I was telling you that a long time ago, the valiant King Vikramaditya of Ujjayini started a new epoch to celebrate his victory over the

Saka invaders, which is known as the Vikram Samvat. Later, his descendant, King Shaalivaahan instituted another samvat after decimating the remainder of Saka resistance which came to be known as the Saka Samvat. The Christians, far to the west, count the years before and after the birth of Christ and the Muslims keep count of time from the year of Prophet Mohammad's journey from Mecca to Medina, which they call Hijri. The Vikram Samvat runs approximately fifty-six years ahead of the Christian era while the Saka Samvat follows it by about seventy-nine years. The Hijri is about six hundred years behind the Christian era.'

Pandijju had already told me that he knew of the Hindu and Hijri systems and had later learnt about the Christian era from white traders, who were frequent visitors to the Mandav court. 'So, according to these different systems, we are now in Vikram Samvat 1606, the Christian year 1550, and Hijri 971.' I had begun to nod off by then, from the sheer monotony.

'Guruji, you'd said that I ought to start learning about flora and fauna, cultural traditions and all… When do you think I could start with that?' I asked.

'It appears you've had enough of time traditions. Well, never mind, we can talk more on it tomorrow. As for the other things, the earlier the better. You could begin right away in your free time. I'm sure your friend Tara can help you with all that.'

Vision 10

By the time Navraatra came again, I was far better adjusted to my life at Garh Dharmapuri. I no longer shut my eyes to the animal sacrifice—I was getting assimilated. But I still had a lingering suspicion that there was something in the air that was not to be shared with me: a sense of being on a short sojourn in the Garh, without citizenship rights and that the community was somehow bearing with me out of pity for an orphan.

I was nearly ten years old now, and thanks to Pandijju's lessons, reasonably well-aware of what was going on in the world around me. I knew a fair bit of mythology and history, and about things past and present. I could see that the men and women of the community gazed at me with a degree of surreptitious awe, as though irresistibly charmed, but none of them seemed quite willing to have a real conversation with me. I could not imagine the reason for their aloofness, but it felt like everyone one was hiding something from me.

My only consolation was that my friends had resumed playing with me. Over time, as we grew older, the sort of games we fancied began to change: hide-and-seek, thief-and-guards gave way to planning and conducting the nuptials of dolls; swaying recklessly high into the air on swings; visiting fairs to pick up bangles and rings and scores of other fripperies like that. Eavesdropping on older women chatting and gossiping had become infinitely more thrilling, and whispering into one another's ears the saucier bits that we overheard, even more so. In fact, whispering and giggling for no apparent reason was fast turning into our favourite pastime. It seemed as though we were about to break into a secret, magic world, even half of which had not yet been unveiled to us.

Ah! My dear scribe, you would have to be born a woman to really understand how tantalizing that time between the known and the unknown was! The four of us hadn't even reached puberty yet. But I could not have imagined that my entry into that phase of life would be so humiliating an experience.

Oh my, look at me running so far ahead of myself all over again!

Vision 11

The next day I told my friends, smiling cheerfully, that Pandijju had asked me to familiarize myself with the local flora and fauna, and that I could go out of the Garh with them. Indeed, I was happy, but also a bit apprehensive at heart. The jungle was fearsome, thick with foliage and bramble, and fraught with unpleasant possibilities. I had often heard of tigers and leopards raiding the barns and carrying away sheep, and of outlaws roaming the forest. Would a rogue take me away on a horse again and muffle my cries?

But Tara jumped with joy at the news and embraced me. All four of us started giggling for no reason. However, Tara sensed my fear as I asked her whether it was safe to go out without someone escorting us. She began to soothe me, 'Oh! Come on, don't be afraid. I'm here to guide you. I know all those jungle tracks like the back of my hand.'

It took a great deal of persuasion on Tara's part to overcome my fears though. 'If you fret so much, you'll certainly be devoured by a tiger, or worse, kidnapped by some dacoit,' she said, chuckling, 'Come now, let's leave. We still have a good three hours of daylight left. You'll feel so good, the greenery will go straight to your heart.'

Leaving the Garh, we walked some distance on the narrow, cobbled road to Mandav before turning onto a jungle-path to the west. Soon we were deep in the woods, crickets and birds chirping noisily. There were huge trees all around, some that rose straight up skyward while some others spread out with round canopies on top, interspersed with tall bamboo groves.

'You see that tree with little fruits beginning to come out, close to its trunk? That's a jackfruit tree, soon they will grow as big as watermelons. And that one there with fruits hanging like rats by their tails, that's Khorasani tamarind, and that one with black berries is jaamun.' Tara was holding forth as I looked around mesmerized. Teak and aakaash-chaandni scraped the sky and bushes of custard apple grew like untended hedges all over the place. Tall grass dotted with tiny white and yellow flowers and plants with thorny leaves with crimson flowers and green pods that looked like miniature conchshells, all grew wild.

'What are those red flowers called?' I asked, fascinated. Tara laughed out aloud. 'Oh, those! They give the folks here their herbal medicines as well as their leisure drug. Its pods, called doda, yield opium.' I kept gazing at the cup-shaped flowers with delicate red petals and the drooping pods for the longest time.

By the time we turned back, dusk was falling. The chirping of crickets and birds had suddenly become more pronounced. We were passing through a bamboo grove when it happened. Tara broke her stride abruptly, shushing us with a finger to her lips, the other arm extended, motioning us to halt and stay quiet. A black cobra, four to five arms long, slithered across our path and disappeared in the undergrowth on the other side. We watched it go with bated breath, shaking with fear, until we were sure it was safe to go forward. Even Tara seemed ruffled. She said hoarsely, 'Well…I'd quite forgotten to warn you about vipers. You must make sure never to step on one. Those bitten stand little chance!'

I heaved a sigh of relief when we were back at the Garh a little while later. But Tara had been right. The greenery had found its way straight into my heart, and it stayed. The safe return from that first outing made me bold and roaming the wilderness soon became my favourite pastime.

VISION 12

After that day, Tara would show up practically every afternoon, and we'd be off, roaming the jungle for hours on end. In the quiet green of the forest, I felt so calm and fulfilled that no sooner had I returned than I would yearn to go back to it. Although the wilderness proved harmless, Ketki did throw tantrums initially. 'Where do you disappear for hours on end?' she asked archly.

'Guruji has told me to learn about local vegetation, flowers and such. So, I just stepped out with my friends for a while,' I said.

'Are you done with the trees and flowers now?' she said, and then her tone leapt up several notches all at once. 'Look, Kunwarani, you'll end up in the claws of a tiger, or an outlaw if you carry on like this, do you hear?' She went on muttering, 'Hunh! As if all this will make her a panditaain or something!' Then making a horrid face, she stomped out of the room.

Her disapproval had no effect on me. I had fallen in love with the white and yellow grass-flowers dappled in the afternoon sun that filtered through the bamboo leaves, swaying ever so slightly in the cool forest breeze, and eagerly waited every afternoon for Tara and the others to accompany me out of the Garh.

One day, Tara said, 'We've had enough of these neighbourhood bamboo groves. Let me show you some real forest for a change. Adhpadam Talao in Champaareni is indeed a bit far, but...' she stopped in the middle of the sentence, as though wondering whether to go on.

'Champaareni...Adhpadam Talao...what kind of names are those?' I asked.

'Oh, let's go.' Tara had decided to take the plunge. 'You'll know why it's called Adhpadam the moment you see it. If I tell you now, it will spoil the surprise.'

'Where is it, how far?' I was instantly drawn to the idea, anticipating something exciting.

'It's about a couple of kos, not very far from the river. There're so many champa trees just short of it, the air hangs heavy with their sweet aroma, and then the lake of deep green water. It's like a small piece of heaven on earth. Once you see it, you wouldn't want to come back, but I suspect your legs won't stand up to the long trek, almost five kos, to and fro!' Tara said.

'Nonsense! What's wrong with my legs? If yours can, why can't mine?' I countered, feigning offence, then whispered excitedly, 'Are you sure we'll be able to return before sundown?'

'Very sure. And there's nothing to worry about even if it

were to get dark, I have a fire-torch we can use.' The mention of a torch made me a bit uneasy. Savita and Kishori hadn't come that day. It would be only the two of us with a fire-torch in the gloom of the forest! But I was so smitten with exploring the wilderness that I was simply drawn along in Tara's wake.

We had gone no farther than two hundred steps out of the Garh when we heard it: the rhythmic thudding of hooves on cobblestones. My heart skipped a beat as Tara hurriedly drew me aside, behind thick foliage. We peeped out and soon two heavily armed riders, wearing steel armour and helmets, with a spare horse in tow, passed by us and dismounted hastily at the Garh's entrance. They half ran into the courtyard as though to avoid a pursuing calamity. I had never before seen armed soldiers come to the Garh. My throat felt choked from fear, and apprehension of something terrible about to happen. Even the normally unflappable Tara seemed rattled, and had quite forgotten the expedition, as we both sat hidden behind the shrubbery waiting for a chance to somehow sneak back into the Garh. Just then, the soldiers returned with Baba and got onto their mounts. Baba, whom I had never seen ride a horse before, jumped onto his ride with the aplomb of an expert horseman. As they passed the spot where we sat, I noticed Baba's forehead, creased with anxiety. I couldn't make out who might have sent soldiers to fetch him, for it was clear that they hadn't taken him prisoner. On the contrary, they had come with a spare horse for him.

Curiosity felt like a bone stuck in the throat, but I knew from experience that no one would likely be forthcoming on what was happening. Before long, I had a confirmation of this.

'Where did the soldiers take Baba to?' I couldn't help asking Revadiya, who was the first person we ran into, upon entering the Garh.

'What? Who told you?' Instead of answering my question, he countered me with one of his own, seeming a bit surprised.

'We saw them leave with Baba. Has there been an accident?'

'No, no...there is nothing to worry. Maybe he has gone to Mandav on some errand. You know, one has to obey the

Sultan's summons. He'll be back soon,' he said reassuringly. I could see that he wasn't prepared to share any particulars, if he had any. As he made to walk on, I said, 'Pandijju told me that you're a music maestro, and he would ask you to teach me music. When can we begin?'

Abashed at the implied compliment, and a bit taken aback by the sudden change of track, he smiled benignly. 'Yes, he told me about it. We'll start in a day or two, for certain,' he said, walking away briskly, as though he was late for some important rendezvous.

Rao returned in the evening, and it was business as usual for everyone but me. My curiosity refused to die down.

Vision 13

I kept wondering every now and then what Adhpadam Talao looked like. I would try to picture it in my mind, but no clear images emerged. I had had the benefit of some education, so I reasoned that Tara's Champaareni must actually be Champa-aranya, a champa forest, and Adhpadam Talao must be the local dialect name for Ardhapadma Taal, the half-lotus lake. But what did Ardhapadma mean? In order to keep my curiosity simmering, Tara had stopped short of explaining what half-lotus actually meant, and lately, she hadn't come to see me either. I was dying to know more about Ardhapadma, if not actually go there myself.

Meanwhile, early one misty morning, Revadiya turned up.

'Come, let's begin your music training today. Come with me.' He turned and began to walk towards a deserted section of the Garh to the north of the forecourt. First, we went through a couple of gloomy little cabins built into the thick rampart-like wall, and then climbed several short flights of steps zigzagging upwards. I did feel like asking him where on earth we were headed, but Revadiya's quiet, decent ways were so guileless, it didn't seem right to begin on a false note. So, I just kept following him. When we reached the top of the wall, I was simply amazed. There was a pavilion enclosed on three sides by exquisite latticework in stone, and open on the side overlooking the slopes outside the Garh, with just a balustrade for safety. The panorama of undulating grassy slopes gently descending to the river and then climbing up towards the massive Mandav Fort walls, with its battlement-crest and domes caressing the clouds, was so breathtaking, I can hardly put it into words.

The neat orderliness inside the pavilion was no less remarkable. The floor was covered from one end to the other with a cushioned mat, spread over with a white sheet. Musical instruments were kept in a row to one side of it. One of them had a round head as big as a melon and an arm-long shaft, along which ran several wire strings that were hooked to small wooden pegs at the other end. There was another with round heads at either end, connected with a shaft and wire strings similarly affixed from one end to the other and two more instruments that I recognized right away as they were played in the Devi's temple every Navraatra, a duhul and a nai.

'Have a seat, Ruupmati,' said Revadiya politely, sitting down cross-legged on the cushioned mat. As I sat down facing him, he fumbled inside his pocket and took out a length of red-coloured woven string, and proffered it to me.

'Tie it on my wrist. If you have to learn music from me, you must first make me your Ustad, according to our custom.'

I did as instructed, though a trifle hesitantly for some inexplicable reason.

'See, this is a tambura, and this is a beenn,' he said pointing to the first two instruments, 'duhul and nai, I'm sure you already know.' I nodded in the affirmative.

'If you remain so distant and sort of intimidated, how're you going to learn music from me? Music is the stuff of the soul being bared,' he said looking closely at my face.

'Are we going to have the music sessions here…every day?' I asked, clearing my throat that felt parched.

'As a matter of fact, yes, but why do you ask? You don't

like this place? I practise here whenever I have the time to. The view is lovely, and the breeze coming across the grassy slopes remains cool all through the year. Indeed, it's a bit far from the inhabited parts of the Garh.' As I remained mute, my head bowed, he chuckled and added, 'In a way that's good, isn't it? At this distance, we wouldn't be a nuisance for tuneless ears, nor would anyone interrupt our sessions.' Then his voice assumed the serious tone of a master, 'You see, the quiet of solitude is essential to the quest of true music. Now, listen to me attentively. I'll vocalize the seven notes of the ragini, you have to note and memorize the subtle differences.' Then he proceeded to sing saa…re…ga…ma…pa…dha…nee…saa, repeating the notes for me.

As Revadiya sang, I was overwhelmed with the feeling that his voice was the abode of Shaarda, the goddess of learning. He was truly gifted. I heedlessly fell in love with his voice.

Vision 14

Coming down the flight of steps, as I emerged from the dark little cabin into the courtyard, my heart skipped a beat. On a crumbling ruin of a platform sat Bhaunda, his jaws hanging open, steadily gazing at the door. From where he sat, he must have heard Revadiya sing.

In the last four or five years, Bhaunda hadn't grown any taller but he was well into his teens now, a soft line of down beginning to show on his upper lip. By now he had given up hope of ever being allowed to play with the girls, but he still tended to hang around, watching us silently.

That day, seeing him so forlorn, I was overcome by a strange mix of compassion and abhorrence. I stopped a step short of him, and as he looked up in surprise, I saw that his eyes were brimming with tears. I had never started a conversation with him before, but I could not help accosting him that day.

'What is it, Bhanwar? Why are you looking so distraught?' I asked softly. He looked me in the eye for a long moment, then began in a voice choked with emotion, 'Ruupmati...' He fell silent.

'Yes, go on. What happened?'

'She slapped me...' He stopped again, and as he lowered his head, tears began to fall to the ground.

'What? Who slapped you?' I was stunned. For a moment I thought maybe it was Tara. I put my hand on his shoulder in silent commiseration. He sprang to his feet with a start.

'Ruup, you're very...' he began diffidently but stopping abruptly, turned and left, as though he had seen a ghost. As I looked back over my shoulder, I saw Revadiya emerging out of the same doorway which I had exited from a little while ago. As he passed by me, he threw an instruction my way, 'Come for the session at the break of dawn tomorrow, that's the best time for music.'

Back in my room, I tried to divert my curious mind while trying to read a book of poems—kavitas, dohas and kah mukarnis by Amir Khusro, my favourite, which Pandijju had allowed me to borrow after considerable persuasion, but alas, even that failed to hold my attention. I just could not stop wondering who might have slapped Bhaunda, and what he had been trying to tell me towards the end when that bizarre conversation was cut short by the sudden appearance of Revadiya on the scene.

The mystery of the slap was soon revealed on its own.

I felt thirsty and decided to go down to get a glass of water. Even before I could enter the kitchen, I heard the tongue-lashing that Ketki was giving Bhanwar. I stopped and eavesdropped.

'You only deserve to be slapped! You can't even keep your eyes and ears open and let me know what's going on, you're good for nothing! Now, don't you glare at me like that. Go away.'

I quickly retraced my steps, thinking hard. Who was Bhaunda supposed to watch—us girls? What was there to see and report about us? I was filled with sudden indignation. We simply roamed the jungle a bit, taking in the greenery and the like, whispering in each other's ears and giggling mindlessly. That wasn't such a catastrophe, was it? But by and by, it did turn into one.

Vision 15

That night I dreamt of a place I'd never visited: the Adhpadam Talao in Champaareni or the Ardhapadma Taal in Champa-aranya, as I had renamed it in my mind. The images were hazy, as though veiled in mist. I saw a longish lake, with a variety of branches and creepers hanging over the surface, and thousands of lotuses and buds that were yet to bloom. My dream was perhaps a subconscious reflection of Tara's rudimentary description, but when I woke up I was breathing heavily as though I'd just been through a harrowing ordeal. There was nothing fearful about the dream, though.

There were still a couple of hours to dawn. I turned on my side and tried to go back to sleep, but to no avail. Just as well, I thought, for I didn't want to be late for my music session with Revadiya.

'Today you will have to sing the notes of the sargam along with me. Do you think you can do it?' Revadiya asked, just at the start of the session.

How would I know? I thought to myself. 'I'll try my best,' I said, my head bowed.

'Try is all one can do, the rest is all in His hands,' he said, pointing a finger skyward. Then, as he began to sing, it seemed to me that the rays of the morning sun emanated from his vocal cords! Soon, my own voice joined with his, following the notes in tune. After repeating the notes together for what seemed an endless number of times, Revadiya looked at me, a trifle surprised.

'Ruup, do you think you could repeat the notes on your own now?' he asked.

'If you wish I can try...' He waved his fingers impatiently, 'Yes, yes. Go ahead.'

I began the solo, and suddenly I had goosebumps all over me: the same voice, a bit husky but absolutely steady, flowing without a trace of strain even at the highest pitch—the very same voice that sang the prayer for liberation to the idols of Radha-Krishna.

That day, I was convinced that the woman with whom I had lived in the maulshri mansion, the one who'd called me sonchiraiyaa in my previous life, was indeed my mother.

'Bravo! Let's have an encore,' Revadiya said, beaming. He kept listening for a while, as though enchanted. Then, putting a hand up to stop me, said, 'Ruup, do you know? Your throat is the abode of Devi Shaarda! Can you guess how long it took me to catch the notes of the sargam when I began to learn? Three whole months! But you seem to have been initiated already. We can begin to practise the ragas straight away.'

I looked at him, astonished.

'Why are you looking so bewildered? You find it hard to believe, don't you? So do I, if you ask me. But believe me, you're not only beautiful but also truly gifted.'

When the session ended and I descended to the courtyard, I felt as if I had grown wings, there was no need to walk the earth!

I was so happy, and yet my happiness sliced through my heart. There was no one in the world, absolutely no one, with whom I could share my joy. In sheer desperation, it occurred to me that I might tell Bhanwar all that Revadiya had said. Then I laughed, he would immediately go and repeat all of it to his sister, who would no doubt make a stupid face and mumble something like, 'Hah, besides being a panditaain, Ruupmati is also training to be a songstress, is she?'

I silently cursed Tara. She hadn't shown up since our aborted expedition to the Ardhapadma. I could have told her how happy I was.

Vision 16

Tara came after several days, with Savita and Kishori in tow. Pretending to be more annoyed than I was, I said to her crossly, 'Where have you been all these days? You had no time to even check if your friend was still alive!'

'No, no. I was sick, that's why!' She lowered her eyes in silent apology.

'What happened? Fever?' I asked.

'No, my stomach kind of ached,' she vaguely replied.

Out of the blue, I smiled wickedly and shot off the usually whispered jibe aloud, in front of the other two, 'I hope you haven't gotten yourself pregnant!'

Kishori and Savita burst out giggling. Tara turned a beetroot-red.

'Go away, have you no shame!' Tara said.

For some time now, we had started to whisper the jibe 'Go, and get yourself pregnant!' when one of us wanted to be funny or to cuss. By then we had learnt of its hidden implication from whispered conversations between married women of the community. The first time one of us used it, a doha I'd read in one of Pandijju's anthologies flashed through my mind:

The brute's so persistent
Hunting female deer:
The last barely a toddler
The next in the womb, almost here!

I couldn't make any sense of it back then, but now when I recited it to the others, we kept giggling at it for a long time.

In relation to Tara's indisposition, the jibe had sounded a bit awkward though, and I regretted it the moment I'd spoken. But she had the knack of easing such tensions without much ado. She replied smiling, 'I know why you're putting a child in my tummy! I haven't been able to take you out to Adhpadam

Talao all this time, but I'm hardly to blame. After the time the soldiers arrived unexpectedly, I came to fetch you but you were nowhere to be found. Only Bhaunda sat moping on a ruined platform in the courtyard. And later, I fell sick. Shall we do it tomorrow?' She made it sound as though she was yearning to visit more than I did.

The next day, crossing over to the other side of the familiar neighbourhood woods, we found ourselves in the heart of the dense forest. Daylight suddenly dimmed as though it was dusk already. The unknown pedestrian track climbed so steeply upward, in complete desolation, that we were soon out of breath. Then it suddenly levelled. Down the slope before us was an enormous bowl-shaped valley covered in tall grass where a large herd of deer grazed peacefully. Startled by instinct, some of them stopped, craning their necks to look back. The view below was breathtaking, the descending path bisecting the grassland perfectly like a neat parting on the head. We followed it down and climbed again to the plateau on the other side, and when we crested it, Tara said, 'We're almost there.'

After a short walk, we were in the middle of a large grove of trees with leaves like the mango tree, except that these were a lighter green. The trees were full of lovely champa flowers, their yellow petals spread like the wings of a butterfly. The air was heavy with a cloying aroma.

As we crossed to the other side of the grove, I was stunned. The lake was almost the same as the one in my dream. The near side of it was thick with blooming lotus flowers and buds swaying in the breeze. On the round lotus leaves, the size of large plates, droplets of water gleamed like pearls in the afternoon sun. Surprisingly, the far-side of the lake was a clear blue with a tinge of emerald: no lotuses there at all! Across the lake stood the ruins of an oblong pavilion, its basic structure and domes intact, but the decorative pitchers on the dome-tops had crumbled and hung loosely downward, and the knee-high latticework railing around it had given way at several places. The stone platform for seating inside appeared to be solidly in place though. On either side of the pavilion, there were trees of a species whose branches meandered a long way out, parallel to the water surface. Ardhapadma Taal was indeed ethereally beautiful, richly deserving of Tara's fancy epithet, a piece of heaven on earth!

'Do you see now why they call it Adhpadam? See, half the lake is full of lotuses, and the other half has water so clear you can see the rocks and pebbles at the bottom. Come, let's walk to the other side.' A preening Tara was pulling me by the hand. Coming out of my trance, I turned and embraced her earnestly, 'Tara, I'll never forget this favour. It's truly a piece of heaven as you said, but what's the secret of half and half, flowers and clear water? And whose pavilion is that?'

'Ah, only if you let me breathe can I tell you all that,' said Tara, squirming to get out of my tight embrace. 'There isn't much of a secret. Half the lake has a rocky bottom while the other half has mud underneath. What else were you asking? Ah yes, the pavilion. Well, my father says his grandfather told him that a long time ago a sultan named Hoshang Shah had it built as a pleasure resort for his harem.'

It took us a good quarter of an hour to get to the other side. I was so excited I walked right down to the water's edge and sat down on a rock. Tara was right. I could make out the pebbles lying at the bottom. Then I jumped onto another rock in the shade of an overhanging branch, where the water was so still and opaque, it shone like a mirror. I had known of mirrors more from books than actual experience and I certainly had seen none at the Garh. Now I knew what it could do to you if you had one. As I looked down, a clear reflection stared back at me. Ah! So this is what my face and body look like. No wonder they all keep staring at me. I'm beautiful, exceedingly lovely to look at. Is that what Bhanwar was trying to say the other day?

Then I ran back to where the lotus part began, and descending to the water level, plucked a couple of lotus blooms and smelled them. It was the most delicate of fragrances. I hurried back to the pavilion and circled it, wondering whether it had been there in my dream. Tara broke my reverie, 'Come, it's time to go back.' I was feeling so happy there, I didn't want to return, but it was late afternoon already.

We were halfway through. Including Tara, it was the first time for us all in the forest after dark, and we were afraid of predators, but even more, of losing our way back. Tara lit the fire-torch she'd brought along. Savita and Kishori walked briskly ahead while Tara and I followed, perhaps a score of paces behind them. When we finally reached the high road to Mandav uneventfully, we breathed a collective sigh of relief.

Well before that, however, Tara had returned my jibe from the previous day. When the two of us had fallen behind and out of earshot, I'd confided in Tara and told her all that had passed between me and Revadiya in the music sessions, so full of myself with his compliments that I whispered to Tara our conversations verbatim. That's where I went wrong!

Tara looked alarmed by what I'd told her. 'Beware, Ruup, take care that your Ustad doesn't get you with child, charming you with such compliments!' she said earnestly.

'What nonsense! So, you're getting your own back for what I said yesterday, aren't you?' I said gruffly.

'No, no! I'm telling you the truth. Revadiya used to take music lessons from an old hag, some songstress in a village across the river. Young women there simply swarmed and swooned around him, they say. I overheard Kishori's mother telling someone that many toddlers there have the same features as him...' She stopped midway, sensing that I was sceptical. I felt crushed and fell silent as well. I was sure that she was slandering Revadiya simply to get even with me. And yet I couldn't help wondering if all that she'd said might be true.

Once I'd arrived at the Garh though, there was hardly any time to think about it anymore!

Vision 17

It was two hours past sundown when I entered the Garh. My heartbeat rang in my ears: how would I explain returning so late if I ran into Ketki? My legs ached from walking briskly to avoid being inordinately late. And to top it all, I was depressed because of Tara trying to run down my Ustad.

I wondered whether Ketki would have looked for me at supper time. Probably not, for it was not the custom. I went down to the kitchen at mealtimes, unbidden. But who could tell for sure? She might just have sent Bhaunda to check on me. Anyhow, it was nearly time for dinner and I thought I would go straight to the kitchen when someone whispered urgently from behind a verandah pillar, 'Ruup, Jiji has been looking for you, come quickly! She asked me to find you earlier too, but I told her you had an upset stomach…no appetite.'

I came to a halt with a gasp. So, he had lied for my sake and now came to claim credit, but what could I say?

That night Rao ate dinner with us, and later, for a long time he kept asking questions on how my lessons with Pandijju were going, his arm lightly encircling my shoulders. He would ask questions and keep gazing at my face while I replied.

Ketki, standing some distance behind us, was looking daggers at me.

After a while, I went up to my room and lay down. The dull ache in my calves had crept up to my back and lower abdomen. Soon, it became so acute that I could barely suppress my sobs. What followed this was something no one had prepared me for; neither Ketki, nor any of my friends, nor any other woman in the community.

Later Ketki washed her hands off the matter, saying, 'Look, how on earth do you expect me to guide you when you choose to avoid my company?'

My lower garments were soaked wet by a sudden onset of

haemorrhaging. I was scared witless, but the idea of seeking help from a woman forever breathing fire was unacceptable to me. I did what occurred to me instinctively: tore up an old skirt and bandaged myself. At the break of dawn, I was at Tara's. Usually, it was she who came to the Garh. Although I knew which of the hutments her home was, I had neither been invited nor had ever visited before.

'Oh, it's you! Here, so early in the morning!' said Tara's mother, who opened the door, looking bewildered, not knowing what to do next. By then, Tara had appeared at her side and within moments she understood what had happened.

'Hadn't Ketki bai spoken to you about this?'

'What do you mean…? She didn't tell me anything,' I said.

'That this could happen anytime now, and that it will recur every month now onwards?' I stared at her, dumbfounded.

I felt low, with my back aching terribly and the haemorrhaging still on, but returned to the Garh, fuming at Ketki.

'Why didn't you tell me anything about it?' I said, seething with rage, quite forgetting to preface my question. Her look of surprise wasn't really out of place.

'Will you at least tell me first what you're talking about?' she said, matching my tone.

In any case, our exchange ended with Ketki putting the blame back on me, 'Well, well, when do you ever spend time with me for me to tell you about such things…'

Back in my room, I lay down on my bed and didn't get up for three whole days, not fasting like the last time, but still suffering intermittent bouts of helpless weeping. Only Tara would come and bring me some food from time to time. I never felt so orphaned, alone and helpless in my life as I did in the days that followed. I knew I had lost my mother forever, I didn't know even her name, background…nothing! I did call Rao 'Baba' but what could an orphan rescued from the river be but an adopted daughter. As for Ketki, I might as well have not existed. And Bhanwar—he was just Bhaunda. He probably liked me a good deal and wanted me to return his affection in kind. But Bhanwar! God help me!

Among my friends, Tara was close to my heart but she had vexed me to no end by casting that shadow of suspicion on my Ustad, whom I revered. That left me only Pandijju, his chest of books and discourses to keep my sanity unimpaired. And yes, I was quite forgetting the music that helped keep my soul humming.

Among musical instruments, I was partial to the been. I found it the most pleasing to the ear and loved playing it the best.

Vision 18

While the passing of time is indubitably uniform, variety rules our sense of its passage. If you're anxiously waiting for something or someone, an hour might feel like a whole year, like my longing to go to Ardhapadma again. Likewise, if the days are a joy and the nights even more so, a year might seem to have passed in the blink of an eye, like my first year with Baz!

We will only come to that after I'm done with the remainder of my life at Garh Dharmapuri.

Presently, I yearned to visit Ardhapadma again and spend more time in its serene solitude, perhaps even make some music there.

My mornings up until noontime were a breeze, with music sessions with Revadiya and Pandijju's lessons, but the rest of the day seemed to hang heavy as a millstone. My friends no longer came to the Garh as regularly as before. Perhaps they had begun their training for household chores. But now I knew for sure where Tara lived. Indeed I didn't feel as close to her as I used to, but I have to say that she was very affectionate to me. I had to plead with her, but she eventually agreed to go, and the other two never questioned her decisions.

That second time around, we left for Ardhapadma rather early in the day. Pandijju was in Ujjayini, and Revadiya out on some business. Before leaving I beckoned to Bhanwar to come closer. His jaws dropped and his face lit up. I whispered to him, 'I'm stepping out for a while with my friends, and I may be a bit late coming back. Can you manage it here, for me? You know what I mean, don't you?' He gave me a worried look, but after a moment nodded yes.

O, that magic of Ardhapadma Taal! It had an intoxicating effect on me.

My dear scribe, you'll never know what it was like to be there. The unceasing wheels of Time build things, and destroy them, too—forts and palaces, mountains and forests, lakes and rivers, everything! The Ardhapadma no longer exists. If you visit Mandav, you'll have to make do with the ruins of our fort and palaces alone.

Our second visit to Ardhapadma will remain etched in my memory forever. Truly, the moment we crossed the champa grove, looking at the lake full of those lovely lotus flowers, I sort of lost my balance for sheer joy. Or, perhaps the time of youth by itself is so magical that I had no control over myself.

I looked all around, scanning the foliage. No, there wasn't a soul in sight.

'Come on, get rid of your clothes, all of you. We will act out the scene in which Krishna steals the clothes of the gopis bathing. Put your things here on the overhanging branches. Let's find out if he will come for them!' I said, smiling crookedly.

'What…have you gone crazy?' Tara looked at me, her eyes narrowed; Savita and Kishori were aghast. After a moment, though, Tara said in a conspiratorial undertone, 'There will be hell to pay if anyone were to see us, mind you!' as though already reconsidering her initial reaction. Savita cleverly came up with our punchline for such occasions, 'I only hope it won't make us pregnant!' We all laughed so hard, there were tears in our eyes.

We did, however, bathe in the jade green waters of

Ardhapadma that day, soaking up the afternoon sun between dips and giggles, splashing water over one another and constantly looking over our shoulders to make sure that no intruder had crept up in that time. We made acquaintance with our changing bodies, the budding lotuses on our torsos and all.

Of course, Krishna did not appear, but the suspicion that someone might be watching from behind the foliage would not go away.

'I hope Bhaunda didn't follow us here, I saw you speak to him before we left,' Tara quipped sardonically. The slapping incident flashed through my mind, and my heart kind of lurched. Did he actually follow us? No, that wasn't possible. He'd expressly agreed to be at the Garh and cover for me. It was surely the inhibition of bathing in the nude that was making us imagine things.

Coming back, I kept noting the turns we took and the landmarks on the way, just in case I were to visit Ardhapadma on my own sometime, though it was hardly likely that I would ever venture so far out, all by myself.

Vision 19

Revadiya returned the next day and Pandijju the day after. My music sessions and lessons resumed.

By now I'd mastered several ragas. My Ustad patted my back, complimenting me on, what he said was, a flawless rendering of Bhairav, a raga meant to be sung in the morning. I can't say why, but I shrank at his touch, like a snail into its shell. Then, for a few weeks, he made me practise raga Kalyan and raga Maalkauns until I'd perfected them to his satisfaction. Revadiya was generous with his praise. He would keep saying things like, 'Wow! You're not merely talented, you're a genius. What wonderful grasp and memory you have!'

I was indeed pleased by his compliments and took pride

in my accomplishment, believing that he meant what he said, but I didn't let it show, keeping my head bowed humbly, and at times meekly suggesting, 'Ustad, don't you think it's time for us to play some instrument for a change?' He'd laugh pleasantly and say, 'I know you want to play the beenn! All right, go ahead.'

Pandijju was no less pleased with my progress. He was now more generous with discourses on poetry and aesthetics. I said to him one day, 'If you permit, I want to show you something I scribbled.'

Dear scribe, paper, pen and ink were hard to get hold of in our time. More often than not, we had to make do with dried leaves for paper, nibs cut out of hardened grass stems and ink made with kohl, stirred in water. It was only after I came to Mandav that I had the luxury of real paper and feathered quills. 'Certainly, carry on,' said Pandijju, encouragingly.

I proffered the leaf on which I had penned my first two dohas:

My paper is awash with tears,
And blotted by shaken ink,
And my pain-tortured mind forbids
Me to write or think.

You are the whole of life to me,
And separation from you is death:
Only the memory of your face
Keeps me drawing breath.

Pandijju looked a long time at the dohas, and then said with a smile, 'These are excellent. Are you sure you haven't picked them up from some book?'

As my face fell in embarrassment, he laughed and added, 'No, no, I was just joking, the dohas are very good. If you keep practising, you'll become a competent poetess someday.' He, too, patted my back, but I did not feel inhibited as I had when Revadiya had done so. Tara's words, it seemed, had driven home!

My days passed in music sessions and Pandijju's lessons, and an occasional walk in the woods, turning into weeks and months, and once again it was Navraatra time. The rituals in the Devi's temple were repeated as before, except that this time around Pandijju didn't invite me for the ceremonial meal like he had in the years gone by. I was replaced by Tara's younger sister. I couldn't figure out the exact reason but suspected it had something to do with my recent ordeal. Rao had also stopped seating me close to him or putting his arm around my shoulders. My childhood seemed to be slipping away farther and my previous life in the maulshri mansion turned hazier by the day.

I was growing up fast. In the last few months alone I had grown taller than Pandijju, my long legs looking like those of some awkwardly-tall animal species, but the tendency of people staring at me was becoming even more pronounced, and most of all, Bhanwar's jaw seemed to drop more often.

By and by, it dawned on me that I was no awkwardly-tall animal specimen, but an exceptionally beautiful, statuesque young woman and reasonably well-educated by the norms of the times as well as trained in raga and raginis. People were beginning to be both enchanted and awed by me. It is very likely that a degree of hauteur arising from my sense of my own beauty and accomplishments was beginning to take hold of me, though I wasn't conscious of it at the time. Nor did I have any idea of the immensity of misfortune that my beauty and talents were going to cause. I was immersed in myself; it was the heady sense of self-importance that adolescence brings with itself.

I reckon I was in my fourteenth year then, a year that would bring great anguish and turmoil as well as the pure joy of being someone special; a time when mysteries without count were to be suddenly laid bare in a cascade of silken veils. What a transformation awaited my life!

Vision 20

The hauteur induced in me by my beauty and intellectual refinement gradually began to make me feel even bolder. I thought that by merely glaring at someone, I could stop them in their tracks. No one could step up and dare to touch me; no man, no bandit, nor even a ferocious wild predator. I wasn't afraid of the woods anymore. I would step out at will, as though for a walk in the park. But Ardhapadma Taal…that was a bridge too far to cross alone!

I had to plead with my friends again, and the four of us went for another visit. This time we decided to take a dip in the holy waters of Reva, rather than the Ardhapadma. It wasn't far from the lake, just about five hundred paces by a rocky pathway that sloped through the foliage to the riverside.

On our way back that third time, we saw a panther walk regally across the path to the bushes on the other side, just a stone's throw from where we had stopped in our stride. Once again it was Tara who had spotted the danger, putting a finger to her lips and signalling us to stop and be quiet. Within moments, the panther had disappeared into the undergrowth not far from where we stood. The last time I was terror-stricken to see a snake but was now unafraid to see a beast up close. The pride I took in my newfound fearlessness had doubled. How could I have foreseen what a disaster my next trip to Ardhapadma was going to be?

Vision 21

Talking of different regions and places, Pandijju once told me that none could match the mornings of Benares nor the evenings of Oudh and the nights were nowhere better than in

Malwa. Truly, the beauty of nights in Malwa, particularly in autumn, is almost impossible to describe: the lush foliage after the copious monsoon rains, all varieties of flowers blooming in the wild with the moonlight seeming to dance a delicate turn, caressed by cool breezes blowing ever so lightly.

It was the night of Kartik Purnima, the autumn full moon. Revadiya was out again, and the early morning music sessions were on hold. On a sudden whim, I decided to sneak away to see the ethereal beauty of the Ardhapadma by moonlight. Ah! How elegant it would be to play the beenn sitting on the pavilion platform, the gleaming taal spread out before me and the heady mix of champa and lotus fragrances wafting through the night!

No sooner had the thought occurred than another voice inside broke out protesting, 'Have you gone crazy? You will walk into that deserted wilderness all by yourself, at night?' I knew I couldn't possibly persuade my friends to join this mad escapade in the middle of the night. I would have to do it alone.

After a brief struggle, the bolder part asserted itself, sneering, 'Come on, don't be such a coward, just come along and see what great fun it will be!'

I made up my mind. I would go and play my beenn at the taal by moonlight. I couldn't care less if a snake appeared, or the panther devoured me, or a rogue horseman kidnapped me. I will go, come what may!

As I was moving stealthily towards the storeroom to borrow a fire-torch, I saw Rao, sitting on his usual settee and Pandijju standing by him, aarti platter in hand. They seemed to be having some sort of an argument, and Rao instantly jumped at the chance to make a witness out of me. 'Did you hear what your guru is saying, Ruup?' he said in a tone steeped in consternation. 'I've never been able to understand why he is always intent on hurting our self-esteem by taking sides with the mlechchhas…look at him saying "Whoever wins the war is the king, no matter whether it is a Hindu or Mussalman!"'

'Rao, how can you talk of self-esteem when…' Pandijju

began a bit hotly, but he looked at me and checked his retort, then taking a deep breath, he resumed in a level tone, 'All I was saying was that men have killed one another for turf and territory from times immemorial, even before the very ideas of religion, community and caste were conceived! Why only blame the mlechchhas, didn't Hindu kings and emperors kill one another to satisfy their egos and build empires, before the infidels appeared on the scene? History is full of princes who killed brothers, even fathers and grandfathers, for the throne! How could we forget that the Mahabharata was fought in this very land, Rao? Wars have always been with us and will continue to be with us in the future as well. He who can slaughter most ruthlessly and come out victorious will be the ruler, whether he be an infidel or one of our own.'

'Still, Pandijju, it doesn't behove you to be singing paeans to mlechchha prowess, even by implication, after witnessing your father's beheading by a mlechchha's sword...' Rao fell silent abruptly, as though sensing that he had hit below the belt to win the argument.

'All right, Rao, it's time for my evening prayers...' Pandijju turned and left.

Stunned by the disagreement, I stood rooted to the ground. Rao looked at me, as though noting my presence afresh.

'Where were you headed at this hour?' he asked.

'Nowhere particular, Baba,' I replied diffidently, acutely aware of my clandestine designs. Rao patted a place on the settee a little away from where he sat. 'Come, sit. I have to tell you something,' he said. Suddenly his tone had turned serious. I sat down tremulously wondering what had made him so grave.

'I've sent a formal offer of your hand in marriage to Chittorgarh. It's been my dream to have you wedded to a prince of that line. Remember, you're a big girl now. Take care not to be wandering around all the time. Do you understand what I'm saying?'

I was alarmed, suddenly overwhelmed with anxiety. As

much as it was a small little fortress going to seed, Garh Dharmapuri had by now started to feel like home. Chittor, I knew a bit about it from Pandijju's history lessons. It was a mighty fort some three hundred kos to the north, the seat of the Rana of Mewar. The very same where Rani Padmini had jumped into the fire and committed jauhar to escape the clutches of Alauddin Khilji, and whose Ranas had fought with the rulers of Malwa for centuries, whether Hindu or Mussalman, for regional hegemony. Baba would send me to an unknown man there! My heart quaked at the thought. For a moment I seemed to have lost my voice, and just sat there with my head bowed. Rao, too, was silent, perhaps not even expecting a reply. I felt weighed down by the uncomfortable silence hanging in the air, then my instinctive curiosity took over, 'Baba, what was it you said about Pandijju's father being beheaded right in front of him? Was it…' I fell silent again. My eyes had misted, perhaps as much from Pandijju's misfortune as from the anxiety about my own future.

'Ah yes, that! Pandijju himself gave me the details of that gruesome incident soon after he came to Malwa a long time ago,' said Rao.

Vision 22

Rao narrated to me the story of Pandijju's boyhood and his flight from Mithila to Malwa in such great detail that it was nearly midnight by the time he finished. My yearning for a glimpse of Ardhapadma by moonlight was practically gone even before I got hold of the torch from the store.

The story itself was fascinating, though, in a macabre sort of way.

'Your Guruji is not an original inhabitant of Malwa. He was brought here as a brahmin boy orphaned in distressing circumstances, and in desperate need of asylum. He never returned to Mithila, where he came from. You know where that is, don't you?' Rao said.

'Yes, while telling the story of Ramayana, Pandijju had mentioned that it is six or seven hundred kos to the north-east in the southern foothills of the Himalayas,' I replied.

'Yes, the very same. Mithila, the kingdom of Raja Janak in ancient times, had a great tradition of Sanskrit learning and Shakti worship—Devi Kali. Pandijju was born in a village by the name of Singhdwar, on the southern border of Mithila, and lived there for the first ten years of his life before coming to Garh Dharmapuri. I wonder if you even know his formal name: Sankarshan Sharman. You might find his first name rather strange, it's one of the thousand names of Lord Vishnu.

'Pandijju's father, Chakradhar Sharman, was a profound scholar of various disciplines of Sanskrit like Vyakaran, Jyotish and Darshan, and was also young Sankarshan's guru. There were only the two of them, Pandijju's mother having died soon after his birth. By the time Pandijju was ten, his father had passed on all his knowledge and erudition to young Sankarshan. But then they had to suddenly flee Singhdwar, you see.

'By then Bang-des and Mithila had been captured by the forces of the Delhi sultanate, and the orders of the mullahs accompanying the army to the Hindu populace were clear: either convert to Islam or prepare for summary execution. People by the thousands converted to save their lives or fled into jungles of the Himalayan foothills to the north. Those who converted under duress usually continued to venerate their Hindu deities at heart for a long, long time, while also offering namaaz according to their new faith. Married women went on wearing the vermilion mark in the parting of the hair, under their veil, and secretly observing Hindu customs and fasts while celebrating Eid and other Muslim festivals alongside.

'One dark night it was the turn of Singhdwar. Heavily armed soldiers surrounded the village. They had wised up to the easy escape routes by then and were determined to show the kafirs that they were no fools. The routes leading to the forested areas in the north were hermetically sealed by a heavy deployment of troops. If you decided to run, it could only be southward, where, if fate spared you from drowning in the eddying currents of the Ganga, hordes of sultanate soldiers waited across the river to get at you. Most Singhdwar residents surrendered, accepting to go through the motions of reciting the kalma to save their lives.

'But to the conscientious Chakradhar Sharman, the idea of a dishonest, dual life under false pretences was unacceptable. He had few worldly possessions, little more than a few bags of dusty clothes, some books and a walking staff. He picked them up, and leading the boy by his finger, he fled Singhdwar in the dark of the night.

'Chakradhar was nothing if not canny. He knew that if they went south, they would run into soldiers and be put to the sword. He walked a kos to the east, before turning to cross the river Budhnad that lay to the south of the village, at a spot he reckoned to be deserted. It was so dark that he could barely see his own hands. How could he know that the narrow stream ran red with the blood of fleeing men slaughtered upstream! As he emerged out of chest-high waters on the other side, carrying little Sankarshan astride his shoulders, his body looked as though he had been through a blood bath.

'As he moved ahead after a few moments to catch his breath, he ran into two men barring their passage. Only wielding laathis by way of weapon and rather tentative with their challenge, they clearly were not regular soldiers, but as Pandijju senior tried to pass them, a scuffle of sorts took place in the dark. "Whoever you are, aren't you ashamed of manhandling a brahmin for no reason? I just have to utter a shraap and you'd be doomed for seven lifetimes to come, mind you!" Chakradhar Sharman knew well that there was no mention in the scriptures of such a curse, but he played the conman to the hilt with an indignant shout. Suddenly the grappling of the strangers was stilled, they hurriedly let go of his arm. "Pandijju…is that you?" the voice was tremulous with fear. The two soldiers bent down to touch his feet. "Who are you?… Oh, Mahendra…and Shravan! What on earth are you two up to?" Then it dawned on him how they came to be there, and he ended up his question with just a whispered "O…!"

'The two boys were already grovelling to be forgiven, "Pa… pa…Pandijju, what could we do? There was no other way to save our lives and as soon as it was done, they put us on guard duty here. Please spare our souls from damnation, Pandijju, carry on wherever you're going," one of them said, and both of them bent again to take his blessings. "Go in peace, may you have the blessings of Mother Goddess!"

'Father and son walked for two whole nights, passing their days hidden in ditches, covered in tall grass and thistle, afraid of running into troops combing the countryside for fugitives, trying to forget that they were hungry and thirsty beyond measure, for there was not a soul they could ask for succour in the small hamlets on the less travelled paths they chose. Villages were deserted, corpses of people executed swaying from the branches of banyan or peepul trees, regarded holy by the Hindus. Even the normally stoic senior Pandijju was unable to keep his emotions under control. Tears flowed from his eyes at the devastation. He would tell the boy to shut his eyes when they happened upon a particularly gory sight, but there were so many of them, how long could he possibly keep his eyes closed! In the small hours of the third night, the two of them reached the north bank of the Ganga. After performing their rituals and morning pooja on the riverbank and seeking the blessings of the holy river, they began to look for some fisherman who could ferry them across. There was no one in sight. A long frustrating wait followed, but eventually, at the far end of the riverside, they spotted a fisherman with a small boat.

'"Will you take us across? If you'll put us down on a deserted jetty on the other side, I'm prepared to give you a whole silver crown," offered Chakradhar Sharman.

'The boatman looked reluctant. Perhaps the amount offered was too meagre, senior Pandijju thought, but he had no more money on him, and he told him so. Eventually, the man agreed.

'When they got off on the other side, they found a large contingent of sultanate soldiers swarming across the place. The boatman stood with his head bowed, like a guilty man before a judge. It was clear that he had betrayed them under duress. As the mounted soldiers tied the hands of the brahmin and his boy and prepared to ride back to the garrison, Chakradhar Sharman whispered to him, "I can sense your helplessness! Go in peace, I absolve you of the Brahma-hatya, sin of a brahmin's murder!" The boy cried out bewildered, "What Brahma-hatya are you talking about?"

'The horses trotted to the Patna Fort, not far from the riverbank, the captives walking behind them. They were incarcerated in a dungeon underneath the ramparts. The stench of human waste was so foul that it was a miracle they could breathe at all! They were given no food for three days and water barely enough to survive. Although the two of them were used to the rigours of fasting, they had no previous experience of walking such great distances, taking in the horrific sights on the way, and being tied up and dragged behind horses. Both lay comatose, all but dead at the end of the third day, when they were summoned to the presence of the deputy kotwal. A tall, barrel-chested mullah in a flowing white robe stood behind the deputy, prayer beads dangling from his fingers. The deputy himself reclined on a settee, his back resting on a velvet-clad bolster and his sword in its scabbard lying on a side table.

'"Take off your damned threads, wipe that mark off your forehead and recite the kalma, and I'll spare your lives," the deputy growled.

'Chakradhar Sharman said nothing.

'"Can't he hear…is this kafir deaf?" the deputy kotwal shouted.

'Still, the brahmin remained mute. The boy beside him, only half-conscious, was shaking like a twig in a gusty wind. It seemed that any moment his knees would give way and he would crash to the ground.

'"Aijaz, you take his thread off and wipe that goddamn

tilak off his forehead," the deputy, seething with anger, shouted a command to the soldier standing by. As the soldier moved to comply, Chakradhar Sharman, no less imposing a figure than the soldier—tall, robust, with a broad forehead—held up his hand, palm in front, to stop him. Breaking his silence, he addressed the deputy kotwal, "No, Amir, he may do no such thing. Do what you will, I'll follow my conscience."

'"What did the pathetic brahmin say? He has the cheek..." The deputy's face was a flaming red with outrage. Suddenly he sprang to his feet with the agility of a leopard, his sheathed sword held in his left hand. Shoving aside the unnerved soldier, he gnashed his teeth, "You get out of the way... I'll take care of this myself." Striding forward, he made to grab at the brahmin's sacred threads. Chakradhar turned his upheld palm towards the kotwal, and the kotwal's fist landed on it with a thump.

'"Did I not tell you, Amir? I won't let it happen. Think of what you want to do next," said the brahmin with quiet determination.

'The deputy kotwal had never seen such defiance before. No one present could later remember when he lost his patience, what he said, or when he drew the sword out of the scabbard. It all happened in a flash. All they could recall was seeing the decapitated head of the brahmin rolling on the ground. Only the wide-eyed boy would recall every detail as long as he lived, as though it had all taken place in slow motion. He even remembered what the deputy had said before swinging his sword, "It's pointless to argue with a kafir as wretched as this!" The sword whistled through the air, the headless body came crashing to the ground like a felled tree, the severed neck sprouting jets of blood that splashed the faces of Aijaz and the boy, and continued to flutter and splutter before finally falling still. Mercifully, the boy was spared these later details. As he saw his father's head falling, he fell with a banshee wail suddenly cut short by loss of consciousness.

'The deputy kotwal returned to his settee and sat down, breathing heavily and muttering under his breath, the sword dripping blood. He casually put his hand out, and taking a piece of maroon rag proffered by his valet, started carefully wiping his sword, the beheading seemingly no more significant than the usual disposal of a petty case brought before him. Suddenly he shouted menacingly, "Take this wretch's head and hang it at the fort wall and clean up this ungodly mess here." The mullah, who had obviously been summoned to administer the kalma, emitted a throaty "Al…laaah!" that sounded like an echo from a deep, dark well, and retreated through a door behind him. A bunch of soldiers touched their fists to their chests and began carrying out the deputy's command.

'"Wh…what shall we do with…th…the boy, Amir?" stammered Aijaz, in a hoarse whisper.

'"Do? What in hell do you mean, *do*? Take him to the Maulvi. If he regains consciousness, have him read the kalma, and if he's dead, just bury him somewhere!" barked the deputy.

'Aijaz miyaan, himself a recent convert, had kneeled and taken the kalma no more than a few months ago. Domraj Rameshwar of Benares in his previous avatar, he had been a devotee of Lord Vishwanath, prostrating to the shrine fervently every morning and evening, but from a distance. Being an untouchable, he was not allowed to enter the precincts. Even now, he heard the temple bells tolling in his dreams, and after incidents like the one he had just witnessed, he instinctively murmured "Hey Shiva! Hey Shiva!" Even as he picked up the unconscious boy, he was praying silently, "O Mahadeva! I had no hand in this Brahma-hatya! You're omniscient my Lord, you'd have seen it all! Please don't condemn me to the fires of hell!"

'Trembling in mortal fear, as Aijaz came out of the deputy kotwal's chamber with the boy in his arms, he took a quick look around and heaved a sigh of relief. There was no one in sight. He slipped into an alley, then through a dark hovel into another one. A maze of bylanes later, he was still praying, "My Lord, guide me… What do I do with this poor boy? He is a brahmin too; I noticed the sacred thread on him."

'He was thinking hard, "If I could save his life and faith, maybe the sin of my association with the mlechchha would be forgiven, my soul saved from eternal damnation!"

'Just then, he recalled having heard of a band of defeated soldiers from Malwa hiding in the ruins of an old mansion and waiting for a chance to head home if they got lucky. They had come hoping to join forces with the Hindu resistance of the Magadhans against sultanate troops. It hardly mattered now that they had ridden roughshod and ruled over Malwa long ago. There was no denying the fact that the Magadhans were great warriors.

'The band of Malwa soldiers hiding at Patna had gone to Magadh that night in high spirits, but for once fortune did not favour the brave. During their very first engagement with the sultanate troops, their commander had suffered a deep arm wound that never healed. For three days and nights, he lay in high fever, septicemia eating into his vitals, and on the fourth, it took Rao away. Yes, Ruupmati, my father died at Patna. I am reminded of it after a long time, recounting the story of Pandijju's escape to you. I was here at the time. I didn't even have the privilege of giving him his last rites.' Rao's voice was suddenly choked with emotion.

'You can easily guess what followed. When Pandijju arrived here, he would have been about ten or twelve. I myself was eighteen then. He was in trauma after seeing the awful beheading of his father. He didn't utter a word for almost a month. He would only look around, his eyes glazed, like a mentally challenged child's, stupid and illiterate.'

And what of me, I thought to myself bitterly. Even I had gone mute after being brought out of the river. Did that not count for anything? Indeed, I was illiterate, but was I also stupid? I seethed with an inextricable sense of resentment, for I loved Pandijju like a father I had never had.

'Once Pandijju rediscovered his tongue, we realized how knowledgeable he was. We at the Garh had wanted a pandit of his sort, and over time he became one of us. All right, enough of him for now. Go, get some rest. And yes, do not forget what I told you before,' Rao said, getting up to retire for the night.

Vision 23

It was past midnight by the time Rao had finished, and his curfew weighed me down. I was beginning to doubt whether it was a good idea to go out at all. But I guess I was made stubborn, not to be deterred from a decision once made.

When I was sure everyone was asleep, I tiptoed down to the store, got hold of the fire-torch, quickly made a makeshift carry bag for my beenn, and left with it slung over my shoulder.

The high road to Mandav was bathed in bright moonlight. The torch was not needed. But a hundred steps down the jungle path, as I stopped to rub the flint, my fingers shook from a mix of plain fear and the excitement of my mad expedition. It only took a few moments perhaps to get the fire-torch going, but it felt like an hour. Then I began to walk briskly.

It took me an hour to get to Ardhapadma. As I emerged out of the ring of champa trees, the view simply took my breath away. It was an unforgettable sight, a moment of pure ecstasy. One half of the lake shimmering in the moonlight was spread out like a wrinkled sheet of black silk embroidered with silver threads, and the other half was packed with lotuses, each flower standing out in focus. The pavilion and the treeline beyond it stood shrouded in a light mist. One could distinctly hear dewdrops pattering on fallen leaves, but besides the call of peacocks somewhere far, the forest was eerily quiet. It was, to be honest, a bit intimidating, but deeply moving. I stood mesmerized for the longest time, taking in the beauty of the tranquil lake and then began to walk slowly to the pavilion.

As I prepared to sit down on the stone settee, something seemed to move underneath, like something slithering through dry leaves. A snake! Revadiya's warning flashed through my mind. Don't ever play on the beenn in deserted ruins or the forest. Contrary to common belief, it's not only the snake charmer's beenn that attracts vipers, but the stringed beenn as well. But I hadn't even begun playing yet! I hastily lowered the torch to look down, but there was nothing there.

I put my feet up, though, to sit cross-legged on the tablet, but even before I had taken my beenn out, there was a sudden rustling noise, now in the foliage to the far left, as though a sudden gust of wind had passed through it.

By now, my daredevil expedition was beginning to turn a trifle sour. I no longer wanted to play on the beenn! Maybe some other time, I told myself. Yet, my rebellious streak refused to be denied altogether. Now that you have come all this way, at least sing a few strains of raga Bhairav!

I started hesitantly, fearing my voice would break from sheer nerves, but it came out loud and clear, and perfectly in tune, echoing in the silence of the night. Entranced by my own voice, I lost track of the time for a while. I was beginning to feel relaxed now, my hauteur resurfacing. I don't give a damn if someone hiding behind the bushes has been watching me. Poor man doesn't have the guts to show himself to me! I've done what I wanted, to hell with the consequences! It was an exhilarating thought. I laughed out aloud.

But then as I lifted my head, I saw that the moon had sunk low, hanging like a golden orb above the treeline. It was time to go.

It was nearly dawn by the time I reached the Garh entrance. Thank God, I thought, my music teacher is away, I can sleep in till late. I stretched myself languidly, suppressing a yawn, and moved towards my room.

Vision 24

The door was ajar, throwing an oblong of murky light on the floor outside. All of a sudden, my confidence evaporated, and my heart jumped right into my mouth. What was this now? I had put out the lamp before leaving. My room should have been dark! Had Rao seen through me and was waiting for me to return, to catch me red-handed, so to say? How on earth could I face him after his recent warning? I would very likely drop dead the very moment I saw him! Or was it Ketki lying in wait? It must be Ketki, I tried to reassure myself, for Rao had bid me goodnight and gone towards his room. Bhanwar must somehow have seen me leaving, and told Ketki, who was waiting to confront me. Would she let go, as usual, after some sarcastic jibes, or make a big ruckus, wake up people? Indeed, I had been out the whole night, as she would put it. Let it be her though, not Rao, please God!

I stood at the door for what seemed an eternity, my mind swirling with dreadful scenarios. After a while, I regained some of my lost composure, the same feeling coming to my rescue. What I had to do is done, to hell with consequences now! I pushed the shutter open. Bhanwar sat on the edge of my bed, looking intently at the door, perhaps having sensed I was about to enter.

I was appalled by the intrusion into my private space! Despite my trepidation which I'd barely got over, I felt a wave of cold consternation wash over me. My haughtiness returned with a vengeance. Screwing up my eyes, I asked him archly, 'You! What are *you* doing in my room?'

'Ruup, you…you…shouldn't be doing…all this,' he said stammering, looking at me unblinkingly all the while.

'What shouldn't I…' I began, then leaving the rhetorical question unfinished, I said even more crossly, 'Never mind! First, you tell me what you're doing here? How dare you? If Rao were to find out—' He cut in to finish my thinly veiled threat for me.

'If Rao finds out, it will be very bad, Ruup!' It was clear from his conspiratorial tone, though, that he wasn't taking advantage of me, but merely advising me in an effort to help. It suddenly dawned on me that he hadn't only seen me going out, he'd also followed me all the way to Ardhapadma, and taking a short cut on the way back, was waiting for me. He must have been the rustling I had heard in the bushes. I guessed he hadn't told anyone about my escapade, and didn't mean to either. Nonetheless, I was aghast that he had practically risked his life venturing out into the forest at night, without even a torch. Why would he do something so silly?

But my confidence was now fully restored. Instead of listening to his counsel, I started to chide him, 'Bhanwar, why did you have to come after me, risking your life? And now, all this drama, "Ruup, this, Ruup, that!"' He seemed about to say something, but I held up my hand and continued, 'Go on, you tell me, what's wrong in what I did? I went to the lake, sat for a while in the pavilion there, singing a few strains of the Bhairav, that's it! Go and tell everyone, if that will make you feel good.' I heard my voice come out like a petulant child's.

Actually, I wanted him to admit in so many words that he'd followed me and hadn't yet reported on me. For the first time ever, I saw his mouth closed and eyes lowered.

'Now, will you say something?' I persisted.

'Ruup, I did follow you because you might have been at grave risk, alone in the jungle at night... I...I...' Then it seemed as though his voice had failed him, or his thoughts gone off at a tangent.

At that moment, I knew I held him in my thrall!

I stepped up to him, and taking hold of his wrist, I placed his palm on my head. He gasped, as though touched by red-hot iron. Then I said coolly, 'Now take an oath on my head that you'll never again follow me. I only need your friendship, not your patronage. Look at me! Do you understand?'

As he raised his eyes, I could see they were beginning to shine with tears held back. Looking him in his eyes, I reiterated, 'Swear by me that you'll never risk your life for my sake, and then we can be friends.'

'I swear by you…' he trailed off as if he couldn't bear to go on. He gently withdrew his wrist from my hold, turned and left, but not before I had seen his eyeballs film over with a deep sense of loss. He hadn't refused to take the oath on my head though, I thought, almost congratulating myself.

Little did I know at the time, that such oaths could spin back like a boomerang in no time!

Vision 25

As I opened my eyes the next morning and looked to the window, I knew it was at least a couple of hours after daybreak. A gust of cool autumn breeze came rushing in. Recalling the events of the previous night, I felt as though something that might have been a bittersweet memory had turned into a nightmare. I had taken advantage of Bhanwar and had manipulated him into taking the oath. I didn't know that I had a streak of cunning in me, and knowing that I had one was not a good feeling. Some part of me kept arguing though, 'What if I am a little devious? Making him promise that he would not meddle in my business in the future was not such a big deal, was it?'

But still, I felt uneasy about the way I had gone about it. A meek voice kept repeating from a corner inside me, 'Ruup, you aren't a good-hearted person. You may be good-looking and bright, but you have a devious mind.'

When I'd had enough of introspection, I shook myself out of it, admitting candidly that I was cunning and devious. If I were not, how on earth would I survive this cruel world and its wicked ways?

My dear scribe, you would probably know what our

times were like. Any well-muscled thug, who could muster a following of a hundred armed horsemen, could merrily run around causing mayhem to set up his own fiefdom. He could kill, rape and abduct at will. A dark shadow of uncertainty lurked in every corner. No one could tell when a ruthless bandit might become king, and continue to behave like the villain he had been, even after being crowned. Given the nature of the times we lived in, a bit of cunning was essential to self-preservation.

It was only after I had silenced the voices at odds within myself that I heard the loud laments coming from the courtyard. At first, I thought it was a group of women singing something that sounded terribly off-key. Then I realized they weren't singing at all. They were wailing, with a hubbub in the background. My heart lurched. I rushed down to the courtyard, taking the stairs in twos. A large gathering of the Garh community, men and women, stood whispering, their faces ashen, around a woman lying prone on the ground and other women bending over her, seemingly trying to revive her by sprinkling water. The chorus of wailing sounds had stopped. Rao sat on his settee, bent forward with his forehead in his palms.

I moved towards them to have a closer look, trembling. Oh my, it was Tara's mother lying unconscious on the ground! Savita and Kishori stood behind the women trying to bring her around, sobbing inconsolably, covering their mouth in their dupatta. There was no sign of Tara around! What had happened?

And a thunderbolt struck!

'Tara! O, my mother… Tara's gone, Ruup,' said Savita miserably, before her speech was chocked by a fresh bout of sobbing.

'Tara… What happened to Tara?' I was stunned.

Suddenly Rao stood up, his eyes red as hot coals.

'Leave! All of you can leave now,' he said in an anguished voice. 'Take her home and try to revive her. Come, Kalu, we'll not rest until we find her, and then we'll kill the dog.' He put his arm around Kaluram's shoulders, trying to comfort him. Tears flowed from Kaluram's eyes incessantly.

'What good is a search now, Rao? My Tara's gone!' Rao's affectionate gesture was making Kaluram hiccup even more audibly. Rao led him towards his private apartment inside. Some women carried away Tara's mother, still unconscious, with the help of some young men. The gathering melted away soon.

Traditionally, from ancient times, a large annual fair was held around the Omkaareshwar jyotirlinga temple on Kartik Purnima. Thousands of devotees thronged the shrine for darshan and a dip in the holy waters of river Shipra. In our time, the Omkaareshwar fair was infamous for such incidents. The rulers of Gujarat and other neighbouring states were so envious of Malwa's prosperity, that the tiniest lapse in security resulted in enemy horsemen, disguised as bandits, swooping down on the fair from across the borders. Hundreds would be killed or maimed in the stampede it invariably caused. The villains would loot and snatch before vanishing as quickly as they had appeared.

The retreating horsemen often pulled up young women on to their mounts and made away with them as part of the loot. They didn't need to even silence their prey with iron fists. Who would hear their screams amid a shrieking melee!

Tara's nani, her mother's mother, had planned to visit the fair and had sent word to her daughter and granddaughter to join her there. Tara's mother had gathered a small group from Dharmapuri and gone. After the raid at Omkaareshwar, everyone had searched endlessly for Tara, but she was nowhere to be found.

Ah…Tara, the dearest of my friends! Lost forever!

For some time, I almost went mad with grief, thinking all the time that some cruel monster must have been snatching Tara as I sat gazing at the Ardhapadma, singing the Bhairav.

Life was never the same again without Tara to keep me company, nor could I ever forget what she had meant to me.

Vision 26

Tara's disappearance had a rather unexpected impact on my psyche. I turned bolder rather than apprehensive.

I cannot quite put into words how anguished I was to have lost my best friend. It seemed as though something very tender inside me had shrivelled and dried. With the greatest of efforts, I eventually found some solace in Pandijju's maxim that each one of us has a destiny cut out even before one is born, something that none of us can escape. Everyone must carry out their karma. My mother, if she survived the night I was kidnapped and is still alive, must be carrying out hers somewhere. Tara must be passing her days somehow, being mauled by some brute without relief. And so, I too must live out my prison term in this desolate Garh. If I'm destined to be kidnapped by yet another villain or devoured by a predator while roaming the forest, so it shall be. There's no doubt that Pandijju's lessons had shaped my thinking, for he would often repeat between lessons, 'If someone's able to circumvent bad karma by his or her effort, then the success of such effort is what was destined. That's why we must strive to take the right path, but knowing well that, eventually, it is God's will that shall prevail.'

My feeling of loneliness became intense after Tara's disappearance. I saw so little of Savita and Kishori now that they might have disappeared as well. Apart from talking with Pandijju and Revadiya during my lessons, whatever little conversation I had was solely with Bhanwar. Yes, I had stopped thinking of him as Bhaunda, or Bhaunra even. At every turn where I'd suspected him of spying on me, he had actually been trying to help me out. Of course, I still had nothing for him in return for the feelings I suspected he harboured for me. And perhaps, there was also the thought of him being a relative of mine, considering Pandijju had asked me to treat Rao and Ketki as my foster parents.

My biggest worry at the time, however, was what Rao had said about the proposal that was sent to Chittor. Truth be told, the mere thought of it made me feel sick with dread. God alone knows what millstone of a princeling would be tied to my neck! What if he turns out to be a head shorter than I, and stocky, mouth always open, like Bhanwar's? Is the golden lotus of my beauty destined for an ugly duckling? I would be consumed by extreme anxiety. The more I thought of preventing brooding over such possibilities, the more I did.

I tried my best not to let my mind ramble. I'd sit for hours in the music pavilion trying out different instruments and ragas, even when Revadiya wasn't there. After Pandijju's lesson was over, I'd take out books from his chest and keep turning pages at random. I'd compose poems and dohas. If time still hung heavy, I would walk straight out to Ardhapadma Taal.

Time simply flew when I was strolling around that little piece of heaven on earth. Didn't I say earlier? Time feels like a load of stone if you're anxious, but light as a feather if you're enjoying yourself.

I went to the Ardhapadma so many times in those few months, I lost count of the visits. So often, in fact, that I began to feel that I could reach there blindfolded, without missing a step.

What I'm about to recount now, my dear scribe, would perhaps make you wonder how I could possibly lose my way with my eyes wide open, and in broad daylight too!

Vision 27

In my later years, I often thought, had I not become so obsessed with Ardhapadma Taal, my life would not have been so complicated, but then it would not have been so dramatically exciting either! It was most likely that I would have lain suffocating in the embrace of some Bhanwar lookalike prince in a gloomy chamber of Chittor. How could any prince ever have the style and charm, and the musical genius, to match my Baz? He was one of a kind.

The day I'm talking of, I was on the right path until after crossing the grassy vale full of deer. I've no idea when, lost in the fragrance of champa and humming some tune, I took an entirely unfamiliar jungle track. By the time I realized I'd taken a wrong turn, I was woefully lost and found myself walking an undulating ridge that surrounded a flat valley sans forest. As I looked down, I was stunned by what lay before my eyes.

It was an unbelievably bizarre sight. The valley ringed by the ridge was a sort of flat oval, somewhat like an arena, that might not have been visible from anywhere but the ridge. On one side of the oval was a row of single-storey barracks. Horses were tethered in most of its cubicles while a few looked like small enclosed rooms. Directly in front of the barracks was a dais about two arm's lengths high, with a stone settee, and on that—I was looking down from a considerable height, and it took me a while to recognize him with certainty—sat Rao, except that he was not the Rao I was used to seeing ordinarily. He was wearing a gold-bordered dhoti, a fresh orange-coloured angrakhaa that looked expensive, and a golden crown set with precious-looking stones that glinted in the afternoon sun. That wasn't all. He sported a long sword in a finely filigreed golden scabbard, hanging down the side of his waist. His face glowed. He looked like someone acting the part of king in a stage play. On either side of him stood Kaluram and Revadiya, like royal aides, both alert and servile at once. The rest of the oval in front of the dais was dotted by circular pits filled with sand, in which young lads and men of the Dharmapuri community, who went out shepherding every day, were practising fencing skills. In one of the pits some of them were wrestling bare-bodied. Much as I found it hard to believe, there was no denying it that they were indeed local lads.

This was enough to leave me astonished, and yet this was just the beginning!

A few moments later, Rao held up his hand, palm open outward, as though to signal the end of the martial arts practice session, like a king might do, to silence his court. The young contestants all made a beeline to the podium, touched Rao's feet, and stood in neat rows on its sides.

Revadiya bent down and whispered something into his ear. Of course, I couldn't hear what he said, but it had to have been confidential and serious, for Rao's face was instantly creased by a frown. I still had a funny feeling that they were enacting a play to amuse themselves. I nearly laughed thinking of it all as a mime!

The proof of how terribly mistaken I was didn't take long.

As soon as Revadiya's whispered report had been made, Rao waved his fingers in a hand gesture that royals might use for courtiers to carry on further proceedings. Presently, two soldiers emerged from one of the enclosed cabins behind the dais with a captive, bound hand and foot by a thick cord, leading him by another tied to his waist, and then shoved him so hard that he fell to his knees in front of the podium, palms joined together as though begging for mercy. Rao said something to him, his eyes screwed and face distorted by anger. The exchange between the two of them continued for about a quarter of an hour, the pleading prisoner beginning to weep evidently seeking forgiveness, and Rao's expression of anger turning even more intense. Finally, after a whispered consultation with Revadiya, he made another royal sign used when sentencing people to be punished.

The two soldiers jerked at the rope, dragging the prisoner away towards one of the pits, where, I noticed, someone had placed a chopping block sawn out of a thick tree trunk. To my absolute horror, one of the soldiers forced down the struggling prisoner's head on it, like Revadiya used to hold the goat-kid during Navraatra. The other soldier whipped out his sword, and the very next moment that pleading man's severed head rolled out in the sand, the first soldier holding on to the beheaded body until the spasmodic fluttering had ebbed and stopped.

I didn't get to see what happened next as an irrepressible surge of vomit forced me to turn and throw up violently in the shrubs behind. Tears flowed from my eyes, blurring vision into total darkness. I rose to my feet and ran, without quite knowing where I was going. It was a wonder that my feet found their way back, blindly, as it were. Dusk was falling as I reached the Garh. I reached my room and collapsed on the bed, distraught and terrified.

If it was a play they had been performing, surely the dramatis personae deserved to be complimented on their acting skills!

Vision 28

I couldn't sleep a wink that night. My mind was in a turmoil—who were these people I was living out my days with? Were these men in dusty clothes, rough cloth-turbans and rustic shoes merely disguised as shepherds? What about these tough men practising warfare and martial arts, what of the man playing ruler and sentencing another to death? Was it a play being enacted? Which one of the facets was real? Or, were both the facades part of a deeper mystery?

I thought long and hard but failed to make any sense of it. Whatever be the reality, I was filled with an abominable distaste and horrified by the recurring images of the poor man pleading for mercy and his decapitated head rolling on the ground. They left me with goosebumps all over, time and again.

It was pointless asking questions. No one would even acknowledge that such a thing had happened in the first place. Further, how would I ever explain my presence in the middle of nowhere, so far away from the Garh? No, I wasn't going to get any answers by asking the Garh inhabitants! There was no alternative other than waiting and watching for what the future held.

I'm telling you all of this in such detail because I want you to understand what was going on in my mind at the time: the extent of my disorientation and my misgivings about the true identity of the community I lived in, and more importantly, the terrible feeling of being all alone.

My past was all but faded, and my present was shrouded in such mystery that I could not identify with anyone at all, except for Pandijju. Although I was sure of his guileless transparency, I did not expect him to be very forthcoming as to who was who!

My future did not appear very rosy, either. At times, I would find myself yearning for Rao's proposal to the Chittor royals to come through. It would, at the very least, take me away from the mysterious miasma of Garh Dharmapuri.

But like I said, everyone must go through their karma, good or bad and I was not destined to be betrothed to some minor Chittor princeling. The fate-line on the palm of my hand, faint and brief though it was, had Baz Bahadur's name writ large over it.

Vision 29

Distracted by the suspicion that someone hidden behind the foliage was watching me, I had been unable to play my beenn at the Ardhapadma pavilion that fateful night of Kartik Purnima. But in the weeks and months that followed, I went there often, and sat playing, trying out ragas for hours on end. I had, by then, acquired such mastery over the beenn that I could play the most complex of ragas on it. Eyes shut in concentration, I would dive deep down into the nuances of the raga, caring little for Revadiya's frequent warning against serpents. There had been no serpent so far to listen to my beenn, but I admit to swaying like a naagin—a female snake—to my own melody.

So many times did I repeat the routine that I began to have a sense of ownership of the Ardhapadma pavilion, as though someone had built and bequeathed the lake, the pavilion, the stone settee, all of it to me.

When my perturbed mind failed to find peace amidst the recurring images of Rao playing king and sentencing the prisoner to death, my instinct took me to Ardhapadma once again that day, only to find a huge surprise awaiting me there.

As the pavilion came into sight, I saw a male figure sitting and playing on a stringed instrument. It would have made sense for me to beat a hasty retreat, but my hauteur took hold of me instead. This place is mine, how can anyone else usurp it!

Without as much as a second thought, I walked to the front of the pavilion, and stood with my fists at my hips, waiting to confront the intruder.

Yes, I had to wait. Like me, he was immersed in his music with his eyes shut and somehow it didn't seem right to interrupt him. The fingers of one hand strummed the string of the tambura while those of the other rapidly shuffled over the stem modulating the rise and fall of the notes, his head swaying and nodding to keep time.

He must have been in his mid or late twenties, I guessed, fair pink complexion, a beautifully hooked nose, and sensuously full lips. I hadn't seen his eyes yet, but I had to admit, albeit a bit grudgingly, that the fellow was handsome. He had on a kamkhaab angrakhaa the colour of rust and beige silk pyjamas, with a dagger, stuck into the folds of his cummerbund. A reddish-brown thoroughbred stood tied to one of the rear pillars of the pavilion. From his looks, attire and accoutrement, it looked as though he belonged to a noble family. He was playing competently enough, I thought and instantly corrected myself. 'He isn't playing just "well enough", your grudging admission is simply false pride. He's actually playing wonderfully well. He is a maestro! Even your Revadiya may not measure up to him.'

Suddenly, I no longer felt so sure of myself. Perhaps it wasn't right for me to be so pugnacious, the critical voice inside me whispered, chiding. I did not speak, but neither did I leave. I just stood there, waiting for him to finish and open his eyes.

With a final flourish of rapid notes, he opened his eyes, and it was as though the petals of a lotus had bloomed when touched by the first rays of the sun! He looked at me in surprise for a moment and hastily rose to his feet in sheer politeness. I was tall for a woman, but he stood taller by a couple of heads if nothing. I noticed he had a well-muscled, lean frame with long arms, and a neck well clear of broad shoulders, and a head of hair thick with curls. I was inexplicably disconcerted, beginning to regret my decision to take him on, but my unbending arrogance wouldn't let go of me. I stood my ground.

'You are…' he began tentatively.

'I'm Kunwarani Ruupmati, from Garh Dharmapuri. This is my place for practising music.' I wasn't sure any longer that it was mine.

'I see,' his eyebrow arched in understanding, as he went on. 'Well, I didn't know. I'd always been told it was Hoshang Shah's pavilion, but surely it can't be his now. You can have it back.' He picked up his instrument, preparing to leave.

Shamed a little by his good manners, I exclaimed hastily, 'No, I don't mind your sitting here, I can sit over there.' I pointed to the other end of the longish stone settee. I have no clue why I did not just let him leave, but I felt kind of defeated. He was gazing openly at my face, as I was, at his.

'And you?' I asked, instantly rebuking myself. *What exactly are you doing, Ruupmati? Prolonging the conversation with a stranger in this deserted place, in the middle of nowhere!* But I quickly silenced that half of myself.

'I'm Bayzeed, folks generally call me Baz. I come from Mandavgarh, to practise. Music is what I do! So, what instrument do you come to practise, so far away from Dharmapuri?'

'Beenn and the ragas.' I was going on and on.

'Beenn? In this wilderness? Aren't you afraid of snakes?' he asked.

'No serpents have come yet to hear me play,' I chuckled, and as he smiled at my levity, his face lighted up as though by a crack of lightning. My hauteur was beginning to melt.

'So, would you let me listen to you play instead?'

'Would you like to?' I was astonished.

'Well, if you permit me, I could join you on my tambura?' He suggested diffidently. I didn't say no.

I sat down at a distance on the stone settee, as he did, at the other end. I took out my beenn and began playing, a bit tentatively. *Why are you so tentative? Well, what if he didn't think much of my skills?* I worried.

But the notes came out true and pure, like waves rising and falling, and I grew more confident as I went along. He looked at me for a few moments, then, taking a deep breath, he began strumming his tambura vigorously. His eyes were closed again, his slender neck and curls shaking in time with the beat.

Our duet wasn't just good, it was magnificent, I thought.

I had played with such vigour as though my life depended on it. I had never played so well before, nor had the strumming of tambura strings ever tugged at my heart as the stranger's did. *No matter that Revadiya is your Ustad, I thought. Even he cannot fly over the notes as this Baz does!*

I wondered if I was falling under the stranger's spell. It seemed to be something like that. Why else would I have talked to him for so long, and end up agreeing to let him accompany me? And to think that I had come and stood before him to fight over turf rights, only an hour ago!

I have no idea how long I played for, my gaze lowered to the strings. As I looked up, I started. The sun was low down on the western horizon. I stopped abruptly.

'I…have to go now, it'll take me at least an hour to get back,' I said. I rose to my feet, and so did he.

'You're quite a beenn maestro! It was a privilege to meet… to have played with you. I won't ever forget it. Could we perhaps meet again, sometime?'

My heart leapt. It wanted to say, 'Why not?' But I actually said something different.

'What… I don't know… I'm about to…' I was afraid if I stayed even a little longer, I would tell him that I was about to be sent away to Chittor. What was the point in agreeing to a rendezvous! I did not want to tell him anything about it. I wanted to tell him all that and more, everything about me!

'You just have to say the word, and I'll be here same time tomorrow. We could practise together again?'

Suddenly I was very scared. What on earth am I doing! If Rao gets to know, it will be terrible… I don't know why Bhanwar's warning suddenly rang in my ears. The picture of the prisoner pleading for mercy swam into my mind.

'I don't know,' I said firmly. He looked into my eyes for a long moment. 'All right! Whatever you like. I'll take your leave then,' he said, clearly disappointed.

I had already turned and left.

The Ardhapadma was spread before me, the silver mesh of fading rays of the late afternoon sun crisscrossing the lengthening shadows. I had the sinking feeling of having left behind something precious. I half turned, and there he was, his hand raised in adieu, his gold-rimmed shoes already in the stirrup of his reddish-brown mount. He sat as still as a statue, watching me walk away.

Vision 30

What a coincidence! Walking back, I kept wondering, this man, Baz, comes so far to practise music at Ardhapadma Taal, just like me. And what a name! Bayzeed, Baz. I had never heard such a name before.

I was happy, though. My heart felt light as a feather. I hummed a strain of raga Saarang as I walked back. What a wonderful duet we had had together! Or was I alone in thinking so? I wasn't sure that he liked it as much, but my instinct told me that he must have. Why else would he want to repeat it the following day? I had played with all my heart. 'Maestro' and 'privilege' were perhaps just polite words, but his eyes had reflected genuine appreciation in parting, though his own playing was definitely far superior; and he had been disappointed when I refused to meet him the next day. The music we had made together had no doubt been wonderful, but I asked myself whether that was the only reason I was feeling so elated or was there something more to it?

God! Why couldn't you just say, 'Yes, let's meet again tomorrow?' Wasn't it plain silly to be so vague, 'I don't know?' Whatever can that mean! How are you going to find him now, if at all!

All the way back, I kept thinking of him, nothing but him.

It made me forget all the things that I had been agonizing over lately: Rao playing king and the horror of the execution I had witnessed, the intriguing mystery of shepherds-turned-warriors and the dread of a bleak future in the confines of Chittor. Only that last image of the talented, handsome stranger sitting astride his lovely horse, his hand raised in a silent salute, kept hovering in my mind's eye.

Just as well, I didn't mention anything about Chittor. Maybe it would have made him lose hope altogether. What a cultured man he was! Indeed, genuine artists are like that—just the exact opposite of his name: Baz, the falcon, the deadly bird of prey that dives down from high up in the air and takes away innocent little birds in one fell swoop. This Baz was apparently a nobleman, didn't even insist on a second meeting much, quietly taking the disappointment in his stride, as it were.

Thinking and thinking more of him, of his eyes and stature, of the colour of his clothes and his horse and his gentle ways, I began to curse myself for having been so stupid! Why did I not just say, 'Yes, I'll be here again tomorrow!' I could have probably learnt so much from playing with him. How would I ever find him now? I could definitely not go around Mandav asking strangers if they knew where to find the musician named Baz, or Bayzeed!

I even dreamt of him through the night, sometimes smiling, asking whether I was afraid of snakes, sometimes suggesting eagerly that I just had to say the word, and he'd be there the same time the following day, sometimes saying despondently he was taking leave of me and sometimes, just turned to stone, his hand raised in mute farewell.

I woke up the next morning missing Tara miserably. O Tara, my dearest, where did you vanish! If you were here, I could have shared all of this with you, and maybe you would have grinned and said, 'Beware, Ruup, mind the stranger doesn't get you with child!' All of a sudden, I burst out laughing in exhilaration.

Vision 31

I was like clear water, and he was a dash of colour spreading in it. I was like the easterly wind and he was the scent of flowers. He kept seeping into me, almost by stealth, or rather his memory did. I would recall snatches of our conversation, and see him vividly in my mind's eye and shiver with a deep longing. I couldn't say what exactly it was that I wanted but I just could not stop thinking of him.

It was not as if I made no effort to meet him again. I was inexorably drawn to the Ardhapadma more than once. But alas! I was only to be greeted by its tranquil solitude. He was never there, except that miserable night much later, when shattered by the discovery of my real ancestry and nearly driven crazy, I ran to the lake to commit suicide. But all that came much later.

Meanwhile, I was sorely missing Tara. She would know exactly what I was going through, what malady was it that had me on the edge all the time.

At times, strange possibilities flashed through my mind, which, on reflection, I found thoroughly ludicrous. I once wondered whether he had been an apparition. He had said the pavilion had belonged long ago to someone called Hoshang Shah. Was it his spirit that I saw?

Then I chided myself. *Stop being silly, Ruup! By making a ghost out of a living person who made beautiful music, you're only insulting the emotion welling up in your heart—don't you see, there is but the difference of a single letter between prem and pret. Surely, it's love and not a ghost, that is afflicting you.*

A doha I'd read in one of Pandijju's books came to mind:

Kal na parat hai mohe tujh bin
Tohe sumiraun pal-chhin nis din[4]

Love! What is love? Is it what you feel for someone without whom you cannot have a moment of peace? You're inexplicably lonely, lost and pensive? Or, is it the one whose mere memory is exhilarating? Is that what love is? So, am I in love?

But what about the stranger, the handsome musician from Mandav? If he too were in love with me, would he not have come to the Ardhapadma looking for me, even without hope, not once? I ruminated endlessly, but couldn't find a way out of my lovely melancholy.

After the oath I had forced Bhanwar to take, he had almost stopped talking to me. He would only accost me if it was absolutely necessary, and would not look me in the eye as he had taken to doing lately; perhaps a fleeting glance, or maybe not even that. His face seemed forever drawn, anguished. Surprisingly, though, his lips now were pursed, and eyes always lowered. At times I felt sorry for him, wondering if I might count for as little in the eyes of the unknown musician as Bhanwar did in mine!

Thinking of him all the time had turned me into an insomniac, sleep eluding me up until the small hours. I would sit at the window of my small room that overlooked the forecourt of the Garh and its entrance beyond, imagining he would suddenly arrive, riding his reddish-brown thoroughbred, and take me away with him.

What really happened was quite different though.

Vision 32

As I heard the clatter of galloping hooves in the dead of the night, I asked myself, *Is that...could it really be him?* But the rider I saw dismounting at the gate was someone else: Revadiya. Dropping the reins, he made his horse trot away into the wood at the side of the road, and strode hurriedly inside, towards the large rectangular hall in the mid-section of the Garh.

In better times, it must have been a durbar hall of sorts. It had an elevated floor at the far end with a stone settee, which the Raos of yore might have occupied with the necessary decorative paraphernalia like cushions and linen, and bolsters with fancy tassels that were now missing. On the lower level there were stone benches on its sides, perhaps meant for important courtiers and suchlike and high above them were narrow ledges running along its length with stone lattice screens in front, from where the women might have watched the proceedings.

Shortly after Revadiya's arrival, the road from Mandav began to sound again with a more leisurely clip-clop of hooves, accompanied by the rumble of wheels turning on cobblestones. It was a large party this time. Two armed riders in front, and two in the rear, escorted a closed phaeton drawn by two thoroughbreds with hard-leather blinkers and fancy reins and a liveried coachman atop. The mere sight of the carriage and the escort was proof enough that they could not but belong to the sultanate garrison. I was at once gripped by intense curiosity. Who could be arriving with royal guards at this time of the night, and for what purpose? Had the Sultan sent some emissary?

As I watched intently from my window, the phaeton door opened and out came a female figure dressed in a dark cloak, her face covered with a veil. She moved taking small steps towards the durbar hall. Two of the guards had dismounted and accompanied a few paces behind her up until the verandah, but they did not go in. The lady stepped on the verandah and disappeared from my line of sight. I reckoned she'd crossed the verandah and gone into the hall.

Gripped by curiosity, I tiptoed out of my room and scurried stealthily across a couple of narrow corridors to one of the latticed balconies. The hall below was dimly lit by a single torch burning on the far wall, and there they stood: Rao, on the edge of the podium, facing the balcony where I crouched, and the woman in a dark cloak with her back towards me, on the lower level of the floor, silhouettes talking in low tones.

Although there was little chance of being discovered, the latticed balcony being dark, my heart beat like a hammer against my ribs and rang in my ears. I could only hear small disjointed bits of what they were saying. It seemed all my hurrying and scurrying was going to go waste, but I persevered. Kneeling in the narrow space, watching and listening, trying to make sense of the snatches of conversation I could pick up.

'... what is not possible... how... it cannot be...' Rao was saying.

'... please... mercy... have gone through...' the woman said.

'... how dare you come... cannot understand... that I just don't... who said...' Rao flared up, but I had lost most of what he said.

'... well-known... blurted out... the moment... Rabat Khan... for pity's sake!'

That was it!

The mention of Rabat Khan's name sent the tenor and volume of the conversation soaring up several decibels all at once. I could finally hear whole sentences.

'So, you think you can threaten me by name-dropping?' Rao said. 'You had better keep your song and dance for the mlechchhas, don't try to tempt me with them, Ruqaiya. Look at you, trying to force a deal on me!'

'Oh, not me, you're the one who cut a deal with them, and now blame it all on me. There was but one consolation of my shattered life and even that was snatched from me...and now this sarcasm! Have you no shame?' The woman was riled as well.

'It is you who should be ashamed of dishing out entertainment to the mlechchhas,' said Rao, with barely concealed loathing.

'As if you yourself don't serve them! Please don't make me spell it out for you!' retorted the visitor.

'How dare you speak like that to me? Don't get so pumped up on Rabat's backing, you might fall flat on your face and break your pretty little nose. He wouldn't take a second look at you. Now, leave! I'm not afraid of anyone, you know. I'm just waiting for my day to teach a lesson to your mlechchha masters!' Rao sneered.

'I never took anyone but you for my master, but apparently one can't get everything from one's master, that's the tragedy of my life. I didn't come here to pick a fight with you, either. I guess I had better leave,' she replied in an even tone.

When she turned to leave, it took me one long moment and I was stunned! I had begun to doubt if I would ever get to see her again in my life and indeed the last eight years had left crow's feet at the edges of her eyes and lined her face, but the loving eyes, the broad forehead, the mass of hair cascading in curls, the statuesque frame, all of it was just the same. The woman who, fondling my hair, called me sonchiraiyaa, her golden bird… My mother! But, Rao her master? And Ruqaiya!

As soon as I had placed her, a spear of longing seemed to pierce through my heart, to spring to my feet and run to her, and weep with my hands around her neck. I did indeed run down the stairs, but only to find that the dark silhouette of Rao's figure, resting its palm on the verandah column, blocking my path.

My feet turned to stone, as my eyes helplessly watched the woman in the dark cloak retracing her steps back to the phaeton in the forecourt.

Vision 33

After she had left, I began to doubt what I had seen and heard only a short while ago. Did I recognize her right, or was she someone with a strong resemblance to the one I longed to see again? No, that cannot be. My memory of her was not so faded, nor my eyesight so poor. But why would she call Rao her swaami? And why did Rao accuse her of such unspeakable things, like entertaining mlechchhas, singing and dancing? O my God, was my mother some sort of a courtesan? But why am I speaking of her in the past tense as though she were dead? Only moments ago, she walked out of here, hale and hearty. I should be saying, 'Is my mother a courtesan who sings and dances for the sultanate bigwigs?'

My heart was sinking and my ego instantly responded with a treacherous trick. What is the proof that the woman with whom I lived in the maulshri mansion was actually my mother? But my conscience refused to have any of that nonsense. I knew in my heart that she was indeed my mother, and that woman called Rao her 'master'. Her master had accused her of cutting a deal and being a songstress at court.

My heart was breaking. I, Kunwarani Ruupmati, the offspring of a courtesan! I began to step backwards shrinking away from the figure leaning on the pillar that was perhaps my father. Silent tears streamed down my cheeks, and my nostrils felt oozy, about to begin dripping.

As I backed into the farthest corner of the verandah covered in darkness, my back came up unawares against someone else.

I gasped. The person behind me, guessing accurately, stifled my upcoming scream in his fist. It brought back the awful childhood memory of the horseman who had snatched me away from my mother, muffling my screams.

'Quiet! Or else Rao will discover that you have been eavesdropping all this while,' he whispered, loosening his grip on my jaws.

It was Revadiya.

So, he is still here, lurking in the dark, perhaps eavesdropping himself? I was bewildered, my heart fluttered like a caged bird terrified of a hand reaching to grab it.

'Ustad, how come you're here?' I whispered back and

became complicit to his clandestine presence. We stood silently for a length of time that felt like a century. Finally, Rao stirred and moved towards his private chamber.

'Let's go,' said Revadiya, taking my hand, 'we'll go to the music pavilion and talk.'

'There? At this hour?' It was a weak protest. My voice sounding like someone else's coming across a chasm, silent tears flooding my eyes.

'Yes, it's the Shaarda-sthali of our music. I'll tell you everything you want to know.'

Disarmed by shock and compelling curiosity, I followed him without further protest.

Vision 34

As we entered the music pavilion, across the dark cabins and alcoves and up the zigzag of bannister-less stairs, the first thing I noticed was the large earthen lamp burning on the niche, as though Revadiya had known all along that he would bring me here. I was trembling. My muscles ached, breaking into random flurries of spasm. I felt I might faint any moment and my face was wet with tears.

'Ruupmati, please don't cry! It hurts me to see you in such a state,' said Revadiya. Indeed, he had a pained expression in his eyes. It worked like a dash of kindling material on a burning fire. My pent up anguish burst forth with unexpected intensity, punctuated by loud sobs.

'Ustad, you're my teacher, I beseech you with an oath upon my head. Tell me, was…is my mother a courtesan? Was I born of a common songstress?' I sounded every bit as anguished as I felt.

'No, Ruupmati, that's not true at all. This is all just bad karma! Maybe some unatoned sin of a previous lifetime! Why blame it on anyone in particular?'

'But Rao did say—' He didn't let me finish.

'Don't jump to conclusions on half-truths, Ruupmati! And then again, anger makes a man lose control of his speech...'

'Then, you tell me the whole truth!' I said sobbing.

'Ah yes, I know that you have been anxious to find out about many things. Pandijju told me that, and...' he stopped midway as though wondering whether to go on.

'And what, what else did he say?'

'He forbade me to let you have any details. He has your best interests at heart and feels that your family's past on the maternal side might upset you a great deal. But I feel that perhaps it would be better to tell you everything now. After all, how much more upset can you be than you already are! And today I also have something important to tell you that I haven't even reported to Rao yet. But before I go on, you have to tell me that you'd be able to calmly bear the hurtful truth. Unravelling a tainted past can be a painful experience, you know.'

I wiped my face with a corner of my dupatta, trying to regain my composure.

'I understand, Ustad. It's better by far to be blinded by the sun of truth than to go on suffocating in the dark bliss of ignorance. You can go ahead, no need to hesitate. Pandijju has formally trained me to be sthitpragya. I can face any unpleasant reality with composure. I am prepared...' But before I could finish, clattering of hooves on cobblestones, much louder this time, shattered the silence of the night a third time in succession, and within moments a large posse of armed cavalrymen rode right into the forecourt. Revadiya sprang to his feet with a start, exclaiming, 'Arre! What's this now?' Then turning quickly to me he said, 'I'm afraid it will have to be some other time,' and hurried away to the stairs, leading down to the courtyard. I stood nonplussed, looking down from behind the lattice.

Fifteen, maybe twenty, horsemen milled around down there. Revadiya now stood talking to the man in charge, who hadn't bothered to dismount. Clearly, they were in a hurry. Meanwhile, Rao appeared on the verandah and strode over to them. Both of them jumped onto spare horses, wheeled them around and exited the Garh.

I was left wondering, for the longest time, as to what on earth was happening around me.

Vision 35

When Rao and Revadiya returned the next morning, the Garh community was instantly gripped by panic at the news they had brought. Shujat Khan, who had ruled over Malwa for close to fifteen long years, had died the previous night. The air was thick with whispered anxiety and uncertainty.

In our time, the ruler was the cornerstone of the state. He alone was responsible for governance and peace in the realm. And whenever a longstanding pillar fell, the kingdom, more often than not, was instantly seized by terrible tumult and violence. More than one claimant from within the ruling family and many ambitious nobles and military commanders began eyeing the throne. Habitations and bazaars wore a deserted look for weeks, months even, apprehending a prolonged war of succession and the lawless strife, wanton killing and plunder that it entailed. Commoners would down shutters and wonder with bated breath what calamities were in the offing until a clear successor emerged to take control of things.

That morning of the year 1555 AD was such a day in Mandavgarh.

There were three likely successors to Shujat Khan: His adopted son Daulat Khan Ajiyala, and two of Shujat's own sons—each prepared to kill for the throne. Ajiyala had the backing of most of the nobility and the army brass. He had been Shujat's favourite. After the accidental death of Sher Shah Suri, the emperor of Delhi, during the siege of Kalinjar, Shujat was removed from the governorship of Malwa. It was with Ajiyala's help that he was restored to the position and later declared himself the independent sultan of Malwa. For all that, however, Ajiyala was only an adopted son. Why would the blood princes give up their claims in his favour! Each of them had their followers and the backing of some section of the nobility. Malwa was headed for civil war.

You're surprised, my dear scribe, aren't you? Where did I learn so much about the contemporary politics of Malwa?

God! She can read my thoughts just looking at my face! Am I also falling under the spell of some spirit? Then recalling what she'd said about Hoshang Shah's ghost, I was abashed and lowered my gaze.

Well, I'll come clean and tell you. I was getting into the habit of eavesdropping at closed doors. What could I do? When one's future is in the hands of others, there's no other way but to hide behind closed doors and listen.

When Rao and Revadiya returned that day with the news of the Sultan's death, they went straight to Pandijju in the subterranean temple. My lesson for the day was nearly done. I was dismissed, but I hid behind the door to listen.

'Pandijju,' Rao was saying, 'just have a look at what the stars tell: I think the time is ripe.'

No one spoke for a while, then Pandijju replied gravely, 'No, Rao, don't get into anything complicated. Let's see what the future brings.'

Even after racking my brain over it for long, I could not make head or tail of what was said between them. Neither could I understand what either Rao or Revadiya had to do with the dispute over succession, or why they were running around in circles.

Three or four weeks later, as Rao sat peacefully on his settee on the verandah, Pandijju came up to him, his aarti platter in hand.

'You look relaxed after quite a while, Rao. Good news?'

Rao told him that Badi Begum, the senior dowager of the late Sultan, had somehow brokered peace between the warring princes by a partitioning of sultanate territories and jagirs.

'Our area has fallen to Bayzeed. Baz is quite cunning though. Let's see how long he remains content with a mere part!' said Rao.

I missed a beat, and my right eyelid fluttered involuntarily—an inauspicious sign! Hearing both the formal name as well as the shorter alias together, I caught on instantly. Ah! So, the unknown musician turns out to be a mirage in the desert of my lonely heart! He is, in reality, Bayzeed Khan alias Baz Bahadur, the elder of the two biological sons of Shujat Khan, and now, the ruler of one-third of Malwa.

I suddenly felt as though I had mislaid something precious that wasn't mine in the first place!

Vision 36

Once again, I was sucked into a vortex of depression. Sometimes I missed Tara, sometimes, I shuddered at the memory of the venom Rao had poured on my mother, and sometimes, I felt intrigued about what the aborted conversation with Revadiya might have revealed. Revadiya had been so busy lately that the music sessions were practically on hold, and I'd had no occasion to speak with him in private.

Pandijju had remained unaffected by the succession affair, carrying on with his routine, including my lessons. But other than that, time tended to hang heavy on me. I often made plans to walk over to the Ardhapadma, but I never actually went. I was kind of disenchanted with it. After discovering the true identity of the musician, the exhilarating feeling that the memory of our meeting had evoked earlier, was lost now. Bayzeed Khan was one of the successors of the late Sultan, and I, just a minor chieftain's daughter. Friendship is a game only to be played between equals, after all. Besides, my favourite haunt had also come to be associated with the brutal execution of the prisoner whom Rao had sentenced to death. I often wondered what the poor man might have done to deserve such a cruel end.

Most of all, my wandering thoughts tended to dredge up the bitter conversation between Rao and my mother. I, Ruupmati, was born of a songstress. So, what did Rao have to do with me? Merely the fact that the woman who was my mother addressed him as 'swaami' did not make him my biological father, did it? Would I be jumping of joy if Rao did turn out to be my father? And what had she come begging of Rao that night? Me? Does she want me back to train me to be a courtesan too? Why do only some people address me as Kunwarani, why not the rest of them?

My thoughts hovered over questions such as these for hours on end, like a dry leaf swirling in gusts of wind before eventually getting stuck in a cobweb of the unknown. I would shut myself up in my little room and weep at my helplessness, but shedding tears brought no relief, there was always more from where they came.

It was during those days that I first thought of suicide as a way out of my misery. How long could I go on with my meaningless existence? I had emerged out of Mother Reva, I could always go back to a watery grave inside her.

Sunk deep in similar thoughts, I was sitting on the edge of the verandah that day when Bhanwar turned up to stand near me. I first noticed his feet and looked up at him. In the last few years, he had grown into a short-statured, stocky young man with moustaches and beard beginning to come out. He was openly gazing at me.

'Ruupmati… I… I…want to go away somewhere very far… There's nothing left for me here…' his eyes were filling up with tears, as he struggled with what he had to say.

'What do you mean, there's nothing left? Far away? But where exactly do you intend to go?' I asked, surprised.

'Perhaps I'll return to Hadoti. These people here will never accept me as one of their own. Now, even more so than ever before… Rao had my brother murdered in front of my eyes!'

Oh! So, Bhanwar was also there. Breaking the oath, he had followed me into the forest again, I thought to myself. The thought left me seething with rage, but I decided that I would not let it show. I wanted to know everything he had seen and knew. So, I went along, prompting him to go on.

'Brother? I didn't know you had a brother,' I said, genuinely surprised.

'Yes, he had come from Hadoti, looking for us. We're from a village near Gagraun. That's where they brought us from.'

'What kind of riddles are these! Why can't you speak plainly?' I said, pretending exasperation. It made him plunge into the story, exactly as I wanted.

'It is twelve years now, a whole yug. The festering border disputes had turned into a large-scale conflict between Hadoti and Malwa. My father and brother-in-law, Jiji's husband, were both expert swordsmen and fought alongside Hadoti troops. Both were killed in action. My brother, Kanwar, sixteen at the time and had been learning to fence. He picked up my father's sword but was felled with a deep cut on his arm. He nearly died, but before falling unconscious, he managed to slip under dead bodies, and mistaken for another dead Hadoti soldier, he somehow survived. He was destined to live another ten years, only to keep looking for the two of us, as it were.'

'But how did you and Ketki come here?' I asked.

'Why, these people did all the horrible things that a victorious army does! They killed most of our innocent kinsmen before setting fire to our homes. Jiji and I were hiding under a heap of shredded wheat-stalk in the barn. When we heard the burning timber crackling and smelled smoke, we knew we were done for. We came out, looking like clowns, covered in shredded hay, and made a run for it. But Rao had seen Jiji. He came galloping after us and forced her onto his horse. Of course, she struggled to get away and they nearly fell off the beast. Her resistance failed, but she continued to scream wildly, 'I'm not going... my brother, he'll die! I'd rather die than leave him alone!' Rao winked at Revadiya, who wheeled around and dragged me up onto his mount. We were brought here.'

'But you've now been living here for so long without any restrictions. Why didn't you try to escape?' I asked in a voice choked with genuine emotion. Perhaps at the back of my mind, I was reliving my own plans to escape from the Garh when I had recently arrived.

'Where would we go, even if we escaped? All our kin were gone, if they had survived at all, and we had no idea where to find them. Then there were these fearsome forests all around here, and to top it all, the spies of Rao disguised as shepherds watching all escape routes night and day. Even so, we did try twice, and both the times we ended up in their hands.

'Spies disguised as shepherds! What spies are you talking about, Bhanwar?' I prompted him again.

'You really know nothing about all this, Ruup, or are you pretending?' asked Bhanwar, suddenly beginning to sound more articulate than ever before.

'No, I really don't know anything,' I said.

'These men who fan out in every direction seeming like shepherds grazing their flocks are Parbhar fighters. Spies, all of them.'

'I've also lived here for several years now, but I had no idea at all of any of this,' I said looking at him amazed. 'How did you—' Bhanwar sighed and cut me short in an anguished voice, 'I know, Ruup, you have always thought I was dumb, ever since we were children, but I know all the dirty secrets of these two-faced scoundrels! On the one hand, Rao keeps rubbishing the Muslim rulers. Mlechchha this, mlechchha that, and on the other hand, he lives off them as well! He is the chief spymaster to the Sultan, just in case you hadn't heard! Indeed, he also nurses secret ambitions of capturing power and ruling over Malwa someday, as he says his ancestors did.

'Poppycock, that! It is a mirage he's chasing, but he doesn't know that. It's the reason why he keeps enacting those silly plays, practising to play king. Nothing will come of these little flares of ambition!' Bhanwar's eloquence surprised me. I'd never really understood he was so deep, I thought, a little guiltily.

'So, you were saying, your brother—' He cut me short again.

'I'll tell you. I've come determined to tell you all I have to say. Well, after my brother's arm wound healed, he started looking for us. Asking around, he had learnt that we were taken alive by enemy soldiers, but that was about all. For ten years he searched every nook and cranny of Malwa: Mandav, Ujjayini, Maheshwar, Vidisha. He made enquiries everywhere. Eventually, he lost hope and was about to return to Hadoti when destiny dragged him here. Exactly two days after the night you made me take the oath, he came here. There was absolutely no one here at the Garh. You were also out, probably roaming the woods. Kanwar embraced us, bawling like a child for the longest time. Then, promising to come back for us that night, he went out to hide in the jungle until dark, but what can you do about the cruel hand of fate!

'While I was still watching him go, he was caught by two of Rao's thugs. As soon as they saw a stranger in their area, they decided to take him straight to where Rao was staging a sickening play that day. Trembling with fear, I followed them. They took my brother to a flat oval surrounded by hills where Parbhar fighters were practising martial arts in sandpits. Rao sat on a dais, with Kaluram and Revadiya standing on either side of him. Behind the podium, there were tenements with small cabins. My brother was kept confined in one of those. As I stood with my back close to the wall near a window, I could see him being mauled and interrogated.

'"Where exactly in Mandav did you want to go? Who did you have to see?" The interrogator roared, slapping him hard.

'"I'm a trader. I had business to transact in Mandav bazaar."

'"What do you deal in? Who is your contact? Out with the truth, or we'll have your head off! From your intonation, it seems you're from Hadoti, aren't you?" Another punch in the guts!

'"Search him," the man in charge said. The other man took his time about it, first landing another blow on Kanwar. He was now bleeding at the corner of his mouth.

'"Hadoti coins and a knife, too. What's the knife for?" Another blow!

'By this time my poor brother could see the writing on the wall. If he carried on lying, he would soon be dead. He spilt the truth, perhaps in the hope that he'd be forgiven, being related to Jiji. I thought so, too. Suddenly they dragged him away to the front of the dais, and for a while, I could see nothing. The next thing I knew was that two men were dragging him to one of the sandpits, and before I could understand what was happening, the monsters had beheaded my brother, right in front of my eyes. I was stunned and unarmed. Still, I felt like snatching someone's sword and rushing at Rao. But the thought evaporated instantly. If I were to die as well, as I certainly would have, Jiji would be left all alone, with no one to take care of her. But she is beyond any need for caring.' Bhanwar's face was dark with despair.

'Why? What happened to Ketki bai?' I said alarmed.

'Nothing, except that she won't go with me, and I will not stay here any longer at any cost. But she doesn't want to have to face our folks back home. She's afraid of all the bad things they'll say to her: "A Malwa Rao, a slave of the mlechchhas, kept her as a mistress for years, and this wretched woman didn't have the courage to even take her life. She'd have been far better off dead", and things of that sort. But there is nothing left for me here! You don't know this, but years ago, Jiji had begged Rao, "My Bhanwar also wants to learn to fence. My father was a famous swordsman." But Rao snapped right back, cutting her short, "He'll not touch a sword ever in this lifetime! Try and get this into your head, the sooner, the better, do you understand?" And now, after the cold-blooded murder of my brother, Rao doesn't even look at me. I suspect if he knew I saw it all, he would have got rid of me too by now. No, no one can stop me from leaving now. I'll be gone tonight after it is dark.'

Then, looking me deep in the eye, he asked, stressing each word, 'Ruupmati, will you go with me?'

'Where, Hadoti?' I countered, not a little amazed.

'Yes.'

'What will we do there?' I asked inanely.

'What do you mean, what will we do there? Well, we will live together and die together, eventually!' He said this with such grave simplicity that I couldn't help laughing out loud. He continued to gaze at me.

'I will die right here, Bhanwar!' I said zestfully.

Suddenly he laughed, too. It was perhaps the first time that I ever saw him laugh so heartily. It seemed to brighten his plain homely face.

'All right, then. I won't go anywhere either. I'll also die here!' he said.

Vision 37

Barely two months after the compromise arranged by Badi Begum among the feuding princes, Revadiya arrived one day at the Garh, and went trotting hurriedly to the private quarters of Rao. He seemed to be panting as much from excitement as from riding hard. The sweating coat of his mount showed that it had been made to gallop a considerable distance.

Within moments I spotted both of them emerge from Rao's chamber and rush towards the staircase to the Devi's temple. I followed them quietly to try and find out what it was all about.

'Pandijju, Baz has breached the terms of the compromise!' Rao was plainly excited about it.

'Why, what happened?' asked Pandijju.

Rao nodded to Revadiya, who launched into a summary of the news that he had brought:

'Well, Baz Bahadur lured Ajiyala into going on a hunting trip with him. The trip being on short notice, Ajiyala's full complement of bodyguards couldn't accompany him. In any case, he is so vain about his physical prowess, he agreed to go with just two of his aides to escort him. Baz led them to the part of the forest where he had already deployed a large contingent of his soldiers. What did three men, however strong and skilled, count for in the face of such overwhelming force! They were easily overpowered and beheaded. Later, Baz and his men rode back to Mandavgarh, and surrounded the palace of the younger prince, Malik Mustafa. But it seems he had got wind of what was coming and fled with his men. He's now hiding somewhere in the heavily forested area to the east of the capital. Baz Bahadur has gone after him with a large force. There will be a showdown between the two brothers for sure. Mandav is relatively unprotected at the moment.'

As Revadiya concluded his report, Rao asked eagerly, 'Pandijju, what do you say now?'

'Rao, the number of troops deployed to protect Mandav even in Baz Bahdur's absence would likely outnumber by far the men you can muster. And let's not forget, they have cannons and guns, recently acquired from Christian and Turkish traders, which are entrenched inside the fort walls. The few hundred of your men would be annihilated in no time.' Pandijju gave his assessment in a measured tone.

'But we have free access to the fort, Pandijju! We'll have the advantage of surprise!' said Rao, his voice already sounding defeated.

'The free access you speak of is limited to you and one or two of your close aides. The moment they see you coming with an armed contingent, mayhem would start at the entrance itself. The gates would be banged shut and guns would be raining fire from the ramparts! No, Rao, I don't see your timing being right, but the final decision, as always, rests with you!'

'But Pandijju, Mandav is ours! It is without a master at the moment!' Rao sounded like a petulant child being denied his favourite toy.

'No, Maharaj, Mandav is not without a master. Baz Bahadur is its master. He just happens to be temporarily absent, out hunting his younger sibling,' Pandijju said calmly.

'Yes, that's all these mlechchhas are good at, fratricide!' said Rao bitterly.

'Rao, you forget. Princes of royal lines, whether Hindu or Mussalman, have for centuries killed brothers, fathers even, for the throne.'

Rao laughed raucously instead of being annoyed, as was his wont in a discussion such as this.

'Ah! If ever someone needed a lesson on how to defend mlechchhas, you would indeed be the man, Pandit! I, for one, could never give them anything but venom even though I earn my livelihood by serving them.'

Back in my room, I was once again racked by conflicting emotions, clashing inside my head.

So, it turns out that your handsome musician, cultured and polite on the surface, is a cunning and cruel man—a murderer under the veneer of all that sophistication! Another part of my mind came up arguing, calmly. *Oh! Don't be stupid, Ruup, they are all murderers. Rao, Ajiyala, Baz, you name anyone! As Pandijju says, whoever can kill the most ruthlessly is the one who rules.*

Look at you! Love seems to have blinded you. You only want to defend your precious Baz. Shame on you, taking sides with a mlechchha! Then the other voice came back, seething with fury. *Who is a mlechchha? Isn't he a mlechchha who abducts the helpless widow of a fallen adversary and makes a concubine of her? At least, the musician prince didn't take advantage of you in that deserted jungle. If he wanted, he could easily have dragged you onto his horse. Ah! What a lovely reddish-brown thoroughbred that was.* The other part shouted, *Stop! That's enough. You should be ashamed of calling your father a mlechchha, and the real mlechchha, a gentleman!*

Vexed to distraction, I put my palms tightly over my ears to shut out the squabbling voices, as though they were coming from somewhere outside of myself!

The day after, it was common knowledge that Malik Mustafa Khan's forces had been routed, and he had fled with his troops. They were chased but had disappeared into the forest and could not be found. The khutba, read out in the weekly Friday congregation of the Jami Masjid, had declared Baz the undisputed sultan of Malwa.

I thought to myself, *So, your musician is no longer a part-owner, but the sultan of Malwa now.* I can't say why, but I wasn't exactly pleased. Or, maybe my mind was playing games with itself, for that reddish-brown thoroughbred kept prancing around in my mind!

But the purity of the duet with the stranger at the Ardhapadma—it seemed such a long time ago—did appear to have gone a trifle off-key!

Vision 38

Once again, I was in the grip of insomnia, what with the fierce debate going on constantly in my head! I would be half-asleep, my eyes closed, yet my mind would be wide awake, wandering, flitting from one thought to another. At the slightest noise, my eyes would open instantly.

It was nearly two hours after bedtime when there was a shuffle of feet, followed by a tap on my door. Who could it be? Bhanwar, come to say goodbye before departing for Hadoti? I got out of bed, and opened the shutter, just big enough to peep out: Revadiya!

I shivered involuntarily.

'Come with me. Our conversation was interrupted the other night, and then there's also the other matter. I have been holding it back from Rao,' he said.

For the first time, I found his demeanour dubious, though I couldn't put a finger on anything specific.

'Where do we have to go?' I asked, knowing it was a foregone conclusion.

'Why, the music pavilion, of course. We can talk in peace there. You wanted to know the truth about your mother, didn't you?'

I was reluctant but seduced once again by curiosity that wouldn't be denied, I followed Revadiya.

'Now, ask me what you wish to know,' he said as we sat down.

'Everything,' I replied, 'you've already told me it's a long, painful story. I have come prepared to listen to it anyhow.' I felt far less confident than I pretended to be. I guess in order to cover it up, I assumed a haughty expression. Eyebrows raised and a supercilious smile playing on my lips, as though I was doing him a favour by agreeing to hear what he had to say. Revadiya's face lost some of its colour. I jumped to take advantage, 'But you'll have to promise that you'll tell me the whole truth, not just bits and pieces of it selectively. Are you prepared to take an oath on my head?' I asked sternly.

'Well, well, it seems my pupil just lost her trust in me!'

'I'm not your pupil in this conversation, just Ruupmati,' I said, drily.

Revadiya extended his hand and placed his palm lightly on my head, 'All right then, I swear I'll tell you everything without editing or pruning, then you can decide for yourself whether you're the daughter of a courtesan or a princess of Parbhar lineage. Our guru-shishya relationship is in any case nearly over. I have taught you more music already than I perhaps know myself!'

As I sat quietly, saying nothing, he sighed and continued, 'The unfortunate story of your family on the maternal side began approximately thirty years ago. The Khilji sultans had by then consolidated their hold over Malwa, but several recalcitrant bands of Parbhar and Purabiya Rajputs were still active, making life difficult for them. On the pretext of looking for resistance leaders, sultanate troops routinely raided and plundered homes, summarily executing suspects and carrying away their women for the harems of their masters.

'The cruelty and excesses of Bakhtawar Khan, the deputy subedar of Ujjayini, were legendary. On the slightest suspicion, and at times with none, he would enter a house and personally behead the 'suspects', and then parade through the city with the severed heads skewered on spearheads, before having them hung over the city wall.

'Your maternal grandfather, Khadga Singh Parbhar was a famed resistance warrior. His ancestral haveli was in a narrow lane of the old part of Ujjayini. After being seriously injured in a raid on a sultanate army camp, he had disappeared. After trying out several hideouts, he had concluded that hiding in plain sight, might be the safest option, and now lay confined in a secret underground chamber of his own house, waiting for his wounds to heal.

'Bakhtawar Khan hated entering narrow lanes, but that day he just happened to turn into the one in which Khadga Singh's haveli was. Khan's troops, holding aloft severed heads of men on their spears, entered the lane and sheer fright made people run helter-skelter, banging doors and windows shut. But the gory sight was so diabolically mesmerizing that before your grandmother could shut the window she was standing at, Bakhtawar got a glimpse of her. I myself have obviously never seen her, but I have heard that Gauri bai was an extraordinarily beautiful woman and Bakhtawar simply loved beautiful faces!

'"Whose house is that?" He turned and asked his deputy, who after a whispered consultation with his aides, said, "Khadga Singh's, Khan, but he isn't here."

'Bakhtawar was peeved. "Have the door broken down!" he roared.

'The alarmed deputy touched his fist to his chest and passed down the orders. Six or eight men immediately got down to complying with the command.

'In those days, the entrance to noblemen's havelis was designed like a tunnel, so in case of a forced entry, the enemy could only come in single file.

'There was no one home except your grandmother and your ten-year-old mother when Khadga Singh heard the noise of cracking timber. He rushed up the stairs from his underground hideout, sword in hand, and took position at the far end of the entrance tunnel. They say that despite his arm wound, he hacked down the first four intruders, but the fifth struck out his sword at Khadga Singh's legs even as he fell to the ground. The next soldier beheaded Khadga in one clean swipe of his sword.

'Your grandmother, trembling and weeping, was watching all this happen from a window upstairs. She took out her dagger to kill herself as Khadga was slain, but then she remembered her only child…what would happen to her? As Gauri bai lamented the cruel destiny that had befallen her and her daughter, she considered giving her daughter the same honour-death she was choosing for herself. While the widow pondered over her grievous dilemma, the girl was bawling, "Mother, mother!"

'The delay proved costly. Two or three soldiers ran up the stairs and caught hold of her. One of them twisted her wrist, the dagger fell clattering to the floor. By then, Bakhtawar himself was upon them. Your grandmother was struggling to get away, screaming expletives and curses, while the child's wail struck like a banshee at the highest pitch.

'"Gag them and bring them along," said Bakhtawar, with practised ease.

'The soldiers, well-equipped for duties such as this, tied their mouths up with coarse cloth—and the loud lament and the wailing stopped.

'Your grandmother passed several months of living hell in Bakhtawar's harem. She did make a number of attempts to put an end to it. She broke her glass bangles for want of anything sharper, and slashed her wrists, but no sooner had she done so than the dark-skinned eunuchs watching over the harem night and day, noticed what she'd done. She was bandaged and reprimanded. Another time, she bribed a eunuch with her necklace, set with priceless gems, to bring her a lethal dose of poison. She fed it to her daughter and took a generous helping herself, and went off to sleep thinking that she would soon be done with the nightmare. When she woke up the next morning, though, the eunuch she had suborned was making faces at her, grinning wickedly, pointing to her chandrahaar around his neck!

'Eventually, her resistance broke, and she made a deal with Bakhtawar. "Whatever happens to me, no one should touch my daughter." Bakhtawar was infatuated with her; he agreed but with a condition—a holy duty. The next morning, the maulvi was there to administer the kalma to mother and daughter. Your grandmother Gauri bai became Gauhar jaan, and your mother, Rukmini, became Ruqaiya!'

By then, I was sobbing inconsolably, my head resting on my knees. Revadiya extended his hand to my shoulder in commiseration, but he had barely touched me when I shrugged it away. Wiping my eyes with my knuckle, I said tartly, 'Carry on, I'm fine.' He looked at me quizzically and continued, 'After a few months, Bakhtawar was ordered to rush to the Gujarat border to deal with a sudden enemy offensive. As soon as he left, the security arrangements of the garrison and the harem fell into disarray, what with the minions sunk deep in drink and debauchery, night and day. Taking advantage of the situation, a band of Purabiyas raided the complex and in the ensuing confusion, your grandmother managed to escape from the harem. But where could they go? If they tried to run home, they would most likely be caught, even before they reached there. They decided to go in the opposite direction. The night was so dark, they could barely make out their hands, far less the part of Ujjayini they were in. Although, even if it were daylight, your grandmother and mother—'

Suddenly interrupting Revadiya, I sharply exclaimed, 'Ustad, would you please do me a favour and just say their names, Gauhar or Gauri and Ruqaiya or Rukmini, as you like, instead of repeating "your grandmother and mother" over and over again!' He looked up surprised, studying me, before picking up the thread again: 'They were both tired and terribly thirsty, their throats were dry with fear in any case. There was no telling when they might run into soldiers on night patrol and be accosted with questions, "Who are you? Where are you headed at this time of night?" It was the third watch of the night. Not a ray of light came from any of the houses they passed. Eventually, they spotted one with lights on, a little away from the road and set in a large compound with high walls. As they went closer, they heard voices, and came to a large gate that probably opened into a forecourt...'

My mind swam to a distant memory. I couldn't help interjecting, 'Was there a maulshri tree in that courtyard?'

Revadiya smiled.

'The haveli I'm talking of, I had no occasion to see, but the one you're apparently recalling will come later. Anyway, Gauhar rattled the iron fastener and waited. After a while, a deep-throated female voice asked from behind the shutters, "Who is it?"

'Now, how do we introduce ourselves, thought Gauhar to herself!

'"We're two of us, mother and daughter in distress... looking for a night's shelter," she finally said in a hushed voice. A pedestrian inlet built into the big shutter opened a notch, just enough for verification. A fat old woman, moon-faced with large eyes, salt-and-pepper hair billowing down to the shoulders, stood peering at them, her face lit by the fire-torch in her hand.

'"What's your name? Where are you from?" she asked, scrutinizing Gauhar and Ruqaiya, her eyeballs bulging out so prominently that they seemed to pop out of the sockets.

'Gauhar didn't know what to say. If she revealed that they were fugitives from Bakhtawar's harem, the door would most likely be banged shut. Ruqaiya was little but had enough presence of mind to sense that her mother's long silence was spoiling the only chance of refuge that had come their way. She spoke up, "I'm Rukmini, the daughter of Khadga Singh Parbhar and this is my mother. The mlechchhas killed my father..."

'"Shush...hh! Don't speak, come in quickly," said the old woman, allowing them in and putting up the heavy wooden bar.

'There was a staircase on one side of the courtyard going up to the first floor. It led to a long corridor with doors opening on either side. The first on the left opened into a large rectangular chamber. As the old woman took them into it, Gauhar noticed that several young women stood outside some of the other doors, whispering and ogling at them. The old woman gave them a look, with a jerk of her head, that sent them scurrying into their rooms.

'The floor of the large chamber was covered in mattresses with white sheets and plush bolsters in velvet covers lay on the sides. There were some musical instruments in a corner.

'As soon as they entered, Gauhar could make out where they had landed. She felt a shiver creep down her spine. Out of the nightmare, straight in the inferno, she thought! With her eyes lowered, she said in a small voice, "Mother, I think we made a mistake, coming here. For heaven's sake, allow us to leave."

'Ruqaiya was intrigued. Why on earth was her mother already talking of taking leave!

'"If you're truly who this little girl said you are, then you just happened to have come to the right place. But first, you must tell me who you really are," countered the old woman, her bulging eyes still scrutinizing their faces.

'"I swear on my daughter's life, what she said is the truth!" She put her palm on Ruqaiya's head.

'"But Khadga Singh was murdered some four or five months ago. I distinctly remember that, because the day he was slain, we didn't cook here. If you truly are his widow, where have you been all this while? I can only help you if you tell me the whole truth, otherwise, you're free to go, why would I stop you?"

'The old woman had concluded by then, that the two of them were indeed from some good family, poor souls in distress.

'Gauhar felt she would die of shame telling her all that she had gone through since her husband's death, but there was little else she could do. She said in a tear choked voice, "Yes, I'll tell you everything, but first, you tell me why you went into mourning the day my husband was murdered."

'"Well, Khadga Singh was the khadga of Parbhars, the sword that symbolized their pride. Besides he was also distantly related to me in a previous lifetime. That's why I said, you might have come to the right place. Now tell me about yourselves."

'Gauhar sat weeping silently for a while, her tears dripping down and making damp rings on the white sheets. Then in an anguished tone, she told the woman the ordeal they had gone through.

'"So, you're now Gauhar, and this here is Ruqaiya. Then I, too, better tell you who I am. I'm Razia, but in my previous lifetime, when Khadga was my relative, I was Rajeshwari… but all that is over, no point going into trivial details. To cut a long story short, your tale is no different than mine. It's indeed a disgrace to end up being a brothel-keeper, but I'll tell you something, I might also be reaping some reward points for the next world. Those girls you saw earlier, I'm keeping them from hells worse than the one I run here! I'll take in the two of you as well. No, no, don't worry, you will never have to do anything that might taint the fair name of a braveheart like Khadga Singh."

'Gauhar was torn between conflicting emotions.

'"Mother, I've lost everything. My chastity's gone, but my daughter! Who can tame the lust of the sort of people that frequent a place such as this? I won't let her be here, allow us to leave! We'll go where destiny takes us, perhaps die somewhere with no one to weep for us!" she pleaded miserably.

'"Where will you go?" Razia said. "It's entirely possible that the moment you step out of here, you'll be taken by villains. They might even separate the two of you. You wouldn't know where your daughter is, what's happening with her. You would be far safer spending the night here. Just sleep over it, and tomorrow you can decide whether you want to take up my offer and stay on or leave. But let's be clear right away that in case you decide to stay, Ruqaiya will have to spend most of her time hidden in a secret underground chamber."

'Gauhar could not get over her apprehension. Could she

trust Razia? Would she keep her word and save them from rank prostitution? Or, was she a cunning, bawdy house madam and would break them into it slowly? She was unable to make up her mind.'

Revadiya had paused. He seemed to be pondering over something. I was, by then, exhausted by his long-winded descriptions.

'Would you do me another favour, Ustad? Could you skip the finer details and just tell me what happened to Gauri bai and Rukmini?'

His face fell at my tone, and he retorted, 'I had forewarned you that it's a long story, and details are relevant. If I abridge it, surely you would end up accusing me of having given you a cherry-picked version!'

'No, no, please carry on the way you like. I don't know what got into me. I spoke without thinking through the whole thing.' I was embarrassed by my peevishness.

'There isn't much left anyhow,' said Revadiya, before resuming. 'Gauhar and Ruqaiya spent seven long years in Razia's mansion, an upscale bawdy house for the elite. Gauhar would sing a few songs, fully veiled, and withdraw. She had a wonderful singing voice, just like yours. Access to Razia's establishment was limited to high-ranking officers of the sultanate and some select affluent clients. Razia was feared, being well-connected, and if ever someone showed any particular interest in Gauhar, or wanted more than just to listen to her songs, the old woman would whisper something into their ear that instantly made them go pale in the face, and withdraw.

'Ruqaiya spent most of her time confined in the dark basement, as Razia had said right in the beginning, but Razia proved true to her word, and protected Ruqaiya as dear life, taking great pride that she was saving the only living child of a Parbhar legend. She hadn't lied to Gauhar. In her previous avatar as Rajeshwari, she'd indeed been the sister-in-law of Khadga Singh's mother's cousin.

'From noon through night Ruqaiya would remain hidden

in the basement. In the morning Razia, like a prison warden, let her out for taking a bit of sun and air for an hour or two. There would be no one moving around the house at that hour. Her girls would be sleeping in, after being up until small hours. Ruqaiya quickly got used to passing time alone in the gloomy chamber, humming the devotional songs she had learnt from her mother.

'When Ruqaiya was about sixteen, Rao happened to visit Razia's house with some sultanate military generals. He got on very well with them because...'

'I'm well aware of the reason for his being friends with them. Carry on,' I interrupted Revadiya's wry smile. He gave me a quick glance of surprise but didn't say more on it.

'Rao was in his prime at the time, very suave and handsome. Although he came and went with the Mohammadans, Razia could make out that he wasn't one of them. One day, she caught up with him alone, and asked, "Who're you? What do you have to do with these people? I know you aren't one of them."

'Rao had a surprise for her. God knows, he had this uncanny knack of digging out people's past.

'"Well, Rajeshwari," he said with a wink, "all I'll tell you is that like you, I have also made a compromise, but I'm waiting for my day. If I tell you any more than this, believe you me, many Parbhar heads will roll. Take care to hide even the little that I have said, with your sins, somewhere deep inside you."

'Razia fell silent. From that day on, however, Rao came to be close to Razia, visiting her often, and even staying overnight on occasion.

'Early morning one day, he happened to get a fleeting glimpse of Ruqaiya strolling in the garden and was instantly taken head over heels with her. But she was nowhere to be seen afterwards as if she had been an apparition. Indeed, he was so smitten that he began quizzing Razia and did not stop until he'd ferreted out Ruqaiya's secret.

'"What...what did you just say? That girl is Khadga Singh Parbhar's daughter, you mean *the* Khadga Singh Parbhar?" Rao couldn't believe his ears.

'"Yes," said Razia. "I've been hiding both of them for seven years but God alone knows what will happen to them after me, I'm getting on in years, you know…"

'Rao began pestering Razia. He wanted to marry Rukmini. So what if she had been converted? She was, after all, the daughter of the Khadga of Parbhars, no less! He would have her reconverted, sort of redeem her.

'Razia and Gauhar were both in a dilemma. Gauhar kept thinking, *God alone knows who he really is! He does say that he's the Rao of Garh Dharmapuri. By looks and stature, he appears to be an eligible suitor too, but who could be sure of a stranger in this time of Kaliyug! If he's as good as his word, surely my poor child's life would be back on track! Once I'm rid of this responsibility, with Razia amma's permission, I could go away to Vrindavan for penance.* But then she would begin to have misgivings and doubts. *What if he turns out to be a conning rogue? After all, he does visit this house of ill-repute in the company of mlechchhas! What if…* She would shiver, and start thinking all over again. Several months passed while Gauhar dithered, and once again, she paid a heavy price for it.

'Bakhtawar returned to Ujjayini!

'Drunk to the gills, swaying on his feet he staggered into Razia's parlour. Even an eagle would envy his sharp eye: merely glancing at her wrists, he recognized Gauhar in a flash, and growled slurring, "Razia! Take off her veil." Razia's attempted whisper was a disaster. Instead of losing colour, Bakhtawar's face turned red. Shoving Razia aside, he whipped off Gauhar's veil and guffawed, "See, Gauhar jaan, how much I love you! I could feel your pulse by just looking at your delicate wrists." Then, turning to Razia, he said, "She had a daughter, too, if I remember right. By God's grace, she must be a grown woman by now…where's she?" Razia, her pupils dilated in pure terror, replied wretchedly, "Was, Khan! She died last year; God alone knows what took her. One day she was fine, and the very next day she had a few motions and vomiting, and the next thing anyone knew, the poor child was gone, just like that!"

'"Shut up, you old hag. Trying to pull a bluff on Bakhtawar Khan! Search the premises!" shouted Bakhtawar, menacingly.

'His men searched the haveli upside down, every corner and alcove and cabin, but no Ruqaiya! Who could have thought that the step-ladder leading into the basement lay precisely under the mattress on which he sat, giving commands to his minions!

'"Line up all the girls. Maybe she's hiding among them." Bakhtawar was visibly annoyed. He rose to his feet and strolled from one end to the other with pauses, personally studying the features of Razia's girls, lined up like suspects for identification by an eyewitness.

'"No, she's not here!" Looking frustrated, he sat down where he had been. Even as Razia was heaving a sigh of relief, he turned to Gauhar. "Come on, get your personal stuff! We have to go now, it's been such a long time!" he said, eyeing her with undisguised lust.

'"I'll be right back, Khan. It's been so disgusting here," said Gauhar, making eyes at him, delighted.

'Razia looked at her in total disbelief!

'Gauhar quickly moved into a back room at the far end of the corridor where she had lived all those years and never returned. A bit sobered by now, Bakhtawar caught on when she seemed to be taking too long to collect her stuff, and sprang to his feet. But by then, Gauhar had slipped through his fingers for ever. She lay face down in a pool of blood, having plunged the dagger into her navel and dragged it up in a zigzag, severing the large arteries of the heart.

'Bakhtawar was stunned only for the fraction of a moment, then his wrath erupted like lava from a volcano. Hurling expletives breathlessly, he went on and on, "I'll see the bitch in hell but have her damned daughter right here, I'll find her if she is hiding even in paataal!"

'Razia was crying miserably, babbling to be forgiven, her head lowered onto her palms. "Khan… Khan! Please forgive me! I didn't know the wretched woman would be so stupid! Spare my life, Khan, for the sake of Allah…"

'After he was done with his ranting, Bakhtawar wheeled, and taking one of Razia's choicest lasses by the wrist, stomped out, dragging her after him.

'For three whole days, Ruqaiya remained confined without break in her subterranean black hole, with only a leather-bag of water for sustenance. Indeed, she was in a *paataal* of sorts!

'Gauhar's death made a decision about Ruqaiya's future easy. Razia was convinced that Bakhtawar, obstinate as he was, would not give up looking for Ruqaiya in a hurry, and with his men nosing around, it was beyond her to keep Ruqaiya safely hidden for very long. She had to accept Rao Yaduveer's offer at face value!

'The next time, Rao came to her place in the middle of a moonless night all by himself. Knowing how cunning Bakhtawar was, he did not bring even his escort that accompanied him to Razia's, though his aides were never allowed to come inside. He sat Ruqaiya, covered in a dark cloak and veil, in front of his own horse, and rode through the night, taking the less-travelled country trail, to the haveli with the maulshri tree that you recall. In those days, there were many such deserted mansions in this region belonging to Rao's ancestors. The maulshri mansion was one such property, about twenty-five kos from Ujjayini.

'Pandijju and a trusted maid were waiting for them there. Between the chanting of mantras and sprinkling of holy water, Ruqaiya was converted back; from Ruqaiya into Rukmini, this time around. Then, Pandijju formally married the two of them, performing the kanyaa-daan himself. The only witness was the maid, though—'

I cut in, 'What do you mean *was*? What happened to her?'

'She was killed trying to defend.'

A strangely bald reply. Defend who, against whom? But I didn't bother asking Revadiya to elucidate. I was beginning to get a broad idea of how things might have gone.

'You were born in that haveli with the lone maulshri tree in the forecourt and lived there for your initial five or six years.

Rao could not obviously live anywhere but the Garh, neither could he bring Rukmini there for fear of discovery. But he visited every once in a while.' Revadiya sounded as though he were commiserating.

'I never saw him come or go. It was only on coming here that I first had his darshan!' My sarcasm was not lost on him.

'Maybe he visited less frequently after the time you were big enough to register, or perhaps at a time when you were asleep, or something…I can't be sure. Shall I go on or is that enough?'

'No, you have to go on. You're under oath to reveal everything. How did I come to be here and where did my mother go? You have to tell me everything,' I said firmly.

'All right then, here it is. Bakhtawar never gave up. His men continued to sniff around for leads. Somehow, he was convinced that Razia had lied, that Ruqaiya wasn't dead. He tried every Machiavellian trick: bribing, threatening, punishing people he thought might have information. Finally, one of his spies who was close to one of Razia's girls got her to spill the beans. "Yes, there was a Parbhar man, a handsome one, who used to come with military brass frequently. He must have been the one that took Ruqaiya away. No one ever saw her die, that's for sure. I don't know the man's name, though, but maybe Razia does. He seemed particularly chatty with her."

'Bakhtawar himself interrogated Razia. Placing the saw-toothed edge of his scimitar on her neck, moving it back and forth in slow motion, he kept asking over and over, "The name, Razia. Tell me his name. Razia! Do you hear me or have you gone deaf? Don't force me to go on with this. I might yet spare your life! Tell me the guy's name, you wretched hag!" Razia's neck had begun to bleed copiously as Bakhtawar's increasing frustration made his hand more merciless. Razia knew her time had come, whether or not she gave up the name, the lie of Ruqaiya's death would take her to her grave.

'She made up her mind, and moaned, "Razia!… Who is Razia, Khan? Why do you keep calling me Razia, my name is Rajeshwari, I swear!"

'Till the very end, Bakhtawar kept gnashing his teeth and prodding her, "You crazy woman, tell me his name, or I'll kill you!" and Razia kept mumbling, "Believe me, Khan, I'm no Razia. Ask anyone, I am Rajeshwari!"

'Razia was done!

'With her death, Bakhtawar's investigation reached a dead end.'

'But Bakhtawar was nothing if not bull-headed. Once something got stuck in it, it remained stuck. He called all the deputy commandants who had been posted at Ujjayini for the last eight years, one by one, and made them swear on the Quran and asked them about the Parbhar who might have accompanied him to Razia's bawdy house. Finally, one of them came up with the name, albeit rather reluctantly, "Rao Yaduveer Singh Parbhar!" Bakhtawar stared at him in total disbelief.

'"What? Rao Yaduveer! Are you out of your mind?"

'Bakhtawar knew that the Rao had direct access to the Sultan, and taking him on without involving the Amir might be a folly he would regret to the end of his days. No girl, no vow was worth the risk! Bakhtawar knew where to draw a line. He sent a sealed letter off to the Sultan giving details of the alleged abduction of a Muslim girl, Ruqaiya, by Rao Yaduveer.'

Revadiya paused to give me an odd look and resumed, 'Pandijju might have told you in your history lessons that the sultans and their warlords filled their harems with as many Hindu girls as they liked, with impunity, but they couldn't stomach the idea of Muslim women taken as wives or concubines by Hindu potentates and jagirdars. In any case, the mullahs wouldn't let them if they themselves didn't care!'

Revadiya fell silent again, staring at the floor before finally looking up and saying rather earnestly, 'What I'm about to tell you now might be particularly painful. All said and done, no one likes to face up to one's parent's weakness. It's a bit awkward for me to be even mentioning what happened next, you might think—'

I cut him off sharply, 'Don't worry, Ustad. My thoughts will arise from my own mind, not from what someone else says. Just stick to the truth.'

'Being a favourite of the Sultan, Rao was granted a private audience. Shujat Khan came straight to the point, "Rao Yaduveer, you've been charged with the offence of abducting a woman of the Faith, and I have a hunch that perhaps there's substance to the anonymous accusation. It's well known that you have my blessings. No one would dare point a finger at you without a thorough investigation, and surely, you're aware of the penalty for such audacity. So, if you tell me the truth, and return the girl quietly, maybe I can think of a way to spare us the embarrassment."

'It didn't take Rao long to realize that if he lied, it wouldn't stand scrutiny. He might have to pay for it with his life, and among other things, his cherished dream of leading a Parbhar revival would be dashed. He decided to come clean, "But Your Majesty, the girl wasn't a Muslim woman, she is the daughter of Khadga Singh Parbhar. I have—"

'The Sultan held up his hand, cutting him short, "So, you admit to having taken the woman from the haveli of a courtesan named Razia?"

'"Yes, Amir," said Rao, his eyes on the floor, as though studying the exquisite Persian pattern on the carpet.

'I can't say why he didn't clearly say that he'd married the woman and that they even had a child,' said Revadiya, 'but I guess he might have thought that this detail was of little consequence, as indeed Shujat Khan himself confirmed the very next moment.

'"Well, it doesn't matter whose daughter she was before. Having taken the kalma years ago, she is a woman of the true Faith now. If you were not so close and dear to me, your head would have hung from the ramparts tomorrow, but now that you've confessed, I'll let you live. I'll take care of the mullahs. You just have to tell me where to find the woman."

'"Sultan, please give me a day's time!" Rao pleaded.

'"All right, Rao, I understand. Very well, you give me the

location tomorrow, so that she is brought to court the day after, and the matter is settled before it turns into a needless kerfuffle. I don't fancy avoidable confrontation with the mullahs. But mind you, Rao, if you try any tricks, your head will hang from the fort wall, I'll see to that. May you have the protection of Allah!" said Shujat.

'Rao knew that his movements would be under close watch henceforth. He directly came to the Garh, and sent a horseman to get you...'

'And the next day,' I said preempting him, 'he went and revealed to the Sultan where my mother was to be found.' I would have said more but my voice failed me.

'But how would you know that?' Revadiya looked bewildered.

'Ustad, thanks to Pandijju, I've learnt how to put two and two together. Can I say something more, if you don't take offence?' I said with exaggerated politeness, and without waiting for a response, added, 'You're indeed a maestro where music is concerned, but your vocabulary is rather poor!'

Revadiya looked at me aghast, that I could be speaking to him like that, but I couldn't care less. 'Only a while ago, you were hesitating to tell me about my father's weakness, but what he did wasn't an act of weakness. The word is treachery, Ustad! So then, shall we conclude? Rao had me snatched from my mother that evening. The next day he told the Sultan where his soldiers could get my mother from, and the day after Rukmini alias Ruqaiya was produced in court. So, what did she tell the Sultan? Did she say, please Sultan, could you have me retained here, and I'll sing and dance for you! She would have had to say something of that sort to end up as a songstress there, wouldn't she?' I was mocking Revadiya brazenly, but he must have decided to be matter of fact. He went on without taking any note.

'"What's your name?" the Sultan asked.

'"Ruqaiya Bano."

'"Are you married?"

'"No, sire."

'"What do you do?"

'"I sing devotional songs, that's all I know."

'"Can you sing one for us?" asked the Sultan.

'Shujat Khan was very fond of music. No sooner had Ruqaiya begun singing, than his eyes lit up like a jeweller's who had got a rare diamond cheaply. When Ruqaiya finished, he signalled her to approach the royal podium. Then, taking off one of his many necklaces, a precious string of real pearls, he bent down and put it around Ruqaiya's neck, and whispered to her, "You'll henceforth be a lady-in-waiting to Badi Begum. Just sing a few songs for me every day, that's all you'll need to do." Then, resuming his seat, he declared aloud, "We're pleased to confer the title of Gul-e-Bulbul on Ruqaiya Bano. She will henceforth be a lady-in-waiting to Malikaa-e-Aalia. Suitable arrangements shall be made accordingly."

'Since then Ruqaiya Bano has lived in the Jahaz Mahal palace complex at Mandav, and the guard commander of the royal household, Rabat Khan, is under instructions to attend to her comfort and needs.'

'So, what had she come begging for, the other night?'

'Perhaps you,' said Revadiya with a shrug, indicating that he wasn't sure. It didn't matter. Even the possibility was enough to make me feel deeply fulfilled as if a deep thirst was quenched.

'All right, Ustad, just one more thing. Why did Rao have me taken from my mother?'

'What do you mean *why*? You're his only child. It was his responsibility to look after you, that's why!' Revadiya sounded amazed that something so simple needed explanation.

'Oh, and wasn't he responsible for his wife's safety?'

'Don't be silly. His own life was on the line, what else could he possibly do?'

'So, you all have jettisoned those grandiose ideas and the tradition of staking your lives for the sake of honour and pride?' I ploughed on with sarcasm.

'I… I…am just an ordinary shepherd.' I stopped him midway.

'No, Revadiya, I know what you all are, and what you do for a living! All right, let it go. One last link remains missing. Everyone believes that I was found floating in the river, but you said that Rao had sent a horseman and had me abducted. So, who was it and what happened?'

'Look Ruupmati, you are not getting it. Bakhtawar had found out that Ruqaiya was alive, but not that she had been married and also had a child. So, Rao could have you rescued. It was his duty…'

'Because saving me was no threat to his life! But that wasn't my question. What I'd asked was who did he send to bring me and what happened on the way.'

'A soldier was sent but while riding back, you bit his hand so badly that—'

I cut in like a bolt from the blue.

'How do you know I bit his hand and not his ear?' I noticed Revadiya's fingers instinctively move to a point between the forefinger and thumb of his other hand.

'So, it was you Rao sent to get me!' I said bitterly. Revadiya kept looking at his fingers for a long moment, then added in a subdued tone, 'None of us can refuse to obey Rao's command, Ruupmati. We're bound by an oath on the sun-god. You know that we, suryavanshis, are born of the sun…'

'We're all born of our mothers' wombs, Ustad! But some men like you, sunk deep in vanity, choose to think otherwise, merely pretending to revere the Devi! But let that be. If you haven't been able to get it into your head so far, it's unlikely that a pupil can make you think straight. All right, let me give you a chance to reveal that secret, something you've been kind of dying to tell me, ahead of even Rao himself!'

Revadiya gave me a hurt look.

'Yes, yes, I'll tell you, but you must promise you won't misunderstand me. I'm not to blame for it. Rao's proposal of your hand was taken to Chittor by one of my trusted aides. He went to the royal houses of both Chittor and Hadoti. Alas, there was no satisfactory response from either of them. They all know Rao Yaduveer, but the rascals also asked for the mother's lineage and name! Maybe they did so deliberately. God alone knows how such things tend to spread all over! But if you wish, I can talk to Rao…' Revadiya's voice kind of trailed off.

I knew what was coming next, but asked regardless, arching my eyebrows, 'What is there to talk about? Just tell him I'm unacceptable as a bride for any of the princelings of Chittor or Hadoti. Surely, he is entitled to know.'

'No, no, I was thinking of asking him for your hand myself…'

I boiled over with pure hatred!

'Beware, Revadiya, do not speak another word! For some time past, I've had this nagging feeling that you would say something most disgusting, as indeed you just have. But don't even think of it! I have no desire to see a Parbhar head hang from the ramparts of Mandavgarh! Such things spread on their own, or are they insinuated and put in people's mouth? Aren't you ashamed of yourself? You're my Ustad, and more than twice my age, and yet you think of yourself as…' I was shaking in sheer rage.

'Ruupmati, listen! I asked you not to misunderstand me. I've never seen a woman as beautiful as you ever before in my life…and I'm not even forty yet. I'm truly in love with you, I'll worship you, treat you like a queen! Don't spurn me!' he looked down at his hands, as though he were seeing them for the first time. They were shaking as he pleaded.

'Shut up. Not a word more, do you understand? I'm leaving now.' I rose to my feet quickly, as did he. His eyes were clouded by terrible despair. As I turned to go, he said in a tone I had never heard him use, menacing and nasty.

'Oh, come on! Who is letting you leave at all?'

Revadiya lunged forward, his hand extended to grab me and I instead of shrinking back, lunged right at him, and with one flowing swing of my palm, slapped him hard, so hard that a trickle of blood appeared instantly at the corner of his mouth.

Revadiya, stunned by the sheer gall of my response, stood

rooted to the ground for a long moment. Taking advantage of it, I turned and ran like a deer sprinting to get away from a predator. Taking the stairs two at a time, I was down in the courtyard in the blink of an eye!

In a corner of the sky, the scythe-shaped moon of the fourth night of Falgun seemed to rest on the parapet of the courtyard wall. I flitted swiftly into the dark shadow of the battlements above, holding my breath for dear life! Within moments, Revadiya came rushing down the stairs, and pausing briefly to scan the courtyard, ran towards the stairs leading up to my room. As he disappeared into the building, I turned swiftly and exited the Garh.

Vision 39

Tara was right! Yes, she was right!

My head was ringing with the same thought over and over again: Tara was dead right! Revadiya turned out a scoundrel. He wanted to force himself upon me. Bhanwar was right, too. He must have instigated his brother's murder.

His sympathy was a mere facade. By relating to me the misfortune of my grandmother and mother, and my father's treachery, he wanted to demoralize me, bring me down on my knees, so that I would gladly accept his loathsome proposal, and when I did not, he wanted to take me by force! Tara was absolutely right about him.

Leaving the Garh, I snatched a fire-torch from its socket near the gate. My feet picked out the path to Ardhapadma Taal, unbidden.

Revadiya's long-winded narration of the horrendous tale, and what had followed it like a flash of lightning, the accumulated perversity of it all, suddenly turned into deep despair, poisoning my mind with a hundred ruinous thoughts. Maybe my grandmother and mother had been forced to do so by unavoidably adverse circumstances, but they had indeed spent years in a courtesan's establishment. Even now, my mother was a songstress at the sultan's court, and my father, trading off his wedded wife to save his own life in a cowardly deal, had me snatched from my mother and forced me into a lonely existence in the care of his concubine. And now, a skirt-chasing low-life like Revadiya was looking to become my lord and master! Even my father might not see anything wrong with that. What a life, indeed! And the irony of it all was that even a minor prince of the royal house of either Chittor or Hadoti seemed like a bridge too far!

I, Kunwarani Ruupmati, a princess descended from the self-styled suryavanshis, indeed! A lonely nobody with a tainted past, an intolerable present, and a bleak future, all alone in this whole wide world, that's who I really am.

I wondered whether there was any point in going on with such a miserable life. Wouldn't it be far better to put an end to it, forthwith? How deep would be the clear-water end of my beloved Ardhapadma? Or, should I just go back to the benevolent Reva Maiyaa? My cheeks were wet with tears flowing incessantly. I was hiccupping and weeping as I walked to the lake.

The truth, my dear scribe, is that I didn't want to die. I was terribly afraid of taking my life. Perhaps it had been just the turn of phases that I felt suffocated in the confines of Garh Dharmapuri. At the moment, I was trembling with fear of how it would feel when the waters of either the lake or the river, holy as it might be, would fill my mouth and nostrils, and make my heart flutter like a terrified pigeon as my lungs would struggle for one last breath! As I came closer to the Ardhapadma, I began to feel increasingly jittery. Alas! If only I could ride that reddish-brown thoroughbred once, before dying!

I know, you must think what a perfectly ludicrous last wish for someone who's fed up with her life, and one determined to end it! You'd perhaps be right, too. But this 'me' that you see, is of a much later time. The day I'm talking of, I was all but fourteen, perhaps fifteen years of age. Indeed, by the yardstick of the time, I was a grown woman of marriageable age, but look at me also by the standards of your time, and you'll realize that I was little more than a child-woman. How would I not be afraid of dying?

As I crossed the Champa-aranya and the lake came into sight, I longed to touch the lotuses one last time. I walked down to the water's edge and passed my hand over the thick growth of flowers and buds, then picking two half-blooms, smelled them. And then, with a deep sigh, I began to debate in my mind, the lake or the river? The fire-torch was nearly burnt out.

I lifted my head to look at the clear-water end of the lake and gasped. Hoshang Shah's pavilion was washed in lamp-light. My heart leapt in sudden hope. Could it be the musician? No, Ruupmati, that musician doesn't exist anymore. He vanished long ago. Only Sultan Baz Bahadur remains.

My mind was once again agog with voices at odds with each other: *The musician who had accompanied you on the tambura is the very same man, so what if he got crowned sultan. How can the two be separated?*

Are these your heartstrings strumming, or is someone playing on the tambura?

Gazing steadily at the pavilion, I rose to my feet and began walking to it. If it is him sitting there playing, I won't even talk to him. Why didn't he ever come back? Hey, what was happening here? I had begun to sulk already, even before I knew whether it is him! Would he have brought along his lovely reddish-brown mount though? Maybe, I'll take a chance and see if he'll grant me my last wish, and let me ride it before I die. God! What to do? Would he let me just plunge into the water, or take my arm and stop me? The voices in my head were a funny jumble.

All of a sudden, another terrible possibility struck me like lightning and my exhilaration evaporated. O my God! Could it be Revadiya? He might have spied me leaving the Garh, and having taken a shortcut, was waiting for me here. What would I do then? Surely, he would have come determined to strike like a viper stepped on.

Then, I brushed aside the rising apprehension: *Oh, come off it, you have come prepared to end your life, nothing matters now, not even Revadiya!* I resumed walking towards the pavilion.

This time around, his eyes were not closed. He rose to his feet as soon as he saw me.

'Come, Kunwarani Ruupmati, I don't know how, but I was sure that you'd come today.'

I don't know what happened to my resolve not to talk to him.

'I came here so many times that I lost count. It was you who never came, but I can't talk to you anymore. I've only come tonight to drown myself in the lake.' I was beginning to sob again. He smiled ever so sweetly.

'Why have you made such an extreme decision?' He sounded as though talking to a child.

'I've lost my will to live. Just let me have my last wish, and leave. I have to drown myself.'

'Well, how come you lost your will to live? Your life hasn't even properly started, yet! And in any case, drowning yourself isn't possible. I'm not about to leave.'

'Why isn't it possible?'

'Because I'm present here, and as the sultan it's my duty to ensure that none of my subjects commits suicide.' He smiled, and began again, 'As for the last wish you were speaking of...'

I never heard what he said next. Someone was screaming inside my head: *What's with all this childish nonsense! Why don't you just go ahead and tell him plainly, why did you never come, why didn't you give me a ride on the lovely horse of yours? Since you never came and broke my heart, my will to live shrivelled and died, and now, I want to die too!*

I was sobbing even more audibly now, and hiccupping. Suddenly he raised his arms high in the air, vigorously shaking his palms from wrists above, as though fending off moths hovering overhead.

That was the moment! I couldn't stand the screaming in my head any longer. My feet moved as if they had a life of their own. Taking a quick step forward, I stood close to his torso with my face touching his chest. He brought his hands down and took me in his arms lightly, but didn't press them hard. He looked down and tenderly wiped my tears with a finger.

'Why did you never come back? Did I alone keep longing for you?' My voice sounded exactly like a sulking child's.

'I swear by my Allah, I kept returning here, almost every day. And longing, well, it was love at first sight for me. It was precisely the reason that I suggested meeting again the very next day, remember? It was you who refused to say anything that made sense. Then, it was perhaps just chance that you and I both came at different times, only to return disappointed. Eventually, there was no other way but to persuade her to go to the Garh.'

'Who did you send there?' I looked at him surprised, though I had a hunch already. We still held each other close.

'Bano,' he said.

'Did you send her to Rao? So, that means she's not keen herself that I should be sent back to her?' I said, my voice choking with fresh tears.

'Oh no, she loves you dearly. She pines for you, but at the same time, she wants to keep you away from the shadows of her past. When I first mentioned my yearning for you, she thought I was merely talking of keeping you among others in the harem, then I told her the whole truth, and that is when she finally agreed to go.'

'What whole truth did you tell her? Tell me, too!' I said in a whisper as though afraid that someone might be listening in.

'That I'm in love with you, and if I were to become sultan, you'd be my patt-rani, the principal queen.'

'So, will you make me a Mussalman?'

'Whoever said that? I only said patt-rani, you'll continue to be Rani Ruupmati.'

'Ruqaiya Bano agreed to go to the Garh, and you're the

sultan already, but Rao refused to listen to her plea. How will you make me your patt-rani?'

After a fair bit of our conversation had gone, I realized we'd both given up the formal 'aap', and were addressing each other with the more intimate 'tum'.

'There's nothing to worry about now that you didn't repeat you vague "I don't know". Rao will not deny the Sultan,' he said teasing me.

'Just suppose that he refuses to oblige, would you drag me onto your horse and take me away forcibly? My last wish would be fulfilled as well!' I parried.

'Certainly, I would! Inshaallah, I'll do everything that it takes to have you.'

'What else will you do for me? Surely, there must be other queens and women in your harem already.'

'Indeed, there are, but none as beautiful like Padmini as you, Ruup. I'll be yours first, and you, above them all!'

'What more will you do for me?'

'What more, let's see. I'll have a fabulous palace built for you and I hear you're a devotee of the holy river Reva, so, I'll arrange to get Reva water for you in the palace pool. So that you can purify yourself every morning after having spent the night with a mlechchha!' Having said that last bit, he laughed heartily and so did I.

I felt madly happy, kind of liberated. I pulled him even closer to me, and standing up on the balls of my feet, I whispered into his ear, 'Sultan Baz Bahadur, since all your answers were perfect, this daasi presents a reward to honour you,' I said, putting my lips softly on his.

The gift was mine to give, he only accepted it. After all, only I could give away something that belonged to me.

VISION 40

I did not have to walk back to the Garh. Baz granted me my 'last wish' that very night. He picked me up as easily as a child and put me on his reddish-brown thoroughbred. Another horse, a white one, had materialized out of nowhere, the sultan's bounty perhaps! He got onto his mount, and tightened his thighs on the sides, tutoring me silently, 'You have to sit this way.'

The horses walked side by side. I asked him why he had been shaking his palms just before I went into his arms. He revealed the reason without any hesitation: the sultan cannot be anywhere without his jaannisaars—personal guards—certainly not in a deserted place like the Ardhapadma. Shaking his palms, he was signalling them to look the other way since we needed privacy.

As the outer wall of the Garh came in sight, he helped me dismount.

'You'll manage on your own from here on, won't you?'

I nodded yes. He bent down to kiss my forehead lightly, 'I'll come back for you soon, don't worry about it.' Then he got back onto his horse and holding the reins of the other, trotted away without looking back.

It was the last watch of the night, eerily quiet all around. My trepidation returned. Would I run into Revadiya, seething with pent-up fury, right at the gate? As I went closer, my heart skipped a beat. The tunnel-like entrance cut through the thick wall was brightly lit from inside as though a huge number of torches were blazing in the courtyard beyond.

O my God! I suddenly remembered it was the dawn of Vasant Panchami, the special day of Mother Shaarda, the goddess of Learning. Like every year, the spring festival would be celebrated at the Garh. The entire community would gather, bedecked in saffron-coloured finery, and sing and dance to welcome spring and worship the mother goddess. A special pooja would be offered to her later. But arrangements for all that had never started quite so early before. What's the matter today, I wondered. I was trying to remain calm but my heart kept thumping madly.

The sight that awaited me inside the courtyard was truly heart-stopping: men-folk of the community were crammed shoulder to shoulder on either side, leaving a clear path in the middle, as though for someone important to arrive and walk through to the Garh. Then, with a sinking feeling, I realized they were waiting for me! Oh, the way everyone glared at me with silent hostility!

Rao sat on his usual settee on the edge of the verandah. To one side of him stood Kaluram and Revadiya, gazing straight at some point in the direction of the entrance, and Bhanwar on the other, his face lowered to the ground. Behind them, inside into the verandah, Ketki stood motionless alongside some twenty women from the shepherds' tenements. Pandijju was nowhere to be seen.

I had not seen so many fire-torches alight around the forecourt ever before. There was the hint of a smile in Revadiya's eyes, as though saying, 'See, this is how the slap works!'

I shivered involuntarily, but there was no turning back now. As I walked on, folks standing on either side seemed to shrink back, as if I were carrying some contagion.

What has happened? Why are they gathered here, glaring at me so? What do they know? How much?

As I reached the verandah, Rao stood up and placed his hands on my shoulders, as though he was going to embrace me, but all of a sudden his grip turned hard as steel, and he shook me with such violence that I feared my ribs would come loose. Then, his right hand flashed as he slapped me hard. I would have surely fallen to the ground from the blow but for his steely grip, still on my shoulder. My spittle tasted of salt. I knew my mouth had bled inside. That hint of a smile had turned into a smirk on Revadiya's face!

'You're a taint on our honour! You too turned out like your mother!' Rao whispered hoarsely in suppressed rage. Then his voice went up several notches as he called out, making an announcement of sorts, to the gathering—'Mrityudand!'—death penalty. His voice carried to the walls of the courtyard, and was chorused back by many, as though confirming the sentence: 'Mrityudand!'

I was trembling in fear, and strangely, also filled by scorn.

'But, Baba…' I started to say, but was cut short by Rao's whiplash whisper, 'Shut up, you harlot! Never utter that word again.'

Rao gripped my arm and pulled me after him, towards the women on the verandah, and shoved me hard. I fell to the floor with a thud. When I raised my head, I found I had landed at Ketki's feet. She hurried to pick me up, and looking at Rao, mumbled, 'Rao, a girl pretty as a flower…poor thing…'

'Keep your mouth shut, Ketki! Utter a word more, and you'll die too,' Rao roared. 'Take her away and lock her up, and prepare a thick broth of opium, right now!'

Pandijju appeared at the far end of the corridor, leading to the temple stairs.

'What happened, Rao?' he asked in surprise.

'Nothing. Your disciple just returned with my honour in tatters! I've sentenced her to death already. Now, don't you start getting into this.'

Then he turned to the women, still standing petrified, and shouted in exasperation, 'Didn't you hear me? Take her out of my sight, and prepare opium.'

Ketki and the women led me towards the stairs to my room. The gathering in the forecourt melted away; the men quiet, apparently satisfied with the outcome.

Vision 41

After escorting me to my room, all other women, except Ketki, left one by one. Ketki stayed on for a while. I sat sobbing on my bed, my head resting on my knees. That day, Ketki put her hand on my head for the first time ever, gently stroking my hair, as though making amends, and said, 'Don't be afraid, Ruupmati. Pray to the Almighty. He alone can do something, if at all.'

The door was locked from outside. There was no way to get out. The windows had thick iron bars. My tears had dried up. I began to wait for the cup of poison. I was thinking: *Your last wish has already been fulfilled. You had gone to the Ardhapadma, determined to commit suicide, hadn't you? Going to sleep and never wake up again would surely be easier than drowning to death! Ketki's right. Petition the Lord, maybe He will set everything right.*

Half an hour passed. There was metallic jangling on the door. So, this is it, Ruup. Here comes your cup of poison!

The shutter opened: Bhanwar, his eyes lowered and red from all the weeping, and ready to shed more tears.

'Why are you weeping? I had told you, I'll only die here!'

'Please forgive me, Ruup…' his voice, cracking with emotion, trailed off into silence.

'Forgive you? Why, whatever for?'

'I couldn't help it! It felt as though my heart was crushed, my mind set on fire, envy made me blind. I couldn't ever imagine that my…my snitching could have such terrible consequence. I thought…' Tears started streaming down his cheeks again. I stared at him, dumbfounded.

'Oh, it was you! But you'd taken a head-oath, you…you even wanted me to go to Hadoti with you, to live and die together! I thought it was Revadiya…'

'Yes, I saw him going towards your room. Please, forgive me. I realize now I didn't deserve you at all. I did not love you, just wanted to possess you. All of this is my fault. Ask Rao to have me executed instead! That alone can be my penance.'

'No, Bhanwar, only I can be punished for my transgression. You can't do anything for me now, it is too late. You can't even take me to Hadoti anymore. My poison cup will be here any moment.' I had recovered my composure.

'No, not today,' he said.

'What do you mean, not today?'

'They'll bring you the poison cup at daybreak tomorrow. Pandijju said that a Padmini virgin possessed of all thirty-two lakshanas must not be put to death on Mother Shaarda's day, no matter what the circumstances, and that if the Devi's wrath is incurred, all of Rao's dreams would turn into nightmares. Rao raved and ranted, but Pandijju stood firm, "If you carry out the death sentence on the auspicious day of Vasant Panchami, you'll forget the names and gotra of your ancestors whose honour you're trying to save, let alone your skills of warfare. The decision, as always, is yours to make. My duty is only to advise you of likely consequences, and that I've discharged."

'Rao was peeved, but eventually said, "All right then, she will depart with the first ray of the sun tomorrow." Revadiya is guarding the gate with all his men-at-arms.'

So, I have another day to live!

A gust of cool spring breeze rushed in through the window. I took a deep breath and wiped my face with the corner of my dupatta. Bhanwar was still standing, looking down at the floor.

'What should I do? If you don't forgive me, I would rather die,' he said.

'That is bound to happen. Remember, you gave up your resolve to go to Hadoti in order to die with me here? So, what else do you expect now! There's no way my life is going to be spared. After all, you reneged on your oath on my head.' I avenged myself in a matter-of-fact tone and turned my face away.

'If that's all you have to say, I'd rather be the first to go. In any case, I have no will to live any longer.' I started with a sense of déjà vu! Bhanwar could not have heard me from that distance, could he now? But regardless, I was alarmed that he meant it seriously. It set me thinking. Only a few hours ago, I had gone through the trauma of contemplating suicide myself. Why should I be the trigger for this poor fool, tempting fate, only hours before my own execution? Maybe what he did was unpardonable, but I am no Rao, I thought.

By sentencing me to death, my dear scribe, Rao had proved that he was indeed my biological father. I cannot speak for what happens in your day and age, but in ours, only the real father of a young woman would sacrifice his daughter at the altar of his family honour, ego, pride, whatever, as casually as if he was beheading a sacrificial goat-kid! He wasn't bothered about what happened to other people's daughters. They could be taken, held captive, tortured, raped for all he cared. All of that wasn't his business.

No, I couldn't be as heartless as Rao. He'd had Kanwar executed, and now I might be causing Bhanwar's doom. This man in despair might cause himself mortal harm. My heart said: *Ruup, release him from his terrible sense of guilt. Let us go clutching at straws in the wind. A thought had just occurred to me.*

'Bhanwar, do you really want to do something for me?' I asked.

'Anything you say!' His eyes were filled with piteous begging.

I took out a book borrowed from Pandijju's chest that had precious paper pages, tore out the blank one at the end, and wrote:

> The tryst was
> Unconsummated last night
> Now father has given her
> The gift of death!
> Harbouring a thirst for you,
> Your love will depart the earth
> At tomorrow's first light,
> Come rescue if you wish to save
> Come this very moment, My Lord—
> The one that gave last night
> The gift of honeyed lips to you!

Even as I wrote I was thinking: *It's quite unlikely that the missive would reach Baz's hands in time, but at the very least, it would help reduce the guilt that consumed Bhanwar.* Folding the letter,

I proffered it to him, 'Would you be able to deliver this to Rabat Khan, the commander of palace guards at Mandavgarh? If you're able to get to him, say, Rani Ruupmati sent it for the Sultan, care of Ruqaiya Bano. Can you remember it? Don't forget to say "Rani".'

Bhanwar nodded gravely.

'And, if you wish, you can go ahead and read it. If you don't feel like carrying it, you're free to tear it to pieces, and forget it all. But if you decide to go, promise me that you'll not risk your life for me.'

'Are you making fun of me, Ruup? Much like the sword, Rao never let me hold a piece of chalk either. If I could read, who knows, I might have torn it. As for my life, even if I sacrificed it for you, what I've done would still remain unpardonable. How can I be afraid of dying after having destroyed someone who I believed to be dearer than life! May I leave now?'

'But how will you go? You said Revadiya is guarding the gate.'

'I have enough rope to be able to get down to the grassy slope outside your music pavilion,' he said, turning to leave.

VISION 42

The Garh that morning was as silent as a deserted mausoleum, without any of the usual bustle of the festival celebrations. Perhaps Pandijju had already observed the necessary rituals of Shaarda pooja, quietly in the temple.

Two hours before midday, he came to my room with his silver pooja-thaali in hand, and stood for a while at the door, gazing at me with deep compassion. Taking a few steps inside, he put a tilak on my forehead and sprinkled holy water.

'Om Namo Bhagavate Vaasudevaay! Be at peace,' he said.

I said nothing. I simply got down from the bed and bent to touch his feet. Then, he turned and left without saying a word.

The day seemed to crawl in slow motion, endlessly, as it were. I stood gazing at the sparkling stream of the Reva way down the precipice, for what felt like an eternity. Ketki came in with a plate of food, her eyes downcast. She mumbled, 'I pleaded with Rao for the longest time… He just refuses to budge.'

As evening fell, I felt my heart sinking, like the sun setting across the river. Bhanwar hadn't returned. I had no idea how long a round trip to Mandav took. Even if he came back, how would he get in! Then I remembered, kind of lazily, that he had that length of rope. Would he have remembered to say 'Rani Ruupmati' and 'care of Ruqaiya Bano'? As if any of that mattered! Perhaps he didn't go at all, or perhaps the guards didn't let him in, laughing at the idea of a rustic-looking chit of a boy, pretending to be some sort of an emissary come to meet with their commander.

It wasn't as if the letter bore a royal seal or something!

My mind felt disoriented, thoughts strangely jumbled and rambling without any semblance of order. Where had Bhanwar hidden last night? Perhaps on the branch of a tree. It was lucky that none of the jaannisaars noticed him, or else the poor man might have been felled to the ground, a poisoned shaft sticking out of his torso! O my God, what all am I thinking! The embrace flashed through my mind's eye, my body stretched upwards on the balls of my feet. Were we visible in the dim light? How much did he see? The soles of my feet and my palms felt icy. Night fell. Possibly the last night of my life, I thought.

My childhood came back to me. Then I realized, I was recalling Rukmini hidden in Razia's secret underground chamber, humming her petition to Krishna. Suddenly, the image morphed itself into the woman in the maulshri mansion, singing:

> O Radha's Krishna Kanhaiya!
> Help my earthen boat across too.

My calves ached. I lay down on the bed and nodded off. When my eyes opened next, I'd no idea how long I had slept for. A half-hour, an hour, two hours, a whole century? I did not have the vaguest sense of how long it was to dawn. I must have drifted off into a fitful sleep again, for I lay dreaming—and thinking, too, whether it was a dream or something that happened—of a soldier, wearing a shiny steel helmet and armour, on a massive horse advancing towards me, a severed head held upon his spear. As he comes closer, I recognize it is Bhanwar's head. I woke up with a start. The window was flooded with light, as though the forecourt was full of fire-torches, second night in a row.

As I tried to peep out the window, I saw a brightly outlined female figure, standing by the bed, and got goosebumps all over. She whispers, 'Don't be afraid, my child. I'm Reva. Once, long ago, you came into my lap, your life in peril, but I saved you. You're still under my protection. Look for me in better days, your day in the sun. Search for me. I'll await you under a huge tamarind tree, as a perennial spring. If you do care to come looking for me, I'll bathe you every morning…'

The shining figure vanished as suddenly as it had materialized. I could not possibly tell you whether it was real, or simply a figment of my imagination, gone haywire under stress.

I finally got out of bed and peeped out. the forecourt of the Garh was indeed lit up by scores of torches burning on the walls. Was this also a dream? No, not this time around. I pinched my arm to be sure. The courtyard was teeming with Rao's men-at-arms, as though preparing to defend the Garh. Maybe a hundred, two hundred or more of them, I couldn't really say. Their preparatory hubbub was suddenly drowned by a deep, rhythmic sound of galloping hooves, a huge number of them, pounding on cobblestones together.

I noticed that for the first time, the gates of the Garh entrance were shut and barred. The metal studs on them, shaped like lotuses in full bloom, were glinting in the flickering light of torches. A distant memory came floating in. The shutters of the gates of the maulshri mansion had similar lotus-studs on them.

The rhythmic sound of hooves was much closer now.

And then, amidst a terrible noise of men shouting and timber cracking, the ramming logs took the shutters apart, their splintered pieces flying all over the place. Pandemonium broke, as heavily armed cavalrymen with steel helmets and armour filled the courtyard. Rao's men hastily retreated to regroup in a pitiful defensive position, close to the edge of the verandah. It was apparent that they stood overwhelmed. Many of them twisted and turned, as if looking for someone to tell them what they were supposed to do next, but there was no trace of either Rao or Revadiya or Kaluram. Perhaps they too, like Bhanwar, had decided to use a length of rope, to fight another day! Except for the medley of horse neighing and stamping their hooves on the cobbles, a hush had fallen over the courtyard.

The contingent leader stood tall in his saddle, straining his boots against the stirrups, and called out, 'Where's Rao Yaduveer? And throw your weapons down, I say. Surrender forthwith, and you might yet get out of this alive!'

There was a deathly silence, no one responded for a while. Then some of the bravehearts among Rao's men, petrified until now, seemed to snap out of a trance, and charged forward with their swords, to challenge the intruders. But the very next instant, they were felled to the ground, lying motionless. The aim of the archers, already in position on the wall over the entrance, was so accurate that not an arrow had been wasted.

All had gone silent again. The rest of Rao's men stood cringing.

The contingent leader sat back comfortably in the saddle. Then, he leisurely took out a firman-scroll from his saddlebag and began to read out aloud:

> Rao Yaduveer,
>
> First, greetings to you from Sultan Baz Bahadur!
>
> Furthermore, you are hereby commanded to send over Rani Ruupmati, Patt-Rani of the Sultan of Malwa, honourably to

> Mandavgarh in the safe custody of Rabat Khan, commander of the contingent detailed to escort her.
>
> Commander Rabat Khan,
>
> You are hereby commanded to ensure the compliance of the orders as above, at all cost but with minimum bloodshed, two hours before dawn tomorrow. If met with resistance even after due warning, you shall bring to the Sultan the severed heads of those who choose to stand in the way of the mission entrusted to you.

'Is Rao Yaduveer here or not, will someone tell me now?' asked Rabat in an exasperated shout, but there was no one to respond. Rao and his close aides were still nowhere to be seen.

'Is there anyone else who wishes to defy the Sultan's command? If not, throw your weapons down. Now! Rabat Khan's not here to slice carrots and radishes!' Rabat was clearly losing his patience.

The courtyard reverberated with metal-on-metal sounds as swords, axes and spears began to be thrown into heaps. Rid of them, the cowering men kneeled, with their hands clasped behind their necks.

'Now, someone tell me where to find Rani Ruupmati.'

Holding the iron bars of my window and taking in all that was happening, I wanted to shout, 'Hey, look up! I'm here.' But then the saner of the voices in my head whispered urgently, *Don't open your mouth. You're Rani Ruupmati now, learn to behave like a queen. There's no need to shout like a frightened child, everything's going to be just fine.*

But that was precisely when it all went horribly wrong!

There was a sudden commotion amid the cavalrymen milling around. Someone was shouting out in alarm, 'Hey, stop him! Stop that man. He ran off with my sword, catch the scoundrel!' A much bigger pandemonium broke out this time. A hundred voices yelled excitedly, and those who were far away tried to stand tall on the balls of their feet and craned their necks, to get a better view of what was happening. I could see everything from my vantage point, a floor above.

The moment I saw him sprinting frantically, weaving among the horses and men to avoid being caught, the naked sword glinting, I feared the worst. I didn't know exactly what it could be, but something really bad, and I cried out as loud as I could, 'Nooooo, Bhanwar! For heaven's sake, Bhanwar, stop!' But my scream was drowned in the uproar. The noise down there was like a sea at storm.

Before anyone could quite understand what was happening, Bhanwar had reached the side of Rabat's mount, and was shouting at him:

'No one can take Rani Ruupmati from here while I'm alive! Come, fight me!'

Rabat could hardly believe his eyes!

'Hey! Aren't you the one that brought the Rani's letter? What's wrong with you?' he said soothingly.

Bhanwar was so short, his head barely reached the horse's back and the heavy sword kind of swayed in his hand. Perhaps it was the first time ever that he was holding one! *Rao never let me hold either a sword or a piece of chalk ever in my life…*

Looking in dismay at the sword, swaying unsteadily in the hand of an obvious novice, Rabat started chuckling, 'Have you gone mad, young man? Put it down…'

He was only halfway through counselling him, when the sword whistled through the air and came down, off-target, lodging itself deep inside the horse's mane. Bhanwar's face was dyed red with the beast's blood, spurting like a breach in a dam. Suddenly, the horse slumped, and with it, Rabat also fell heavily, landing awkwardly with his elbows to the ground, apparently without any serious injury.

The hue and cry couldn't get any noisier. I screamed loud and long, but it was of no use.

Rabat got back to his feet quickly, with a murderous look in his eyes, but it was clear from the quickly changing expressions on his face that he was trying to control his rage. After all, the dwarf was some sort of a confidant of the Malikaa-to-be. He didn't retaliate, for what did a horse matter, one could always get another.

But what can one do about the hand of Fate, my dear scribe?

Before Rabat Khan could order Bhanwar to be taken into custody, his deputy came sprinting from behind and beheaded Bhanwar with a clean swipe of his scimitar. It all happened in a flash.

Ketki ran down from the verandah, screaming and wailing like a madwoman, and flung herself down on the ground muddied by a mix of animal and human blood. She took the severed head of Bhanwar on her lap and broke into a loud lament, slapping her forehead in frenzy. The silence that ensued the beheading was filled by her wailing.

Pandijju got down from the verandah, walking silently to where Ketki squatted. He paused and patted her head gently, 'Calm down, daughter! Everyone's time is destined.' Then turning to Rabat, 'There's no need for any more bloodshed, Khan. I don't know where Rao Yaduveer is, but I'm his pandit. Come, I'll take you to the Rani.'

When the bolt outside my door rattled, I knew that my time at Garh Dharmapuri was about to come to its end.

Walking through rows of Rao's men kneeling in surrender, I walked to the spot where Bhanwar had committed suicide. Indeed, it was nothing but plain suicide and Ketki now sat lamenting him. I stopped for a few moments near her, but neither she looked up, nor had I the courage to address her. Words of consolation, I thought, would sound so inane, kind of hollow. Instead, I resorted to make-believe. The unfortunate woman sitting on blood-soaked earth, mourning her brother's gory end was a scene from one of my nightmares. I walked on to the huge palanquin draped in crimson silk embroidered with gold thread. Sultan's Khan-e-saamaan stood in front, his fist on his chest, his head bowed in a silent salute.

Vision 43

Eight palanquin-carriers in front and eight in the rear. It was a large palanquin, so large that one could sleep fully stretched in it. The plump mattress was covered in cream-coloured silk sheets, and there were pillows and bolsters in crimson and gold velvet covers, with dainty tassels dangling from drawstrings. The carriers changing shoulders made the palanquin bed sway, as though it were floating on waves.

I wondered what my new life was going to be like. Pandijju was wont to say, whenever you're about to start something new, always remember to invoke Ganesha, the lord of auspicious beginnings, and seek his blessings. I was trying to picture in my mind the Ganesha statuette in an alcove atop the Garh entrance. I've no idea when I drifted off into deep sleep, or how long I slept for. I woke with a start as someone shouted a command to the carriers, 'That's it, put the palanquin down on that parapet.'

I was amazed to find my cheeks wet. Perhaps I had wept while sleeping, racked by some nightmare about Bhanwar's tragic end. I wondered whether Rabat would be carrying his severed head back to Mandav. Maybe not, for it had still been in Ketki's lap when we left. Ah, poor Bhanwar! He truly was in love with me and he couldn't live down the guilt of his indiscretion.

The palanquin had been stationary for some time now. Just when I was beginning to wonder if I should step out, the curtain lifted, and I kept gazing at her face for the longest time. I had not seen such a dark-skinned woman, ever in my life. Head to heel, of a complexion as dark as a moonless night, or coal. Her skin shone like a Shiva-linga of black stone, smoothened by thousands of hands passing over it and a round head full of tightly curled hair, trimmed short. She had large eyes, with whites of eyeballs the colour of alabaster, a small upturned nose and sensuously full lips. It was a remarkably captivating visage, complexion notwithstanding, that I looked at.

'Khushaamdeed, Malikaa,' she said with a bow, her voice as deep as her colour.

'You…?' I could only say as much.

'I'm Nayla. The Sultan has been kind to give me the privilege of serving you as your principal lady-in-waiting. Otherwise, I supervise the harem guards.'

'Why did you address me as "Khushaamdeed Malikaa"? My name is Ruupmati, Rani Ruupmati. I was unable to understand many of the words you just used,' I said in a wondering tone.

'Rani, it would be more appropriate for you to address me as tum. I'm your servant. Khushaamdeed means welcome, and we address the first queen as malikaa. I have to tell you many more things, but you might want to freshen up a bit and eat something first?'

'I want to remain Rani Ruupmati, please don't call me Malikaa. Where's the Sultan?'

'He's out for his morning ride, and might bring some game in.'

As I came out of the palanquin and we both stood together, I noticed Nayla was even taller than I, and her neck stood out from the shoulders, like a startled doe's. She was a rather attractive woman, statuesque and well-endowed.

The palanquin had on arrival been placed on a stone platform in a mango grove. My escorts had dispersed to rest awhile in the shade. The rays of the early morning sun, coming through new leaves the lightest shade of green, gave a sparkling sheen to the crimson satin atop the palanquin. Wildflowers swayed lightly in the spring breeze, on the undulating expanse of the open grassland that sloped down in front of us. There were five huge cottage-tents, pitched in a flatter part of the green, some two hundred steps from where we stood. Big enough to almost be regular cottages, except that they had canvas for walls and ceiling. The one at the centre was red-coloured and larger than the rest, which were all white. On top of the red tent, a dark-green triangular flag, with a crescent and star emblazoned with silver thread on it, fluttered in the wind.

'The large red tent is the Sultan's, and the rest are for his attendants and personal guards, the jaannisaars, men who're expected to die happily protecting the Sultan's life, God forbid, should the need arise,' Nayla said pointing to the tents.

From where we stood, all the way up to the red tent, a narrow strip of red carpet had been laid to make a sort of welcome walkway, on either side of which stood heavily-armed soldiers dressed in black every twenty paces or so, looking outward for possible intruders. The group of tents was also similarly guarded by men in black, with several cannons in a ring all around it.

'All these men in black, the jaannisaars, are here to keep you and the Sultan safe, Rani,' Nayla said reassuringly.

That night when Nayla and I sat chatting by ourselves, she told me a whole lot of things. It was I who got the conversation going since I was assailed by any number of conflicting emotions, apprehensive voices in my head, curious to know what kind of life I was headed for: *God forbid, Ruup, but could you possibly be going from one prison to another, and this one more heavily guarded at that, night and day? How much do you really know about how a Mussalman sultan's harem works? Life at the Garh was like an open jail. You could sneak out at will to the Ardhapadma and thank God for that little piece of heaven on earth. But would it be possible to escape the shackles of the sultan's harem? And then the strict observance of purdah! Wouldn't it all be so suffocating? He has told you already, he has other queens and kept women. They'll be breathing venom down your neck, all the time in the confines of a shared harem!*

Then my other voice would come up: *So, what was the alternative? Having accepted the poison cup ordered by my diabolical father, and depriving myself of a life with the lover my heart yearned for, irresistibly? Or, should I have run away with Bhanwar to a lifetime of destitution, or begged with folded hands that loathsome blackguard, Revadiya? No! Whatever has happened is your providence. You better believe that to be true, and live to the fullest, each golden moment, of this third lifetime with your lover, as handsome as Kaamdev. Whatever happens, is what was destined.*

Nayla and I were in the rear section of the tent-cottage, while the Sultan and his favourite courtiers and generals sat relaxing in a musical soiree out front, each of them with a silver cup in hand. A singer was performing a rendition of raga Maalkauns. The Sultan himself accompanied him on the tambura, their music meeting with generous applause from time to time. While hearing them, we could see the soiree as well, through a square of netting in the canvas divider, while remaining invisible ourselves, as the rear section was relatively dimly lit. But my heart was not in the music that night. I was thinking about my new life. To get a conversation going, I asked Nayla, 'You don't seem to be from here, I mean, origin-wise?'

'Now I belong here, but you're right, Rani. Across the Arabian Sea, there is a huge country that the Arab seamen call Alkebulan. I'm originally from there, Afuraka, the Dark Continent. A large number of Portuguese vessels hunt for slaves in the jungles along the coast there, catching people like animals, with a surprise hit on the head from behind, or by nets thrown down from trees overhead and then selling them in slave-markets in faraway countries. My mother and I were taken in the coastal forests of Ethiop. They brought us to Surat and sold us separately. I was perhaps seventeen or eighteen then. I lived in the harem of Sultan Qadir Shah for five years and then with Shujat Khan for thirteen years. After his accession, Baz Bahadur freed me and made me the chief of harem guards. Now I'm thirty-six and have been living in Mandav for the last eighteen years.'

'Thirty-six years! I thought you'd only be a few years older than I, but you're more than twice my age. You don't look like it,' I said.

'God has been kind, Rani.'

'Nayla, can I trust you like an older sister, to help me?' I asked, almost pleading.

'Certainly, Rani, you can rely on me completely. That's why Baz made me your lady-in-waiting.'

Only Baz! Not even Bahadur suffixed, I thought to myself. It's quite another matter that she was one of his father's women, but still only Baz. After an uncomfortable pause, I asked:

'All right, tell me then, how many wives and concubines are there in the Sultan's harem?'

'As for wives, Khulla Jani's the only one. She and Baz were married about ten years ago. There are some six or eight other girls besides, but their main job is singing and dancing. You know how passionate he is about music.'

'Would I have to live together with them, I mean, in the same apartment?' I asked, dreading what the reply might be.

'No, no, Malikaa! I beg your pardon, I meant Rani. The palace complex is the same, Jahaz Mahal, but the Sultan ordered a separate apartment to be renovated and refurbished, specially for you. It has nothing to do with the rest of the palace. And yes, you'll also have a separate kitchen, and the Sultan has ordered that I'll taste your food before you eat.'

'What do you mean "taste"? Will I have to eat your leftovers?' I must have sounded appalled, for she hastened to reassure me.

'No, no. I will taste the food from the cooking pots in your presence, before serving suchchaa food on your plate.'

'But why does anyone need to taste my food?' I was still bewildered.

'Well, it's necessary, to make sure that no one has poisoned your food.'

'Poison my food! Why would anyone want to do that?'

'Out of envy!' she said nonchalantly, as though it was commonplace to poison people out of envy.

Oh my, what kind of people am I going to live with! I felt a bit light-headed. Even Ketki, for all her tantrums, had never tried to poison me. God alone knows how the poor woman is faring, I thought to myself, as Nayla said hesitantly, 'Rani, I have to tell you something else. You'll have to wear a hijab when there are other men around. It's the custom here.'

'Hijab? What's a hijab?'

Nayla brought out a triangular piece of fine silk netting, 'You will have to wear this tied behind the head, covering the lower part of the face, and it will go with a turban to cover your hair.'

'Even within my Raniwaas you mentioned?'

'No, no, not there.'

'Nayla, are you people going to keep me locked up inside the palace like a prisoner serving time?'

'Most certainly not, Rani. Quite the contrary, the Sultan was saying he'll take you along wherever he goes, riding and hunting and all.'

My heart suddenly felt much relieved, as though it had just escaped being caged. The hijab seemed like a small price to pay!

VISION 44

It's difficult for me to say with certainty who had engineered what followed later that night. Either Khulla Jani, Baz's estranged wife, infuriated by the rumours of a Hindu girl about to replace her as the first queen, had bribed Rabat Khan, or he was driven by ambitions of his own.

By the time the music soiree finished, it was near midnight. Courtiers rose to their feet, bending low to offer kornish to the Sultan, and left one by one, a trifle unsteady on their feet from all the wine they had consumed. Baz sat, putting his tambura back in its red satin cover, and finally got up to offer a pranaam with his palms joined together and head bowed, to the maestro, waiting to take leave of him.

'He is Rai Chand, the seniormost musician at court, and the music tutor to the Sultan. Baz holds him in high esteem,' Nayla whispered to me.

As Baz entered the rear enclosure where we sat, Nayla bent low to greet him, 'Khushaamdeed, Amir, please come,' she said, raising the black satin curtain of another door that I hadn't quite noticed in the dimly-lit rear section. The chamber inside was so brightly lit, my eyes were dazzled. It was much larger and even more richly decorated. It had plush carpets with intricate patterns on the ground, an exquisitely carved four-poster bed in the middle, a huge candelabra above it with no less than fifty candles burning, besides the ones in crystal candlesticks, fixed to tent poles. There were several large mirrors fixed to the poles and the overhead beam above reflected that light, making it even brighter. I was thrilled to see our life-size reflections—me and my handsome lover—in such large mirrors, and kept looking around, rendered speechless for a while. Suddenly, Baz said, 'Takhliyaa!' Nayla bent low again and backed out of the chamber, replacing the satin cover.

As soon as we had privacy, Baz moved towards me, his arms extended. I put my palm up to stop him.

'Why, because I've had wine to drink?' he looked at me, surprised.

'No, that's not it. You're a sultan after all. It's only expected that you'd drink!'

'Why, is it compulsory for sultans to drink?' he asked, clearly amused.

'Yes, my guru, Pandijju, used to say that kings and sultans cannot have sound sleep without drinking. They have nightmares of swords hanging over their heads.'

'Then, what is it?'

'Why were you so late coming to me? I'm in a sulk now.' I smiled.

He lifted me and laid me lightly on the four-poster, decorated with rose petals.

'Ouch!' A number of fine thorn-heads had pricked my back.

'What happened?' he asked in alarm.

'It seems some thorns remained sticking to the petals.'

'Then, I guess we'll have to try out these Isfahani rugs for now!'

We had barely moved to lie on the carpet beside the bed, when the massive candelabra, weighing several maunds, crashed down on the four-poster with a great thud, amid sounds of timber giving way and glass shattering. The bed-linen was up in flames instantly, at several places, from the burning candles that had fallen on it. The tent poles had gone askew at the corners, with the central beam collapsed, and the whole place was filling up with acrid-smelling smoke at an alarming pace. A major fire seemed only moments away.

Baz leapt up instantly, and in the same flowing motion, his sword appeared in his right hand, unsheathed. With his left arm protectively around my shoulder, he brought me out into the rear section, shouting, 'Nayla, take care of the Rani.' Nayla appeared, with a naked sword in hand, too, and took charge of me. Baz hurried away, out of the cottage.

'Jaannisaars.' I could hear him shouting commands, 'Take the tent staff into custody! Disarm the escort contingent, hurry! Make sure, no one gets away.'

In the next half hour, Baz had everything under control. The tent staff in shackles and Rabat's contingent disarmed and surrounded by jaannisaars. Two of them stood on either side of Rabat, though he still had his weapons on him. He looked worried, kind of bewildered.

Even in the midst of that entire hullabaloo, Nayla had quickly put a hijab on my face and brought me into one of the white tents which were still intact. We now sat below a partly enclosed awning, not far from where the Sultan was holding an impromptu court proceeding, under the open sky.

Baz was sitting on the edge of a rock jutting out of the grassy slope, an inexplicable smile playing on his lips, as though nothing out of the ordinary had happened. He called out to the chief of his jaannisaars, 'Mohammad Khan, have the tent-man brought forth, and the chopping block fixed.' Two soldiers came carrying a sawn-off piece of a thick tree trunk, like the one on which Bhanwar's brother had been beheaded, and placed it in the middle of the gathering. Two other men in black brought forth a trembling middle-aged man.

'What is your name, my brother?' asked Baz gently, as though only intending to make his acquaintance.

'Qu...Qu...Qutbuddin, sire,' the man stammered, his eyes widened in fright, hands folded.

'Did you put up my tent-cottage?'

'Yes, Your Majesty.'

'Have his head placed on the block, Mohammad,' Baz said sternly.

'Sire! Please have mercy on me, Sultan, it's not my fault, mercy, sire!' Qutbuddin was shaking violently.

'Then, whose fault is it? Never before has the tent been put up so tardily.'

'For Allah's sake, please have mercy on me, Sultan.'

Baz said nothing. Two of the soldiers forced down the man's neck on to the chopping block. Qutbuddin was now screaming in fright, his tears and saliva wetting his face.

'Brother Qutbuddin, why are you hell-bent on taking someone else's blame on yourself! Whose doing was it, since you're not to blame? Why don't you come clean and name him?'

The Sultan was smiling, digging little holes in the ground near his feet with the tip of his sword and surreptitiously scrutinizing faces around him, from the corner of his eyes.

'Sire, please spare me! I'll tell you everything. It was Naib Parvez Khan, he gave me five gold mohurs for it.'

'He is a liar!' shouted the deputy of Rabat Khan, gnashing his teeth, from the midst of disarmed men.

Qutbuddin loosened his cummerbund, and five gold coins rolled onto the ground, jingling.

'Jaannisaars, take Parvez into custody,' said Baz, slowly lowering the fingers of his right hand in a silent signal. The severed head of Qutbuddin rolled towards the coins.

Pointing to Parvez, the Sultan said, 'Now put this scoundrel's neck on the block.'

'No, please have mercy, Sultan, I beg you!' Parvez trembled like a leaf in gusty winds. Losing control of his bladder, he had wetted his lower garments.

'I only…by Allah, I only carried out Commander Rabat Khan's orders!' he blabbered through a terrible bout of sobbing, but before he could say anything more, Rabat roared: 'Liar!' and rushing forward, beheaded Parvez.

'This is what the kamzarf liar deserved, Sultan!' he said, breathing hard.

'You are dead right, Rabat Khan, he was indeed kamzarf, no wonder he couldn't hold a secret long.'

This time around Baz did not give any command. He merely dipped his right hand's fingers in the same silent signal, as before. Mohammad Khan, the jaannisaar chief, took a couple of steps forward, and with one fell blow decapitated Rabat, standing on his feet.

I shivered at the three beheadings I had witnessed in less than an hour, but unlike the previous time, I neither felt queasy nor threw up. Indeed, the thought that I was changing very fast did cross my mind, leaving me a trifle uneasy.

The next day, when we arrived at Mandav, the jaannisaars hung the severed heads of Qutbuddin, Parvez and Rabat Khan from the ramparts.

Vision 45

It was nearly dawn by the time the summary trial and executions were over. It seemed to me that all that blood had flowed down the grassy slopes and painted the horizon a dark crimson.

After the attempted assassination, Baz was not inclined to stay out in the open countryside, any longer. He immediately ordered the camp broken.

The jaannisaars had divided themselves into two lots. The first surrounded the disarmed soldiers and marched them back to the capital, and the other took us inside a protective ring for the journey.

Mohammad Khan came and bowed to the Sultan: 'Sire,

we're ready to depart. Shall we take the shorter route through Jahangirpura, or Nalchha?'

'The shortcut is rather rocky and uneven, the Rani will be unnecessarily inconvenienced. Let's go through Nalchha, and send an advance party to the commander of Nalchha Fort. We'll halt there for the night. He should prepare to offer a suitable reception to the Rani, and also keep elephants ready for our journey ahead. Let's go.'

Nayla had put the hijab on me for the ride, as also a turban with a sparkling diamond, as big as a large grape, stuck in the middle. Baz had on a long robe of maroon kamkhaab, close-fitting pyjamas, and gold-rimmed, pointy moccasins. His head was protected by a tempered steel helmet set with rubies. Our horses trotted side by side, and Nayla's, a few paces behind us.

Except for that short nap in the palanquin, I hadn't slept for two nights in a row. Soon I began to feel terribly drowsy, and the rocking motion of the horse only made it worse. Baz was cautiously scanning the vistas for any possible signs of an ambush, but every once in a while, he would glance smilingly at me. Seeing my eyes turn droopy, he said, 'Be careful, or you'll fall off the horse!'

Indeed, I was so sleepy, it was difficult to keep my eyes open. I decided a conversation might help.

'You cut off people's head without batting an eyelid. Don't you feel any pity?'

'Running a sultanate is no child's play. If I don't chop off others' heads, I might lose my own, Rani.'

'But I heard you even killed both your brothers for the throne!'

'Yes, I killed one of them, the other fled. Ajiyala wasn't my blood-brother, and he was plotting something similar against me. It's only that I made the first move, and succeeded. But in any case, had all three of us been blood-brothers, it would have made little difference! Each one of us wanted the whole of Malwa for himself and let alone three, even two swords don't fit into a single scabbard, as the saying goes!' Silenced by his plain-speaking, I dropped the topic.

'Rabat Khan read out your firman at the Garh...'

'Hmm!' he made a non-committal sound.

'You mentioned me as your patt-rani in it, but when we were never formally married—' Baz did not let me finish.

'Why, have you forgotten what I said after your sweet little gift the other night? Let me recall it for you. Didn't I say, "With these incredibly beautiful lotuses of Ardhapadma, and the reflection of the crescent moon in its waters, and this reddish-brown favourite of yours as witnesses, I take you as my wife in the gandharva tradition?" All right, let's include Nayla as a further witness. Nayla!' He called out to her with a backward glance.

'At your service, Sultan,' she responded, easing her mount forward.

'With you and these horses as witnesses, I'm taking Rani Ruupmati as my wife in a gandharva marriage. Will you remember it?'

'As you wish, Sultan. I'm deeply honoured, sire,' she said.

'But if the marriage is not made public, who will accept me as patt-rani!' I said petulantly.

'Yes, you have a point there but I'm hardly to blame, Rani. It was you that cribbed "Will you make me a Mussalman?" Now, without making you convert, I can hardly have a nikaah with you. On the other hand, if I were to go around the fire with you, the mullahs won't stop short of reading the khutba in someone else's name! I guess we will have to make do with a gandharva vivaah in the circumstances, won't we?' Baz said laughing.

I was abashed.

'Oh, I said that because I have been worshipping Radha-Krishna and the Devi since I was a child. I couldn't possibly forget them for my own happiness!'

'No, why should you? Even I worship a Devi, for that matter,' he replied smiling broadly. I looked at him amazed.

'But Pandijju always told me that idol-worship is strictly forbidden among...' Baz laughed out loud with a mischievous look to his eyes. I suddenly caught on to what he had meant and my cheeks turned a deep crimson.

'All right, I'll ask you two questions,' said Baz, changing track. 'They will help pass time, and meanwhile we'll have arrived at Nalchha. Tell me, were Radha and Krishna ever married?'

'No, I haven't come across any such thing in the books I've read,' I said.

'Well then, tell me what did your Pandijju say in your history lessons? Did Alauddin Khilji get Rani Padmini for all the troubles he took?'

'No, she committed jauhar.'

Before I could say anything more, Baz said:

'But I have got my Padmini without much ado. Look, there it is, we're about to arrive at the Nalchha Fort.'

The fort was visible straight ahead. There was a large crowd of people gathered at the entrance, waiting to welcome us. As we arrived, the massive arched gates reverberated with an ear-piercing cacophony of duhul-taasha, turhi-nakkaara, jhaal and nai, all combined.

Vision 46

What a striking change my life had undergone, in just two days! There was hardly any point comparing my lonely existence in a shabby room in the Garh, and the two or three pairs of ordinary clothes and plain food there, with the regal opulence of the Nalchha Fort palace complex, the fanfare, and the high-ranking noblemen lined up to welcome us.

The room where we were to stay was beautifully decorated with coloured glass orbs, hanging from the ceiling down to differing heights, large mirrors on the walls, and expensive-looking rugs on the floor. It had a finely carved four-poster bed, huge as a ship, in the middle, teapoy tables laden with fruits and savouries in fancy plates, and silk curtains on the widows wafting in the morning breeze. Six or eight maids hovered around us, obsequiously waiting to jump at any command that Nayla or I might give. It was as though someone had waved a magic wand and transformed my life overnight!

I thought it was going to take me long to get used to all this.

'Rani, would you like something to eat?' asked Nayla.

'No, I'm not hungry, but I would certainly appreciate a bath. After that I would like to sleep for at least a couple of hours.'

Nayla signalled to two of the maids. I thought they would take me out to some nearby pool, or the bathing ghat of a river. Little did I know that I was already a prisoner in a golden cage! There was a bathroom across the corridor, with a steaming marble pool. The maids prepared to undress me. I was disconcerted and told them to leave me alone, that I'd manage on my own. 'Don't be coy, Rani. Malikaas are only supposed to bathe like this,' said Nayla, from across a translucent curtain, her voice laced with a little giggle that sounded like tinkling of bracelets.

Ruup! Ruup, listen, a voice whispered in my head, *forget your old ways. This is a new life. You're no longer the kunwarani of the impoverished Garh Dharmapuri. You are Sultan Baz Bahadur's Patt-Rani, the Queen of Malwa! The sooner you get used to your new avatar, the better.*

'All right, go ahead. Undress me, and make sure you scrub my back nicely.' One of the maids took off my turban and put it on a rack. My curled hair cascaded like a little waterfall right down to my waist. 'Maashaallah!' one of them mumbled under her breath. Meanwhile, the other took to cleansing my back gingerly, fearing her touch might soil my skin. Nayla laughed again, sounding genuinely pleased with what she saw.

'Rani, many will turn green with envy, looking at you,' she said.

The new garments that the maids brought for me felt so light and soft, as though I had nothing on.

Once in bed, I fell into a deep slumber, sleeping like a

log from mid-afternoon right through the small hours of the morning. The spring breeze turned chilly in the hours before dawn. As I opened my woozy eyes, I found Baz sleeping by my side in his day clothes, his shoes still on. His sword in the scabbard lay on a table to his bedside. I thought it might make him more comfortable if I took his shoes off and put a duvet over him, but before I could make a move, a tall, dark silhouette emerged from the curtain, preempting me. Hardly had it touched a shoe, Baz sprang to his feet like a cheetah, and miraculously, by the time he was up on his feet, his sword was already in his hand, unsheathed.

'Shuh…rest easy, Sultan, just Nayla here,' she said in a whisper.

Baz fell back onto the bed as quickly as he had got up. Nayla quietly covered us both with a large duvet and retreated into the shadows behind the curtain.

I had silently kept observing all of this, with my eyes half-closed, pretending to be asleep. Baz fell into deep sleep almost instantly, but I kept tossing and turning through what remained of the night.

Vision 47

The human mind is possessed, in equal measure, by the nectar of trust and poison of suspicion, both holding each other in a critical balance. The moment the former is depleted, the latter begins to encroach.

Only last night I had pleaded with Nayla, addressing her as an older sister. Even until a few hours ago, I was thinking that my new setting was so unfamiliar and intimidating that it would have been tough to come to terms with it but for her guidance and advice. And now, only a while later, how sinister an aspect her character had assumed in my eyes! Could she possibly be Baz's secret lover?

No, no. Surely, I was letting my imagination run wild!

She had already told me frankly what she had been in the past. His father's concubine for thirteen years. Could the father's mistress now...? Well, she was, without a doubt, a well-kept and a rather attractive woman still. But Baz's secret lover! No, that was simply not likely, I told myself, still trying to convince myself that I was imagining things. Wasn't it possible that having lived in the intimate company of the late Sultan for long years, she had come to love Baz in a different way, perhaps?

But there was no denying the fact that as I got up to use the toilet early that morning, my mind was in turmoil. Where did she fit in? My head rang with her name. Nayla! Nayla! Nayla! Like an echo trapped in a vault. I was despairing already. Will that silhouette continue to emerge out of the shadows, like last night, to invade my privacy, leaving nothing secret between me and Baz? The thought soured me towards her, like my bias against Tara, after she warned me off Revadiya. Ironically, though, Tara had been right.

Ah! Tara, my dearest, do you even exist anymore? And Nayla, it appears you're hidden behind every blessed curtain!

As I returned, Baz was sitting up in bed, as though waiting for me. I found it amazing that he could recall every little thing about last night, and that in such a short time together, he was so deeply attached to me already that he read my thoughts, from a mere glance at my face. Apropos of nothing, he said, 'Rani, once you let suspicion get hold of you, it will be difficult to make it go away. Nayla will die before she betrays either of us.'

I lowered my eyes, embarrassed, 'No, no, as a matter of fact, I was looking for her.' I was lying despite being found out.

'She's gone to look at the arrangements for our departure,' he said. I found out much later that he had also lied, at least partly.

As we left for Mandav, that cavalcade of seventeen elephants, their hangings worked in gold and silver threads, glittering in the morning sun, was living proof of the splendour and inestimable wealth of the Malwa sultans. Except for one of them, all the rest had beaten-silver houdahs on their back. The sultan's elephant had a solid-gold houdah covered in red satin curtains, worked in gold thread and flew a triangular green pennant, similar to the one atop the ill-fated tent-cottage that was gutted the night before. The last two elephants only carried my maids, each one of them so beautiful that they could have been queens in their own right!

In my last days at Mandav much later, I wondered at times whether it was the fame of such inestimable wealth and the fairy-like beauty of the women in the sultan's seraglio, that eventually led to the undoing of Malwa.

After Nalchha the road was level for a time. Just before we came closer to the ascent of the Mandav plateau, Baz said, 'Rani, we are about to pass by Suuli Bardi. Don't look to your left for a while, this is where criminals sentenced to death are hanged.'

Beyond that point, the pathway ran continually along a ridge-like formation with deep gorges on either side, so narrow that with each step that the ponderously swaying elephants took, my heart leapt to my mouth for fear that they might fall into the abyss. The gorge near Kaankdaa Kho was so deep that my head reeled with fright.

Baz held me reassuringly with his arms around my shoulders and every once in a while, looked adoringly at me. When he did so, the large diamond on his sky-blue turban and chiselled gold earrings, glinting in the sun, dazzled my eyes. But for me, the intimacy of his passionate glances was far more precious than all the gold and silver and the regal paraphernalia that surrounded us. In mere two days of togetherness, Baz had become a soulmate for life.

Nayla was nowhere to be seen. On our arrival at Mandav, I did find out where she had been and busy doing what. But I had no idea that a long-cherished dream that I'd been nurturing, one that I believed to be on the cusp of being realized, was actually about to vanish forever. As a matter of fact, the very next moment, as it happened.

'Sultan, I wish to request you for a favour...' I began my petition self-consciously, but he cut my formal address short with an affectionate smile.

'Call me Baz, and tum, at least when we're by ourselves.'

I silently pointed to the mahout.

'Ah, you don't know yet; only the congenitally deaf and mute have the privilege to be the sultan's mahout.'

'I want to meet my mother as soon as we reach Mandav.'

'Alas!' he said looking sad, 'that won't be possible now. I myself wanted it, but Bano was so adamant...'

'What's the difficulty in meeting her?' I looked at him in total disbelief.

'She's not in Mandav.'

'She isn't? But she is your mother's... I mean, she's Badi Begum's lady-in-waiting, isn't she?'

'She was, but the day after she returned from that humiliating meeting with Rao, she went away to Vrindavan with Ammi jaan's permission. We tried pleading with her, but she wouldn't listen,' he said, looking down at his hands helplessly.

'Then I'll go to Vrindavan!' I said petulantly, like a child close to tears.

'Rani, Mathura is a major Mughal stronghold. If we went there, we might not return alive. I cannot put my life at risk,' said Baz, softly.

'Why, are you afraid of endangering your life for my sake?' I was in a deep sulk already.

'I wasn't talking of myself. I'm concerned for you. I don't want to lose you now, under any circumstances.'

Teardrops were rolling down my cheeks by then. Taking out a handkerchief from his pocket, Baz tenderly wiped them away.

Vision 48

As our elephant entered Mandavgarh through the three imposing arches of Dilli Darwaza, facing north, we were greeted with a fanfare similar to Nalchha, only the number of people gathered here was ten times more. Under the close watch of jaannisaars in all-black uniforms, countless military generals and members of the nobility, with their fists on their chests and heads bowed, waited to receive us. Behind them was a sea of the common citizenry, jostling to have a look at us and hail welcome, and the usual deafening backdrop, a tuneless mix of musical instruments playing at their loudest, to go with it.

We moved on, the Sultan smiling and waving to the crowds, acknowledging their chorus of 'Long Live Sultan Baz Bahadur!' We took a right turn near the Jami Masjid and passed by the white-marble dome of Hoshang Shah's mausoleum. People lining up the streets were singing and dancing joyfully, showering flower petals on one another, since throwing anything at the royal cavalcade might get them into trouble. The havelis on the way were decorated with flower strings and musicians played the surnai, regarded auspicious, seated in pavilions on top of the entrance portal.

Soon we were at the gates of the Jahaz Mahal sprawl. Here, a more select crowd from higher echelons and palace staff were gathered in welcome.

As soon as the mahout sat the elephant down, Baz jumped down from the houdah and jauntily turned a full circle with his right palm raised, as though blessing all those gathered to welcome us. The crowd roared back 'Long Live Sultan Baz Bahadur' amidst the melodious tune of surnai playing atop the gate.

A maid came jogging with a small silver table and placed it below the houdah, close to the massive side of the elephant, to help me get down from it.

Recalling Nayla's advice, I'd put a hijab on my face. As I put a foot on the silver stool to get down, Baz himself prompted the gathering, 'Long Live Rani Ruupmati!' The domes of the gate echoed back, as the crowd responded in unison, 'Long live Rani Ruupmati!'

At this distance of time, I cannot remember exactly how many collonaded verandahs, courtyards, chambers and corridors of the sprawling palace complex we passed through that first day, but I do remember seeing a well, in a courtyard which smelled of champa flowers. I learnt later that it was called champa-baori. The maids and palace eunuchs were lined up on either side of the way to my new habitat, the Raniwaas, showering flower petals and sprinkling rose water on us, as we walked. I could hear women singing somewhere in the distance. It sounded like a chorus that Hindu women sing on auspicious occasions.

The Raniwaas doorway stood across a pointed-arch portal, the shutters with climbing rose creepers inlaid in gold, with emeralds for leaves and topaz for flowers. The shutters seemed to open on their own as we arrived, as though by magic, suddenly revealing the women who had been singing Ganesha-vandana, an invocation to the lord of auspicious beginnings.

I looked at them in dismay. Fifteen or twenty women awaited us in traditional Hindu garments: long skirts, with cheerful red-and-yellow polka dots, the chunri and blouses with silver-foil borders, their faces veiled in near-transparent dupattas, wearing thick lines of vermilion and gold pendants in the parting of their hair.

The two in the lead had large metal platters in hand. One with an aarti-deep, a bowl of sandal paste, rice grains coloured in turmeric, durbaa-grass twigs, a small heap of rose petals and suchlike, and the other with a thaal, with a raised round edge, that contained a viscous mix of water and aaltaa, the colour of blood.

The bloodshed of the past two days, starting with Bhanwar, flashed through my mind. I rebuked myself silently: *Ruup, don't let your mind wander off to such memories in this auspicious moment; stay focused!* I noticed a pitcher full of raw rice across the base of the door frame.

The woman in the lead did aarti and put sandal-paste and vermilion tikaa on our foreheads, sprinkling turmeric rice and durbaa-twigs. The other said, smiling away to glory, 'Praise be! Our great good fortune our mighty sultan has brought home a Rani! Now wet your palms in aaltaa and put your prints on the wall here.' I did as told. She then sat down on her haunches and said, 'Now stand with your feet in the aalta-thaali. Yes! Now cross the threshold and topple the rice-pitcher down, with your right foot.' As I did that, dutifully, she looked up at me with her eyes gleaming in a mischievous smile. 'Now, you can go right in and feed rice-pudding to your man, to your heart's content!' she said with an abashed giggle and bowed her head.

Baz took off two pearl strings, from the many he wore around his neck, and gave them away to the two women and a gold mohur each to all the rest. They all but jumped for joy, greeting us with their palms together and heads bowed, and left, singing another stanza of Ganesha-vandana.

Leaving red foot-marks on the white marble floor, I crossed the forecourt of the apartment and went towards the corner room they had indicated as the kitchen. Well before I reached the entrance, I could see the tall dark figure of Nayla, almost a man's height, with her hands on her hips, supervising two maids stirring large pots of bubbling rice-pudding. Suddenly, my heart went cold. Oh, so she was the one behind all the elaborate arrangements for the ceremonial homecoming of a new Hindu bride! No wonder she was nowhere to be seen when we left Nalchha. Why didn't Baz just tell me, I thought wryly to myself, the poison of suspicion beginning to spread further.

Playing my mother-in-law to the hilt, isn't she?

I tried to get a hold on my rising bile: *You didn't ask, he didn't tell you, it's as simple as that! You were busy asking about your mother!*

Still, I wanted to say something sharp, but what I ended up saying was something quite different.

'Nayla, I don't know how to thank you enough for all this. The elaborate arrangements for a traditional welcome and all, but I wonder why you didn't tell me anything.'

'Sultan's orders, Rani!' she said, smiling, as she turned.

'But why hide such a beautiful ceremony?'

'He wants to welcome you with a surprise every step of the way. He loves you so…' then leaving the sentence unfinished, added with a shrug, 'Surely, you must know that already. Shall we bring the kheer for the Sultan, Rani? It's ready.'

I was miffed. I didn't want to share my Baz with anyone.

'Shouldn't I take it to him myself today?' I sounded brusque.

'As you wish, Malik… I beg your pardon, I mean, Rani.' She began to ladle out rice-pudding into two small silver bowls placed on a carved wooden tray. The maids stood watching, their heads bowed and fingers interlaced to keep them from trembling. An embarrassing silence had fallen over us. I couldn't bear it.

'Hadn't I told you not to address me as Malikaa? How does this "Malikaa" still come up every now and then! Were you serving some Malikaa before?' I said.

Nayla's eyes were lowered at the bowls on the platter, but her fingers holding the handles were steady. She said almost in a whisper, 'Yes, Rani, I was in the service of Badi Begum.'

'Taste the rice-pudding!'

'From the bowls?' she looked up.

'Yes, from the bowls, where else?' I said sarcastically.

Nayla took spoonfuls of kheer from the bowls by turns and dropped them into her mouth without letting the spoon touch her lips, her head tilted backward, and gulped. Then, she proffered the tray to me.

My dear scribe, you must think what a stupid, ungrateful and suspicious mistress I was to a faithful companion like Nayla, but don't forget that I was only a fifteen-year-old girl who had gone through so many ups and downs in her short life. I had been deceived so often that I did not trust anyone except my beau and was determined not to share the tiniest bit of his affection, with anyone at all.

Vision 49

'The kheer was delicious, but I must be off now, for at least a couple of hours. I've come back after several days and must attend to court matters for a while. Do I have the Rani's permission?' Baz rose to his feet, still looking at me as if enchanted, and left.

My apartment in the Shaahi Mahal, or the Raniwaas, as everyone called it, was truly magnificent. I began to explore it after Baz left.

Across the courtyard from the entrance, there were three large chambers in a row. The first was a reception hall with formal seating arrangement. To its right, across three pointed arches, was a more private living room, with a lotus-shaped marble pool and fountain in the middle. Further to its right, across a single pointed arch with rich carvings and red velvet curtains, was the bedroom with an enormous four-poster bed made of some black-coloured wood, once again shaped like a lotus. Directly above the bed hung a mat woven from peacock feathers, with a cord that ran over a wooden-pulley through the wall to the courtyard verandah. When summer came, I discovered the contraption was meant to be a manually-pulled fan.

The west-side doors of the three chambers gave on to a large rectangular open terrace, screened on three sides by delicate, pink sandstone jaali, with decorative pavilions at the corners. Its entire length was interspersed with small, pointed-arch peephole windows. I looked through one. There was a huge rectangle of well-tended green bordered by manicured flower beds, with a red sandstone fountain in the middle.

Across the park was a small stand-alone mansion, with blue domes and pavilions at either end and beyond it, in the far distance, one could see the pointed arches and arrow-slits of the Mandavgarh ramparts. I wondered who lived in the haveli with the blue domes.

To the south of the open terrace was the Munj Talao, a large man-made lake. The reflections of the domes and pavilions atop the palace seemed to be tossing on its waters all day long.

The entire floor of the living area of the Raniwaas was covered in cushy carpets with intricate patterns, obviously worth a fortune. The courtyard and the rest of the space were gleaming white marble. The sitting rooms were furnished with carved settees and matching chairs and small tables beside them, bearing fresh-cut flowers in green-stone vases. The doors and windows had silk curtains that swayed in the light breeze, coming across the open terrace, the walls adorned with delicate-looking blue-glass candlesticks and enormous candelabras hung from the ceiling, their glass pendants gleaming like real diamonds.

My new abode was marvellously decorated but, I haven't finished describing all of its parts and amenities.

In the north-side wall of the bedroom were two doors, shutters delicately inlaid with gold foil, flowering rose creepers that seemed to be the handiwork of the same craftsman who had done the main entrance shutters. One of them was padlocked while the other opened into a narrow corridor which ended in a giant-sized toilet area, almost as large as the living rooms. Two-thirds of it was occupied by a marble pool about two cubits deep, with water a sparkling crystal, tinged blue. On closer inspection, I noticed that the bluish hue came off the glazed pottery tiles with which its base and sides were paved. In one of the far corners of the bath-pool, there stood a metal cauldron with sturdy legs and a built-in fire-grate. There lay a large heap of round black stones the size of cannonballs by its side. The privy was separated by a latticed screen in black wood, similar to the wood used for the four-poster in the bedroom.

As I returned from the toilet area, Nayla stood at the bedroom end of the corridor.

'All this black wood furniture, the four-poster here and the screen in the bathroom, I haven't ever seen such black wood trees in the jungle around here. Where is this timber from?' I asked.

'The same place where I came from, Rani. The Alkebulan traders bring it,' she said in a matter-of-fact tone.

My face reddened, without a reason that I could make sense of.

'And the glass candlesticks, candelabras and the blue tiles in the bathing pool?'

'There is, they say, a Christian city called Venezia to the north of Alkebulan across the sea. The glassmakers there are magicians. Rani, do you need anything? Can I be excused from attendance for a while?'

'What's in there?' I asked, pointing to the locked door, cutting short her petition.

'I have no idea, Rani. I've never been inside.'

I thought to myself: *You don't know, or you won't tell?* But I said nothing.

'May I be excused for a while, then? The maids will, of course, be here to serve you in my absence,' she tried again.

'Where are you going? Will you not stay here, in the Raniwaas?' I asked, a bit puzzled.

'No, but my rooms are just a little distance away, here in the Shaahi Mahal itself. I'll be back shortly.'

'Yes, alright. If I need anything, I'll tell the girls,' I said, thinking again to myself: *Go, by all means, go, and I don't really care if you don't come back at all.* And still, no sooner had the thought occurred than I felt deeply ashamed of myself. How on earth did I become so haughty?

Equally soon, however, I forgot all about my compunction and fell to rejoicing in my fabulous new home. Ah! A house, a piece of a palace actually, that I could call my own, the very first that was absolutely my own! Wasn't that something!

Vision 50

That day, I thought my life was like one of those famous fireworks of Malwa whose rise to the heavens had been invisible in the dark, but now that it was up there, it had blossomed into a giant flower, its glowing petals illuminating the night sky.

As soon as Nayla left, four of the maids surrounded me solicitously. Indeed, they were most affectionate. I wondered whether Nayla had deliberately handpicked mostly Hindu maids for me—Kamla, Radha, Renu, and Zubeida.

'Rani, have a bath if you please, then we'll serve you lunch,' said Zubeida, the most vivacious of them all, for sure.

Two of them stripped me of my clothes in a trice; this time I didn't feel awkward being in the nude in front of them. It had only taken me a day to begin feeling as though I'd always bathed like this. Two of them began to rub sandal and turmeric paste all over me. By then Radha, having made a fire in the cauldron-grate, was heating black stone orbs and dropping them into the wire-mesh holder, underwater. In a short while, the water was comfortably warm. Meanwhile, Zubeida had found a rabab and had begun to play soulful snatches of raga Basant on it.

When I came out of the bath, my skin glowed like a pink pearl. Doing my hair up, the four of them gazed at me as though they weren't looking at a rani, but some fairy descended from the heavens above.

'Why are you staring at me like that?' I pretended a mild reprimand, and then, looking at my image reflected in the large mirror on the wall, smiled involuntarily.

Oh, dear scribe, you must surely think that I'm patting my own back for what I looked like.

No, no, Madam! I'm looking at you with my own eyes. Is there anything more to say!

By then, two of them had run to the clothes and jewellery

store, in a room to the south of the courtyard, and brought out a dark crimson set of skirt and blouse and dupatta with exquisite zari work, and a navratan necklace set with gleaming jewels.

Lunch was served to me in the private living room with the lotus fountain, on a plate made of solid gold. In the absence of Nayla, Zubeida happily went through the motions of 'tasting' my food. After lunch, I thought I'd take a nap, but that was not to be!

'Khulla Jani is here!' As a breathless Zubeida rushed in to announce her arrival, Radha, who had been massaging my foot, gasped and sprang to her feet as though a quake had been announced.

'What…where's she?' I got up.

'Outside, in the reception room. She walked in unannounced, with only with a maid behind her. She was asking for you!' Zubeida stammered, as though she might have made a mistake letting her in.

'All right, tell her I'll be there shortly.' I walked to the toilet, straightened my dress, patted my hair in place and walking with measured steps, came out into the front room.

She sat with an elbow resting on a bolster on the settee, one of her feet curled up on it and the other almost touching the floor, dangling comfortably. She was wearing a green kamkhaab jodaa, head uncovered and the dupatta hanging down. She had small piercing eyes, nose sharp as a knife's edge, and lips so thin that they appeared to be a single line. She had in her mouth a paan, swelling the right cheek out.

She didn't bother to get up or anything, as though she was sitting in her own house, and I had come to meet her instead. I folded my hands in a pranaam and sat down on the settee opposite hers.

She turned her head back, and the maid standing behind her hurriedly brought out an hourglass-shaped metal container from under her dupatta, extending it forward. Khulla let loose a long thin stream of red spittle into it, and then, chewing on the paan in her mouth, she said, 'So, after all, you're here! I have been hearing things about you for quite a while.'

I said nothing for some time. Then repeating my gesture of putting my palms softly together, I began a short welcome address, 'Rani Ruupmati offers her pranaam to you, Madam…' But she cut me short.

'Oh, come off it. Forget all this mime about Rani and Madam! Baz was needlessly making such a racket at the gates, "Rani Ruupmati Zindabaad" and all! Change your name, recite the kalma and have a proper nikaah with him, I say! Then you'll know. He has abducted you in any case, hasn't he?' she said smiling crookedly.

'He hasn't abducted me. He married me and has promised that he'll not make me a Mussalman,' I replied indignantly.

'Oh, come on, such promises are commonplace when you're new and also, you are beautiful, I see. Well, make hay while the sun shines!'

'But he is in love with me!' My tone was urgent.

'Love? What is that, my dear?' Khulla laughed aloud, scornfully.

'When you haven't experienced it yourself, how can I explain what it is, in a conversation? But you are his senior wife. You're most welcome to visit my Raniwaas, whenever you wish,' I said in a tone meant to end the conversation that seemed going nowhere.

'You speak well, I say,' she said smiling deviously, her small eyes becoming smaller.

Saying nothing in reply, I prepared to rise to my feet, but waving her fingers languidly and pointing to a silver box on the table between us, she said, 'Sit, sit, now that you're here, I've brought you some laddoos to welcome you. At least have some of these.'

I felt sudden panic, missing Nayla sorely. I resorted to a white lie, 'My pooja is not yet done. I'll have them afterwards,' I said rising to my feet, and finally, she did, too. Suddenly I noticed that I had an advantage over her. Khulla was a clear head shorter than I and had to look up as she said, 'Won't you show me around your Raniwaas, I say? I understand it has undergone a, what do you Hindus say…yes, now I recall, it has undergone a total uddhaar! Do you know who used to live here before you? Uncle's mother, Badi bi. She lived here for years with just one maid to attend on her, a real old-world kind, she even stitched her own clothes herself! This part of the palace was almost in ruins. Have you called on my dear Aunt yet?'

'Aunt? I'm sorry, I don't know who you mean?' She had sprung a surprise.

'Why, don't you know? Oh, how could you! You've just about arrived from a village, after all,' she said condescendingly, and went on, 'Badi Begum, Baz's mother, is my father's sister, and the late lamented Sultan Shujat Khan was my uncle.' Khulla's chin had gone up a notch as she informed me of her old royal connection.

After I had graciously accommodated her, taking her around my apartment, Khulla's face darkened and her eyes shone.

I smiled, taking joy in her displeasure! *Just you wait, Ruupmati,* I said to myself, *her ears will begin to let off smoke any moment now.*

'Who has had it renovated? Your habshin?' she asked bitterly. Then, without waiting for a reply, added, 'Beware of her. Indeed, she had my uncle bewitched and now she has Baz eating out of her hands as well! Don't say later I didn't forewarn you. And yes, don't forget the laddoos either. I made them myself, especially for you.'

I knew what she wanted to do to me in parting—kick me where it hurt the most, but by then, I was beginning to enjoy the duel, relishing the fact that she was going bottle green with envy.

'Indeed, I'm a village lass,' I said, pretending sombrely, 'having lived all my fifteen years in rusticity, but in eight years of reading and writing, I dare say I have yet to come across the word habshin. Who exactly were you talking about?'

'Oh, who else but that black monkey from Alkebulan, Nayla. But say, you really know how to read and write, do you?' Apparently, my words had found an unintended mark. I decided to drive them right home.

'Oh yes, I have a smattering of Hindi, Sanskrit, the great epics—all that, and a bit of history, geography and arithmetic as well. I can read and write Devanaagari. Baz was saying I should also learn to read and write Faarsi. I think so, too. It would help pass time usefully.'

Khulla stared at me in helpless amazement for a long moment. Then, she turned her head, and once again the maid promptly produced the spittoon. Having made copious use of it, Khulla turned abruptly on her heels and left without a word in farewell. For a while, I really thought that her ears must be emitting smoke, because a distinctly acrid smell was coming from somewhere.

Vision 51

The smell of smoke was too real to be arising out of just envy! I looked all around. Outside the Raniwaas, there was a square courtyard abutting the collonaded verandah. Thick plumes of smoke were coming out the window of a room on the top floor.

'What's that? Has a fire broken out?' I turned in alarm to ask Zubeida, standing behind me.

'No, Rani, it's not a fire. That is the kitchen window of Nayla bibi,' she replied.

'What kind of smell is this? What does she cook?'

Zubeida hesitated, and then said in a low tone, 'She's very fond of rabbit meat. She traps them in the nearby woods, and cooks them on charcoal.'

'Oh well! Shut the Raniwaas door tight,' I said, as I turned to go back in.

There was no smell inside, but I kept sniffing with a frown

on my forehead, that refused to go away. I kept wondering whether the habshin also practised some sort of black magic. Apparently, Khulla Jani had not returned empty-handed either!

It was an inexplicable quandary. I was unable to get rid of negative feelings about the very person that I needed the most at the slightest sign of a dilemma, even when Khulla asked me to taste her laddoos. Only a moment ago, I was suspecting the 'habshin' of performing black magic, and the very next it occurred to me that if she were here, I'd ask her whether I ought to go see Badi Begum sometime soon. Then again, why her? I could ask Baz, if he had returned from court.

It felt like a century had gone by since he left that morning, and with this thought, I lay down and drifted off to sleep.

When my eyes opened, there they were: Baz sitting on the edge of the bed near my feet, and Nayla, standing a few paces behind him.

'You…when did you come?' I said, rising up in bed.

'Just now,' said Baz. He looked tired, his face drawn. He turned to Nayla and said, 'Nayla, would you arrange for me to have a bath? Ustad Rai Chand is performing this evening to welcome Rani and me. It's a very special concert.'

'Won't the Sultan go to his palace to bathe? Clothes and all?' Nayla said tentatively.

'No, I'll stay here. Inform Suleman and get him to send over my clothes and things.'

'I am at you service, Sultan.' She left.

I took a deep breath, and told Baz all that had passed between me and Khulla Jani, and all that had happened in his absence, mentioning the acrid smell of raw rabbit roasting on charcoal. Although, I stopped short of sharing my suspicion of Nayla performing black magic. I couldn't share the ambivalence towards Nayla, plaguing my mind, even with him.

He heard me out desultorily. When I finished, he said, 'Ruupmati, Khulla is simply insane. She is jealous of Nayla. Naturally, she would be even more so, of you. Whatever you said to her is just perfect. Don't pay attention to her babbling and for heaven's sake, do not have those laddoos! She wouldn't, of course, have poisoned them but they would certainly taste like poison. She doesn't know how to make anything.'

Then, stretching himself, as though to relieve his fatigue, he said with a sigh, 'Ah, the mullah's shenanigans did tire me out today.'

'What happened?' I asked, suddenly concerned.

'The senior imam of Jami Masjid got the kotwal to arrest a brahmin today, and bring him to court handcuffed, demanding that he be sentenced to death.[5] There's a small Devi temple in a lane near the Jami, the brahmin is the priest there. He was tired of booing and jeering, day in and day out, by ruffians, as a kafir practising idol-worship. So, he decided to go and complain to the Imam. Little did he know that the Imam himself was the moving spirit behind all that was happening! An argument followed between the two of them, and it got out of hand. The pandit lost his cool and said sarcastically, "You're right Imam sahib, we're all creatures of Allah, or else wouldn't our blood have been blue instead of red like yours!"

'"There, there, now you are talking," said the Imam with a smirk. "Then why indulge in idolatry, I say! Read the kalma. Allah is very kind, He will pardon all your sins. Say, are you ready?"

'"Imam sahib, you first need to ask your Allah why he made us with blood the same colour as yours but filled our hearts with reverence for the Devi," replied the brahmin.

'That put the Imam in a towering rage. He got the kotwal to handcuff the pundit in public, and drag him through the bazaar, all the way to court.

'"This wretched pandit has challenged the existence of Allah, you must have him hanged now," the Imam declared.

'"Do you have anything to say in your defence, pandat?" I asked.

'"What would he have to say?" growled the Imam, gnashing his teeth.

'"Reverend, please do not forget that you're in the court of

Sultan Bayzeed Khan, for the moment!" At my reprimand, the Imam lowered his eyes, and the pandit said, "May the Amir Sultan be forever victorious! It was only an academic discussion between us regarding religious customs and practices, my Lord. I have never ever caused any offence to any other religion. My head is at your feet, and I shall sever it myself and offer it to you, should you so command, my sultan."

'The argument had taken place in the public square, in front of the Jami. There were umpteen witnesses, and I warned everyone that anyone found to be telling a lie would be the first to hang. Every one of them corroborated the brahmin's version. The Imam, meanwhile, went on demanding immediate execution of the pandat ad nauseam.' Baz paused, beginning to rub his temple.

'So, what was your verdict?' I asked.

Hearing of the pandit's arguments had suddenly put Pandijju in my mind. He was wont to saying things like these. It was a moment of shame as I realized that I had quite forgotten my beloved guru in a hurry, as it were, after my sudden elevation to royalty. God alone knew how he and the other survivors at Garh Dharmapuri were faring in the aftermath of that traumatic night—it felt like a distant dream already! I couldn't believe that it was only three days, to be precise, since Pandijju had saved me from the poison cup, giving me the chance of a new life. Baz was still continuing with his narrative:

'"Imam Nuuruddin, as far as I can see, this pandat has accepted Allah's existence rather than challenge it. Indeed, he entered into argument with you about the rituals and customs of different faiths, but should a creature of Allah be made to pay for something so minor with his life?" I asked the Imam.

'"Certainly so, Sultan. He isn't a follower of the true Faith," said the Imam, still bristling with self-righteous outrage.

'"But he says that his blood is also crimson, like the rest of us, who follow the true Faith," I needled the fellow, smiling. The Imam reddened, silently glaring all around, as though looking for support. No one spoke.'

'So, eventually, what was your decision?' I asked, impatient to know the outcome.

'I banished the pandat from the sultanate for having insulted the Imam in public,' said Baz, studying the patterns on the carpet.

'What?' I could hardly believe if I'd heard him right. 'But didn't you just say that the pandit was only having an academic discussion on religious beliefs?'

'Ruup, Imam's goons wouldn't have spared the Pandat. Within days his body would have turned up in some gutter in a back alley. Once I have had him cross the border into the neighbouring Hindu kingdom of the Chandelas, at least he will walk away with his life. Ah! Why can't religion just be a salve to soothe souls, like music? Why does it have to be so brutally competitive?' Looking drained, Baz was rubbing his eyelids and forehead by now. I felt a deep swell of protective instincts for him that moment. I took him in my arms, asking softly, 'Shall I massage your head?'

'No, Rani, I should be all right in a while. Can I have a bath in your toilet?'

'Of course! I'll see to the arrangements myself,' I said rising.

'No, no, why bother with all that, Nayla will see to it. Get yourself dressed up, for the music concert tonight.'

That snuffed out my sudden burst of affectionate enthusiasm, but I hardly had any time to brood over it. Radha and Zubeida took charge of me, leading me solicitously to the south wing.

'You haven't seen all of the Raniwaas yet, Rani.' They were right, across the wardrobe room, there was another toilet area identical to the one adjoining my bedroom.

When I returned after a while, dressed up for the evening, Baz instantly ordered, 'Takhliyaa!' We were to be on our own for a while. The maids left doing a kornish. My mood lifted as Baz took me in his arms.

'Do you remember your gift at the Ardhapadma Taal?' I felt my cheeks burn, and leaned my head on his broad chest, managing just a whispered, 'Hmm...'

'I, too, want to gift you something today, to go with this Raniwaas. Come with me,' he said, leading me by the hand to the padlocked door. The lock seemed to give to a mere touch of his fingers. We were in a corridor similar to the one that led to the toilet area, running parallel to it, and at the other end of it there was a medium-sized room, with another door that gave on to the open terrace. The afternoon sun filtered through the blue glass panes on its mullioned shutters, giving a bluish tinge to the opposite wall. As I followed Baz inside, I was amazed. On a marble table set against the right wall stood my mother's idols of Radha and Krishna: Radha gleaming white, and Krishna, jet black. In a moment that seemed like a flash of lightning, I was transported back in time, to a previous lifetime, the one in the haveli with the lone maulshri tree in the courtyard. I couldn't quite believe my eyes!

'The day after Abbu gave Bano the necklace and a place in my mother's household as reward, she came back to return the necklace. He was bewildered. Bano said, "The necklace is of little use to me. If you really want to give me a reward, could you get me my idols of Radha-Krishna?" Abbu was so taken with her singing, he immediately had these brought here for her. Alas! I couldn't persuade her to remain until you came, but these idols are now yours, Rani. Leaving for Vrindavan, Bano said she was going to them, anyhow.' Baz fell silent.

Overwhelmed by his gift, I thought there was no way I could thank him enough for his thoughtful gesture. I simply rushed to him and embraced him. My eyes wet with tears welling up, I said, 'If you hadn't sent her to Rao begging for me, she might still be here!'

Baz said nothing but simply bent his head and kissed me on the lips, lingering long over it. Then he said in a small voice, 'What else could I have done, Ruup? After meeting you that first time, and then not being able to see you, drove me mad with yearning. I had hardly any appetite for food, or even hunting, of which I'd been so fond before. Ammi jaan could not bear to see me so forlorn. My father was still alive at the time, she went to him, but he dismissed the matter out of hand, "Counsel the prince to try and learn to respect the women of our Hindu nobility, and apply himself to learning statecraft, instead." But Ammi could not see me suffering, so she persuaded Rukmini Bano to go, without telling the Sultan.'

'Rukmini? She was known by that name?' I said, amazed to hear my mother's Hindu name.

'Yes, she remained Rukmini to my father. He was originally from Sasaram, you know, and spent his best years fighting alongside Sher Shah in the Benares-Jaunpur region. He genuinely respected Hindus, and was very fond of listening to bhajans, as I myself am, perhaps having inherited the trait from him. As a matter of fact, I quite forgot to tell you, in the concert this evening Ustad Rai Chand is to sing a Sanskrit bhajan of sorts.'

'A Sanskrit bhajan! Which one?' I exclaimed excitedly.

'*Madhurashtakam*,'[6] he said.

'*Madhurashtakam* of Sri Vallabhacharya! I've read it many times over. Pandijju had several hand-written volumes of Vallabhacharya in his book-chest. Baz, I shall not forget this day in a long time—first, my mother's deities, and now, *Madhurashtakam*! My word, I can't believe this!'

'Oh, there's a lot more to follow, Ruup,' he said languidly. Then he kissed me again, with great ardour, as though to give me some sense of things to follow.

'I had meant to ask you for something else, but I can't really ask for anything more today. I guess it will have to wait.'

Vision 52

'This evening's concert is in Hindola Mahal, the Hall of Special Audience. A number of high-ranking generals and courtiers will also be there. Women of the family do not sit with them. There is a separate arrangement for them on a screened balcony, the zenana-jaali. Nayla will bring you there. I have to go in advance,' said Baz, and left. He wore the traditional Malwa turban with the usual diamond and falcon feather adorning it. The sight of his well-muscled, lean frame, clad in a green kamkhaab long coat, was so winsome, I said a silent prayer to keep the evil eye away.

The concert that evening was truly a magnificent event: beneath the multiple saucer-shaped domes resting on twenty-five—as far as I could count—massive carved stone pillars, the Hindola Mahal was ablaze from the light of several giant-sized candelabras, and blue glass candlesticks on the pillars, that twinkled like a constellation. Carpets were covered in spotless white sheets, interspersed with red velvet bolsters, embroidered in gold thread. The elite of the sultanate army and nobility, in their best ceremonial dresses, sat in neat rows on either side of the rectangular hall of Hindola's cushioned floor while the Sultan sat on a raised marble platform, on a throne with hand-rests made of solid gold. At the other end, on a makeshift dais, specially erected for the occasion, sat Ustad Rai Chand, the music tutor to the Sultan and the main artist performing that evening. He was surrounded by accompanists on an assortment of instruments: the tambura, duhul, kartaal, beenn, jhaal and nai. In the middle of the great hall, a rectangular space had been left bare, where the marble floor was inlaid with coloured stones, in the shape of a huge blooming lotus.

The Sultan rose to his feet briefly, and announced, 'Bismillah! Ustad Rai Chand, you may begin.'

'Your wish is my command, Sultan,' said Rai Chand, rising to his feet and bowing deeply with folded hands, 'If it pleases you, sire, may I begin by presenting two of my most promising disciples first?'

'Go right ahead.'

For close to an hour, two of the rising stars among Rai Chand's many disciples, performed compositions in raga Basant and raga Maalkauns, one after the other. The domes of Hindola reverberated from time to time as the audience applauded their vocal presentations, with tunefully choreographed instrumental music playing in tandem.

The lyrics of Jaidev Maharaj, the first of the two, were:

Until the sun and the moon
Rise in the sky
May Baz remain our sultan
On high;
As well as our pride
He is our life
May Baz remain our sultan

And Miyaan Guftar's lines went something like this:

Putting the garland around his neck
Ruupmati chose her man
And him she made her own
Forever
Our dear beloved Sultan

As my name came up in the lyric, I noticed that several of the noble lords in the audience frowned, quickly lowering their faces in an obvious effort to hide their disapproval. Even within the zenana gallery, a woman went on staring at me balefully. As she wore a hijab, there was no way I could know who she was, not that I was acquainted with many people until then. But with Jaidev Maharaj and Miyaan Guftar making such great music, I couldn't care less about these distractions. Gazing at my handsome beloved, I kept humming their tunes in my mind.

As soon as the two of them had finished performing, Baz signalled them to approach the royal podium, and taking off two of the many necklaces he wore around his neck, gave them away as rewards with whispered words of praise. Then, holding his hand up for silence, he stood up. The gathering instantly fell silent, obviously keen to hang on to every word he was going to say.

'Indeed, Ustad Rai Chand didn't spell it out in so many words, but apparently, he does not think of me as one of his promising disciples,' he said with feigned gravity but broke into a bright smile within the moment. Several in the audience chuckled and tittered phrases like 'May God protect the sultan!' A shadow of panic flitted in and out of Rai Chand's eyes, over a possible faux pas! Baz was still on his feet and he went on, 'Still, he is my guru, and he is very kind to me and my sultanate stands on an ancient land of learning, where stalwarts like Kalidasa and Raja Bhoj flourished. For centuries past, learned men have been revered here. Ustad Rai Chand is going to perform a heartwarming piece tonight, to welcome me back with Rani Ruupmati, and I can't wait to listen to his celestial song. But before my guru begins, I wish to offer flowers of obeisance at his lotus-feet, with his permission.'

Once again, I could see many raised eyebrows in the audience, chagrined eyes silently thinking: All right, all right! So, you take music lessons from him. But why heap such accolades on a kafir? Come off it, chap!

Everyone knew that Rai Chand was Baz's music tutor, but he had never before acknowledged him as effusively in public as he did that night. How would I know, but Nayla was the one who told me about it later.

Be that as it may, there was pin-drop silence. Rai Chand himself was taken by surprise, looking at Baz in dismay and gratitude. He sprang to his feet as though coming out of a trance, and said, 'Why, sire, please do go on! Grace us.' The rest of the gathering sat gaping, wondering what the Sultan had in my mind.

Baz simply put a hand over his temple, and with the other waving in the air, began to sing—a truly ethereal *taan* rang out to the domes of Hindola:

From your revered mouth
O my Guru
Please sing praises of Lord Hari;
Holding your lotus-feet
In his hands
So pleads Sultan

I could see that many of the nobility in the audience were now clearly annoyed, but for all their disapproving frowns, the hall rang with thunderous applause and loud clapping.

I was thrilled beyond words. Although Baz had accompanied me on the tambura with extraordinary proficiency, I'd never heard him sing before. Ah, what a divine gift he had! And how skilfully had he rhymed his lines with those of Jaidev Maharaj and Miyaan Guftar. He was still standing, smiling beatifically. As the applause died down, he said, 'Ustad Rai Chand will now present a new composition of *Madhurashtakam*. This incomparably beautiful poem is the work of Vallabhacharya, a saint-poet who lived about a century ago. It is the loveliest description, of the charismatic persona of Lord Krishna, that I've come across.' He sat back on his throne.

Ustad Rai Chand rose to his feet and bowed, 'The Sultan is so magnanimous in his praise,' he said, 'that my throat is choked with emotion. God alone knows how I will be able to sing, but indeed, I must welcome the Sultan and Rani Ruupmati. And as I do so, I pray to the Lord that the Rani may forever view the Sultan the way Sri Krishna is described in *Madhurashtakam*.' He sat down and began to sing.

Adharam Madhuram Vadanam Madhuram Nayanam
Madhuram Hasitam Madhuram |
Hridayam Madhuram Gamanam Madhuram Madhura-
Adhipater-Akhilam Madhuram ||1||

As if taking a cue, the moment Rai Chand started singing, a troupe of six beautiful danseuses wearing yellow saris with gold borders and bedecked in resplendent jewellery with jasmine garlands entwined in their braids, entered upon the central part, left uncovered by rugs, and started to dance, miming the description of Krishna in *Madhurashtakam* with gestures so deftly in sync with the lyrics, that even those who did know Sanskrit could easily comprehend what the words said.

I was overcome with a serene sense of joyful bliss. My beloved, my sultan, my Baz was so good of heart, so charming.

I could hardly believe that I, who had been unacceptable for even a minor prince, had the good fortune of having him for a husband.

The music concert that day was something that I could not forget for the rest of my life and neither could I forget the night that followed it.

By the time we returned to the Raniwaas, the maids had decorated the lotus four-poster with strings of marigold and roses. Did I see the hand of Nayla somewhere? Thankfully, no sooner had we arrived than Baz ordered solitude, and the maids backed out, bending low in kornish.

For the first time, there was no one between the two of us, no lurking shadow behind the curtains! Only snatches of the rabab played by Zubeida kept floating in, from somewhere in the distance.

Neither of us slept much that night. Between ecstatic love-making and short naps, we kept humming the opening lines of the *Madhurashtakam*, looking deep into each other's eyes, smiling.

The more we had of each other, the more we wanted to have!

Vision 53

Happy times do have powerful wings! Our golden days were flying away fast, like a stack of loose papers left out in the open on a windy morning.

Baz would only look at really important matters of state, cursorily at that, for an hour or two in the forenoon, and leaving the rest to his trusted elderly vizier, Khan Meerzah, come back to the Raniwaas. As soon as he arrived, he would announce takhliyaa. I felt immensely relieved—at least that tall, dark shadow would not fall between us. From then on, through the afternoons and the night, we would be by ourselves, making love, sleeping and waking up in each other's arms. Sometimes he would sing for me, as did I for him, and at other times, we would do a duet. And when we fell silent, we would listen to strains of Zubeida playing the rabab, somewhere across the courtyard.

An unspoken truce had come about between me and Nayla: I would only accost her if absolutely necessary. She seldom spoke much in any case, mostly when spoken to.

Baz had entrusted her with two special tasks to do with me. One was to teach me how to ride a horse properly, and the second, to read and write the language that was spoken at Mandav court—a mix of Faarsi and the local dialect. I have to say that she handled both rather competently. Within four or five months, I was able to gallop shoulder to shoulder with Baz on his morning rides, without faltering and converse with people in the language of their choice. Baz wanted to assign another task to Nayla—to teach me fencing—but I put my hands up firmly.

'You have enough soldiers to slay the enemy. I'm Rani Ruupmati, and I do not wish to turn into Rani Durgawati. Let me remain what I am. Indeed, if you want me to learn music, you can take me as a disciple,' I said.

'For that, you'll have to take a test. Only then will I know whether you deserve to be my disciple,' he said, smiling broadly. I thought he just meant to tease me.

'All right, I'm prepared for it. You think you can scare me?' I parried.

The day after the music concert, I asked Baz about calling on Badi Begum, his mother.

'No, not now. I've already presented your greetings to her. You go and pay your respects to her in person when she calls for you,' he said.

The summons came two weeks later. Nayla arranged for a palanquin and escorted me to the haveli with blue domes, visible across the park from my open terrace.

My mother-in-law was from Sasaram and had spent long

years in the areas around Benares and Jaunpur. She was married to Shujat Khan there, while he was the right hand of Sher Shah Suri. Even after having lived in Malwa for years now, first as the wife of its subedar and then as the Sultan's Malikaa, her Benares roots were quite evident in her speech and the habit of paan, forever clenched in her jaw. In fact, the first thing that came to my mind on seeing her in person was that Khulla Jani must have taken to chewing paan from her. Tall, fair-complexioned with large eyes, about fifty, maybe fifty-five, Baz's mother must have been quite a beauty in her youth.

I don't quite know why, but on an impulse, I stepped forward and touched her feet in traditional Hindu greeting. She smiled, and putting her forefinger on my chin, lifted my face to have a good look. Releasing me from scrutiny, she touched her fists to her temple, making a sign to drive away the evil eye, and said, smiling even more broadly, 'Maashaallah! We don't have the custom of touching feet, but it's so endearing to see you keep to your tradition, Rani. I'm delighted to see you. Come, have a seat,' she pointed to the settee opposite hers. Cheerily looking at me, she proffered a red velvet string-pouch, 'Your munh-dekhnaa!' she said. Then, looking at Nayla standing behind me, she said, 'Nayla bi, you carry on, I'll arrange to have the Rani sent back in a while.' Nayla bowed silently in a salaam and backed out the door.

Hardly had Nayla left when, from a door at the back, Khulla appeared, kind of imperiously surveying the surroundings, and walked over to sit beside Badi Begum. I cursed silently: so, here she comes to spoil things with her prattle! She began right away.

'So, you're inspecting the new bride today, my dear Aunt! I went and looked her up the very first day. She's beautiful, isn't she? I told her to forget all about vivaah, and get a proper nikaah, then rot inside the harem at leisure. Why don't you also try and see if you can persuade her to understand?'

Vexed by her inane gabbing, Badi Begum hissed, 'It's good to keep your counsel to yourself at times. Why do you always keep babbling so...'

Making a horrid face, Khulla fell silent, but bending to the Begum's ear, she whispered something. She gave Khulla a startled look and asked in a low voice, 'When did he come?

Before Khulla could reply, he walked in briskly through the same back door. It was my turn to be startled. He had the same build, similar facial features and eyes, as though he and Baz might be twins. The only difference was that he had a moustache while Baz was clean-shaven. Entering the room, I was the first to be noticed, as I sat facing the door through which he'd come. Perhaps he had not expected a visitor, and stopped dead in his tracks, gazing at me intently. Before I could bring up a corner of my pallu to use it as a hijab, he had had a good, long look at me.

Khulla looked uneasy, while Badi Begum half turned to look behind and said in a forbidding tone, 'You remain inside for a while, I will be there shortly.' The Baz look-alike turned instantly and disappeared through the door.

Badi Begum turned back to me, 'I knew Rukmini well. She was a good woman, very adept at singing bhajans. I have heard a good deal of bhajan-kirtan. I spent almost half my life in and around Benares, you know. So long, then! Do come and visit me again some day. And yes, tell Baz from me that he should come and take care of Khulla too, once in a while.'

I could see that Badi Begum was in a hurry to go inside, and attend to the man who resembled Baz so much that I was almost sure it must be Malik Mustafa Khan, his younger brother. But where on earth had he come from?

In later days, I often thought that it was only because of this chance exposure to Mustafa that the fame of my good looks reached powerful people in faraway places, people who had never seen me in person before, and was presented to them in a manner that it made them go mad with lust. Eventually, I had proof of it from the horse's mouth, as it were!

Vision 54

'I know about it. Alas! By the time I was informed, he was gone. Well, it's good that the information brought by my aiyaars, the intelligence-gatherers, stands corroborated by what you saw there. I'm not going to rest now until I have found out what conspiracies are being hatched within my immediate family!' said Baz fuming, when I told him what had transpired during my visit at Badi Begum's.

'But isn't it possible that it was simply an innocent visit, to see his mother?' I said, trying to soothe him.

'May it be so by God's will, Rani. But if he is trying to upstage me by any chance, I will not let him. Until now I've been considerate, after all, he is my blood. If he's making a life for himself, hidden in Raisen Fort, so be it. A prince born to my own parents at least needs something to survive. But what does he think he's doing, sneaking into Mandav without my leave? That surely is not something I'm going to ignore. He will have to answer for it.'

'But listen, Baz, until you have irrefutable proof of treasonous intent on his part, please don't be harsh on your brother. I'll be disappointed, and you'll antagonize even more of your noblemen,' I couldn't help playing counsellor.

'Antagonize *even more* noblemen? Whatever do you mean, that some of them are already disgruntled, is that what you're saying?' Without paying much attention to what I'd said, he leisurely took off his turban and put it on a table by the bed, but he did keep looking at me, expecting a clarification.

'I have a feeling that some, if not most, of your noblemen and generals disapprove of your taking a Hindu wife. If you had had me abducted and made a concubine of me, perhaps not an eyebrow would have been raised, but the grand ovation at the city and palace gates, the music concert to welcome us, the fantastic Raniwaas you've had redone for me and the fulsome tribute you pay to your music tutor—these are not things they can easily stomach. And to top it all, the acrimony with the Imam in open court! We had better move a bit more cautiously, Baz. That night when Miyaan Guftar's lyrics mentioned me, I saw a clear shadow of contempt on the faces of many a warlord in the audience. Let's face facts, religion matters.'

'You're right, Rani, but I tell you what, I will be what I am! I praised Rai Chand's talent and will carry on doing so in future. I'll praise Sanwla, too, if I find him to be deserving. Artists must be measured by their talent and skill at their craft, not by the God they worship, I say! Don't be scared, nothing will happen. And if something bad is destined, it will just come without a warning,' he said dismissively. There seemed nothing left for me to say, yet I asked, 'Now, who might this Sanwla be?'

'Sanwla? Well, Sanwla is a painter, and if he's as good as he's said to be, I'll give him a stipend and retain him at my court. He'll make a portrait of us both riding out in the woods, but that will be tomorrow morning. I hope you haven't forgotten you have to take the music test tonight, to see if you qualify to be my disciple?' Baz smiled crookedly.

'I remember it very well. Just tell me what I have to do.' I smiled as well.

'Did you listen carefully to Ustad's rendering of *Madhurashtakam*? Can you repeat it in Kalyan, the raga that he used?'

So, Baz really meant to put me through a test, I thought to myself. All right, so be it! I had indeed listened to the Ustad with such deep concentration, loving every moment of it, that I had the composition almost by heart—the raga, the notes and the words. The only thing I was not entirely sure of was the exact rise and fall of notes at a few places. But it was too late to withdraw.

'Well, I could surely give it a try.'

Zubeida brought the accompanists almost instantly into the lotus-fountain living room. I sat on the settee, and closing my eyes, began to sing—instinctively improvising on the notes I was unsure of—and went along without losing time.

As I stopped and opened my eyes, I saw Baz almost gaping at me. After a few moments, he raised his hands and began to clap in slow motion, smiling broadly, 'Why, that was fantastic, Rani. It was simply wonderful! Without breaking out of the discipline of raga Kalyan, you've practically invented a new variant of it, with those improvisations of yours. We will have to present it to Ustad Rai Chand, I say, and if he approves of it, we will name this new variant raga Bhoop Kalyan.'

Baz kept on gazing at me adoringly for a while, and then, apparently in continuation of our earlier conversation, he said, 'Rani, it just occurred to me that there is a way to silence those jealous of our union, but we'll have to work hard at it night and day. Think about it.' His eyes had a mischievous glint, but his tone was serious.

'So what if it's hard? We'll do what it takes,' I said with conviction.

'Well, we'll have to produce a male heir to the throne, at the soonest,' he said laughing merrily. I blushed a beetroot-red, but rising to the occasion, I replied, miming Nayla's usual response to Baz's instructions, 'Your wish is my command, Sultan!

That night again, neither of us slept a wink.

And yet, with the first rays of the sun still gathering dew-drops on the green, we were astride our horses on a grassy knoll in the woods, trying to keep our mounts still for Sanwla to sketch the outlines of our image.

Vision 55

Six months had passed since I came to Mandav—in the blink of an eye, it seemed. During the peak of monsoon that year—the months of Saawan and Bhaadon—it had poured torrentially.

By now our days had settled into a predictable routine: we'd be awake until the early hours, sleeping in until late in the morning. Then Baz would go out for a while, sometimes for a ride on the grasslands, or a brief hunting trip, or an hour or two to listen in to his spies deliver akhbaaraat, the secret news they had gathered. Then, after the midday meal and a bit of rest, we would begin our daily session of riyaaz, honing our music, often in the lotus-room, moving to a bigger music room only when Ustad Rai Chand joined us.

Yes, Baz had gladly taken me under his tutelage.

A week later, I performed the improvised composition of *Madhurashtakam* in the presence of the Ustad. He made me go over the improvisations several times before giving a vigorous nod, 'Yes, Sultan, no doubt the Rani is beautiful, but it's the qualities of the head and heart that will make her immortal, I mean in the world of music.' He happily agreed to the suggestion of the variant being named raga Bhoop Kalyan—the raga Kalyan for Kings!

More months passed, without a night that Baz had not been with me, and yet I couldn't quite shake off Khulla's taunt. 'Make hay while the sun shines!' she'd said, as though speaking from experience. Nor could I forget Badi Begum's exhortation, 'And yes, tell Baz from me that he should come and take care of Khulla as well, once in a while!'

As Baz and I lay side by side one night, I teased him lightheartedly, 'What sort of a sultan are you? You neither visit Khulla, nor go to any of your other women!' For a while he remained silent, but his face kind of tightened, as though he didn't appreciate much what I'd just said.

'I haven't been to see Khulla for years now, but what other women are you talking about?' he asked tersely.

'Well, you've forgotten, haven't you? Remember, at the Hoshang Shah pavilion, you had said that you have other queens and mistresses. Nayla was also saying that there are five-six other girls...' my voice trailed off, as I thought I had made a mistake raising the topic.

'Oh, those women! Their work is to sing and dance to help me practise music, my dear, or lighten my mood sometimes. Didn't you notice how skilfully they danced, in tandem with Ustad's rendering in the concert?'

'Ah! Those were the women then? So, do you never sleep with…' Baz suddenly cut my question short with a kiss full on my lips. When he was done, he sighed looking directly into my eyes, as though pleading, 'Rani, for heaven's sake,' he said, 'don't dig so deep into me. I'm yours forever, but I am also Malwa's sultan, a marionette in the hands of Time. I have to do a lot of strange things. In the morning, witness the execution of men I have sentenced to death, and then pass the evening drinking, in the company of my frivolous warlords, watching women dance. If you were to look too closely, I'm afraid, I might frighten you! You might even come to hate me, and I might lose you even while you are still with me. If that happens…' His eyes reflected anguish that seemed to arise from somewhere deep inside him.

I put a finger on his lips to stop him, going on in that vein.

'I shall never let anything of the sort happen. I'm yours alone, and will be yours until my last breath. Now, enough of all this serious talk. Come, tell me if you remember the promise you made at the Ardhapadma, or have you forgotten it? You know something? Khulla taunted me saying, "When you're new, such promises are commonplace!"'

'No, no. I haven't forgotten them at all. I'll have a palace built for you, and that bathing pool as well, but you do seem to have forgotten that you said you'll find the site for it.'

'Indeed, I had, but I guess I have been lazy. Well, from tomorrow, would you let me go out riding with you regularly, so that we can look for it together?' I said.

All of a sudden, things long forgotten flashed through my mind: the lotuses of the Ardhapadma swaying in the breeze, that dreadful night that I thought would be my last on the earth, the glittering outline of Reva Maiyaa whispering to me, 'You are still under my protection—look for me in better days, your day in the sun. I will await you under a huge tamarind tree. If you care to come looking for me, I'll bathe you every morning!'

'I'm yours to command, Rani, but not from tomorrow. We'll begin our search the day after. Tomorrow I must sit with my aiyaars to gather the latest akhbaaraat.'

Vision 56

When I ran into Nayla the next morning, I asked her, 'Nayla bi, I find the Sultan closeted with his spymaster rather often, lately. Is something the matter?'

Since the time I had noticed Badi Begum address Nayla as Nayla bi, I'd also taken to adding the honorific. When Baz heard me do that, his face was suffused with satisfaction, which left me instantly vexed, but only for a moment. After all, I had no quarrel with what made him happy. Indeed, he himself had soon started calling her Nayla bi.

'Yes, Rani, the day I took you to meet Badi Begum, the Sultan's younger brother, Mustafa, had come visiting her, apparently without taking his permission. The Sultan is trying to find out whether a family conspiracy of sorts is in the making.'

I was piqued. This clever woman knows about everything that is happening, without exception! It was just as well that I'd told Baz about Mustafa right after returning from Badi Begum's, and yet I found myself asking her for assistance the very next moment.

'There's another matter I've been rather worried about these last few days. I've never really remembered to find out how the remaining people at Garh Dharmapuri have been faring all this while—Pandijju, Ketki and all. I'm afraid they might be starving. Maybe, I should seek the Sultan's permission and send over something to help them out,' I said, more as if I was thinking aloud.

'Rani, if you don't take it amiss, may I tell you something—' Without letting Nayla finish, I cut in tersely, 'Why should I take anything amiss? Carry on, tell me as many things as you like.'

It was another matter that I already sounded terribly peeved, without quite knowing why.

'The morning you left Nalchha, the Sultan sent me to Garh

Dharmapuri to take stock of things, and since then, I have been keeping track of the people left there,' Nayla said, her eyes lowered, as they usually were.

A wave of intense anger washed over me, but somehow keeping my tenor under control, I asked, 'So why didn't you tell me? Or was it supposed to be a state secret of some kind?'

'The Sultan said it might distress you to know all that I'd discovered. That's the only reason it was kept from you,' replied Nayla in a small voice.

'Then tell me now. If it's distressing, I'll deal with it.' My tone sounded like the crack of a whip.

'There are only seven souls left in the Garh itself. There are some women and children in the adjoining hamlet, families of soldiers who were either killed that night, or captured and sent away on punitive assignments. Rao Yaduveer crossed the border into the Chandela country, with his trusted lieutenants and men-at-arms.'

'Who told you all this?'

'The seven left in the Garh, Pandijju, Ketki, who looks after him, and the five Purabiya soldiers who said they were ready to lose their heads rather than leave Pandijju unprotected. Apparently, they came with him as boys from Patna long years ago, and later took their deeksha-mantra from him and accepted him as their guru. They went into hiding, in the jungles around the Garh, as they didn't want to leave with Rao, and returned to be by his side after Rabat and his contingent left with you.'

'So how do they manage to live? They must be starving!' I said ruefully.

'No, no, Rani, it's your old Garh after all. I have been arranging for enough foodgrains and things to be sent to them to keep them going, as directed by the Sultan, of course. I can't claim that they are happy, but they won't starve for sure.'

'And what about Pandijju's pooja material, how does he get them?' I wanted to know whether Nayla had discovered the secret of the Devi temple as well.

'I didn't have enough time to see him at pooja, but we have been sending enough ghee and oil for lighting.' Then she fell silent, looking tentatively at me, as though wondering whether to go on.

'Nayla bi, I'm truly grateful for all this, but perhaps there's something more that you wanted to say,' I prompted her.

'May Allah protect them, I thought those five Purabiyas needed to have their weapons in that wilderness, so I had them restored and they also had a message for you.' Nayla stopped again.

'Carry on, Nayla bi. Now that you've told me everything, if you don't let go of that message, you might burst at the seams!'

I don't quite know what on earth happened to me while dealing with Nayla! If there was anything important that I wanted done, she was the first I would call upon for assistance, but if she had already anticipated my wish and had carried it out, I would be sore with her. Nayla bi, the omniscient, I would think, sarcastically.

'Rani, when I was about to leave, those five men said, "Ruupmati is our guru-sister. Please tell her if she's ever in any kind of trouble, she shouldn't forget we are still alive, that we're always there for her!"'

My eyes welled up with tears. I couldn't even remember what they looked like.

'Didn't Pandijju have any message for me?' I said, sounding a bit disappointed already. I couldn't say why because she was yet to answer my question.

'Yes, in parting he only said that I should tell you to be happy, but to never forget that sorrow exists. Frankly, it went way over my head, Rani.'

'But to me, he only said, "Be happy!"' I blurted out, without really intending to reveal my disappointment to Nayla. I composed myself, and said, changing track, 'I suppose you have shared all this with Baz already.' It wasn't a question, but she nodded silently. Probably that was her fault, too.

Having lived in Nayla's company for almost six years, I

could never quite understand why I blamed her for nearly everything, even when she had done all the right things. Towards the end, when she said for the very last time, 'I will taste it first', it was a little too late to make amends. Everything lay hopelessly in shambles, by then.

Vision 57

My dear scribe, you cannot imagine how enormous and invincible a bastion our Mandavgarh was. I would have to describe it in some detail for you to have some sense of how wonderful and lively a fort-city Mandav was, in our time, for the ruins that lie strewn around, beautiful as they might be, can hardly tell the entire story.

Across the Reva's turbulent stream, roiling with eddies and undercurrents to its north, the four-kos-high steep hillside of the plateau rose towering into the sky to merge with the ramparts and battlements of Mandavgarh. Our capital was spread over the plateau, measuring a staggering seventeen thousand bighas with a circumference of eighteen kos. It had twelve market streets, dotted with scores of inns and public baths. The Shaahi Laal Bagh garden alone spread over two hundred bighas. About a thousand bighas were under the plough and jungles and grasslands spread over thousands of bighas. It wasn't just a fort, but a whole bustling city within the fort walls—a mighty stronghold that would have taken an invading army months of siege to capture it, if at all.

That is why it was brave of my Baz to have exposed himself to an army three times the size of his own, instead of defending himself from within its almost impenetrable walls. But all that came much later.

As of now, the two of us went out riding every day to look for a suitable site for the new palace Baz had promised to build for me. It didn't take us long. On the third day we sighted the round canopy of the large Khorasani tamarind tree. As we came closer to it, we discovered the natural spring gurgling out from under the rocks near its base, and flowing into the meadow and turning into a lively brook. On a rise beyond the tree were the ruins of an old palace.

'Baz, this is it! The exact place I had in mind,' I said, elated.

'Well, I've already said that your wish is my command, Rani. We'll begin construction within the next few days. God willing, you'll have your new palace here in six months. The old ruins of Nasir Shah's palace over there will help, and a small dam over this brook will fill the pool in which you will bathe every day to make yourself pure,' he said, smiling, evidently happy that I had found the site I had been looking for rather quickly.

'But what about the drawings, masons and workmen? Can all that be arranged so quickly?' I said a tad doubtfully.

'The drawings are all in here,' he said pointing to his head.

'And what happens about the rest?' I was still sceptical.

'Rani, didn't I say, I'm not only your Baz but also the sultan of all Malwa!'

'You may be the sultan, but I am Rani Ruupmati. I will certainly break a coconut secretly and invoke the blessings of Ganesha when the foundation stone is laid,' I said tentatively, gauging his response.

'Why would you do it secretly? You're a rani, not a thief. Do it openly, by all means!' he said with the aplomb of someone in absolute control of things.

The work progressed apace. Hundreds of workmen and masons working night and day, and my dream palace materialized in just over eleven months. When it was about to be finished, Baz ordered a grand celebration.

On the inaugural day, people from all over came in droves, thronging the city streets and wishing long life to their sultan and me. Sweets and savouries were distributed to one and all and new clothes given to workmen who had indeed toiled hard. Scores of country bands competed with the official musicians on their duhuls, nakkaaras, seeng, jhaanjh and surnai to create a fanfare that seemed to pierce the Mandav sky. Baz went so far as to order remission of prison sentences of men serving time for petty offences! As darkness fell, the night sky over the city was lit up by the famed fireworks of Malwa, so bright that people could see it from their homes.

Later that evening, a special celebration, for the elite of the nobility and army brass, was held in the palace precincts. It went on until the small hours, and breaking old tradition, wine flowed like water in the Hindola. During the party that night, there was little of classical singing. The courtesans swirling to voluptuous music took centrestage. Watching from behind the zenana-jaali, I could see the celebration turning rather raucous and bawdy in the hall down below. I found it revolting, my mind already perturbed by what Pandijju had said in parting after the inaugural pooja in the new palace…

Hey, wait a moment, did I just forget to say that he came for it?

When I first broached the matter of inviting him and the others at the Garh, Baz's response had been tepid at best. Certainly not as enthusiastic as when I'd suggested breaking a coconut at the foundation. And frankly, I couldn't blame him for it. Looking at the vitiated environment of Mandav—the gaiety of the grand celebration notwithstanding—it would have been foolish on my part to expect him to be as spontaneously generous as before. Even so, he hadn't altogether disappointed me.

'Tell Nayla bi to bring Pandijju in through the ladies' entrance to the rear court, in an enclosed palanquin. In any case, he's elderly and can't possibly come walking or riding a horse. The fewer the people that see him coming, the better,' he'd said. When I mentioned I wanted Ketki and my five guru-bhais invited as well, he had shrugged his shoulders in a helpless gesture, 'Let them come, but I'm afraid they will have to make do with being among the workmen and commoners.'

Truth to tell, Mr Scribe, the Mandav rumour-mill had

gone into overdrive the very day of the foundation laying. I can't speak for your time, but in ours, the common man was so terrified of the sovereign, no one ever dared question what he was doing, what it was going to cost or whether it was necessary at all. But when the clerics and the mullahs, and more than them, members of the ruling family itself, let loose even a muttered protest, it didn't take long for rumours to grow wings and start flying every which way. And in this instance, Imam Nuuruddin was already bristling with contempt over my lavish reception and the imbroglio of the pandit's blasphemy, while Khulla Jani was forever babbling maliciously.

Every second day, a new rumour began to spread and engulf Mandav like a forest fire—swift and destructive. Looking at the scale and speed of construction, the first salvo was indeed fired by the Imam in the shape of a roundabout denunciation of lavish spending, in his sermon to the congregation after Friday namaaz. Baz was promptly informed of it by his spies, but he chose to ignore it. Nayla told him in my presence that the Imam needed to be summoned and reprimanded for his insinuations. 'Nip it in the bud,' she said, but he dismissed the whole thing. 'Even the tiniest of things get blown out of proportion if you give it attention as though it deserves to be taken seriously. Let the old fool babble. I am the sultan, not he. The palace shall be constructed anyhow,' he had said.

With no action resulting, the Imam was emboldened and continued to fan the fire.

After a few weeks, a new rumour began to spread like the plague: The Hindu Rani has sucked the Sultan dry of his manliness. His sword is rusting. For months he's not had time even to inspect the army parade.

Everyone, it seemed, from the mighty to the lowly, had something to say about the new palace. 'This wretched palace is sure to empty the sultanate treasury, what with stones being bought from faraway foreign lands like Dholpur, Makrana, Mewar and Khandesh.' Then someone else would repartee, 'Arre miyaan, you seem to have no idea! Let me tell you, the stones for this elephant of a palace have nothing to do with Makrana. They say there's a Christian town called Carrara, somewhere across many seas. The Sultan has bought marble from white traders from there, and do you know what he's had to pay? A whopping one-hundred-fifty maunds of solid gold! Yessir! You heard it right, a hundred and fifty maunds! His infatuation with this kafir Rani is going to run the state dry, I say!'

All lies! As a matter of fact, marble was hardly used in my palace except for a few adornments, here and there. But rumours have a life of their own. Once spread, they go on feeding upon themselves.

Then another rumour went off, and this one left Baz shaking with sheer rage: 'Arre miyaan, the real fun is about to start now, just you wait and watch! It's only a matter of time now and this kafir-loving sultan will tumble down from his precarious perch. Imam Nuuruddin is already rehearsing the new khutba, which is to be read in Prince Mustafa's favour. Why, everyone in the royal family is so fed up of Baz's shenanigans, even Malikaa Khulla Jani is ready to wed Mustafa, once they get rid of Baz! All they are waiting for is a nod from Badi Begum, now!'

The evening his spies brought news of this rumour being rife in town, Baz was so angry that I was afraid to meet his eyes. After several hours of consultations with his warlords, when he returned to the Raniwaas late at night, he was in a towering rage, his steps unsteady. He entered shouting, 'Nayla, where are you? Bring me my sword, and my armour this very moment. I shall depart for Raisen, now!' Then, he sat heavily down on the settee, his head held in his palms, obviously drunk without measure. I looked helplessly at Nayla, pleading with my eyes: for heaven's sake, please do something to calm him down! He is raring to go on a military expedition, without any preparation, this time of the night!

Nayla did plead, but Baz kept saying, 'It's absolutely necessary to teach Mustafa a lesson forthwith! It won't do to put it off any longer, whatever happens, I'll go at first light.'

'All right, go if you must,' said Nayla soothingly, 'but not in a way that the scale is tilted in his favour. You'll have to play your hand very cautiously. You must realize that the enemy is from within your close family. One misstep, and your very own will be ranged against you.'

'I'll leave for Raisen tomorrow, no matter what! But listen to me, Nayla, and listen well!' he said finally, looking at her in the eye. 'Two things, lest I forget to tell you before I depart. In my absence, the construction work on Rani's palace shall not come to a halt, and you have to see to that. The second, should the worst happen to me while confronting Mustafa, make sure you cut off Khulla's head and hang it from the rampart before you die, if you have to. Got it?'

Silently trembling in mortal terror, I was looking at Baz, mesmerized. He had meant every word of what he had said to Nayla. Suddenly he turned to face me, 'None of this is your fault, Rani. I'm the sultan, all decisions, good or bad, are mine, and I take full responsibility for them. There's no need for you to be so petrified.'

That night I knew how deeply in love with me he was. He had sensed my feeling of guilt without even looking at me.

The next day Baz left for Raisen to teach a lesson to his brother, as he'd put it and did not return for three months. After his departure, I seemed to fall into a black hole of melancholy. It was our first separation for any length of time. My mood was so dark that it seemed even darker than the skin-colour of Nayla! At times I felt like laughing at my meanness. Wasn't it pointless to be so peevish towards someone who wasn't even the 'other woman'!

But Nayla understood me perfectly well. Unlike other women in the household, she never came up with any artifice to divert my mind. If she had, it might well have had the opposite effect. Perhaps she knew this and also that Baz was the very fulcrum of my lonely existence that no one else could supplant. Indeed, she would come from time to time, to bring me news of his well-being, and the progress of his expedition, but that was about all.

This time around, it did seem that the shots in the dark d finally hit a few marks. I noticed that Baz often returned te in the evenings from wherever he had been and was often uite unsteady on his legs as he staggered in. I was afraid for is safety. Assassination attempts on a careless sultan were commonplace. Once I even asked him in a roundabout manner, ut he smiled sardonically and said, 'No, Rani, the day I start fearing for my life at the hands of my aiyaars and sipahsaalaars around me, you can take it that I'm no longer the sultan. Even in this state, I can easily take on at least four or six them at once, and slay them all. I'll tell you something that you might not know, the masters who taught us fencing were not allowed to train anyone other than princes of the royal bloodline, and they were the very best in business!'

Then, as the day of the inauguration of my new palace drew nearer, I tried my best to stop him from making a big event out of it, lest it provide more grist for the rumour-mill.

'Baz, it's just another palace among the many you already have. There's hardly any need for a big carnival over it,' I had told him, and it was after a long time that Nayla and I happened to be on the same side of an argument. But what can one say, when it had to happen this way!

Across the latticed screen, by now the gathering seemed to be getting completely out of hand. After the long hectic day of earth-shaking ballyhoo, my head was thumping with a severe ache in the making, and my thoughts kept returning to inauspicious portents of what Pandijju had said when leaving.

'Nayla bi, please get my palanquin, I want to leave.'

'As you wish, Rani, but Rai Chand's performance is about to begin any moment now,' said Nayla.

'Can't you see how that oaf of a general is vomiting in the flowerpot? Half of them will pass out here for the rest of the night! No, I'm done for the day. Call for my palanquin right away. As it is, Rai Chandjju ought not to be performing at all, for an unruly audience like this!' I said, my bile rising.

It wasn't as though I was unhappy with my new palace or

I would sit in my room the whole day, with a feathered quill in my hand, composing and kavitas—as dark as my mood, my heart qua uncertainties of my beloved being in the thick of could easily swing either way.

When Baz finally returned after those three long we immersed ourselves once again, in the games of l loved to play in keeping with our time of life.

The siege of Raisen had been anything but easy. Had hurried away in a huff without preparation that night, t outcome might have been different. Mustafa had defende himself staunchly, but being short on fighting hands and supplies, he'd had to eventually yield and flee, abandoning the fort. Baz's troops gave him the chase until he was over the northern borders of Malwa. Baz was happy that Malik Mustafa had not been captured, and that he was spared the subsequent dilemma of whether to kill his little brother or to grant him his life.

After the fall of Raisen, Baz proceeded straight to Kadrula. The rumour about his sword beginning to get rusty had gone straight to his heart, and when Kadar Khan, the arrogant chief of a rebellious band of Afghans, in occupation of that small fiefdom-fortress, had sent him his thumbprint on a piece of blank paper instead of the annual tribute, Baz had taken a vow to behead Kadar Khan with his own hands. The subjugation of the distant country cousin at Kadrula had added another month to the campaign.

On his victorious return from the expedition, the Sultan was indeed hailed by jubilant crowds, and a spate of colourful celebratory events followed. But the rumours refused to go away. As I said, once the cycle of idle hearsay is set in motion it's nearly impossible to break it. Indeed, it seemed to poiso the very air that we breathed.

New rumours started. The latest was that the Sultan tiring of the Hindu Rani and that he had taken to drink wildly, immersed in making music night and day with pretty girls of his seraglio.

anything like that. On the contrary, its grandeur was much beyond my expectations. It was an imposing structure with two Rajput-style pavilions at either corner on the front. The spring-stream was dammed to make a pool to a side of the precincts, enclosed by a collonaded courtyard with a latticework screen, and a novel feat of engineering brought running water into the palace bathrooms through an elaborate set of Persian wheel and aqueducts. On a nearby hillock, the ruins of an old stable and watchtower had been renovated, with two round pavilions added at either end for our music sessions.

The day the construction work was completed, Baz himself took me up there. He said, 'Come, I'll show you a wonderful sight.' Reaching the top, I was truly delighted. From the hilltop, the walls of Garh Dharmapuri were clearly visible in the far distance across the ravines, and by its side lay the thin silver line of my benefactress, the holy river Reva.

My palace, my pavilions. Ah! All but quicksilver mirage on the Sands of Time!

Pandijju had been brought quietly through the back door, as agreed. I could not locate Ketki and my five guru-bhais in the crowd milling in the distance. Nayla later told me that they had been there.

Pandijju kept gazing at my mother's Radha-Krishna, while I, bending to touch his feet, kept waiting for his words of blessing. Those few moments seemed like a long time.

'May you always have the protection of your man, Ruupmati. Be happy!' he said, and lay before the deity in a dandavat pranaam, fully stretched face down, to offer obeisance. After a while, he rose to a kneeling position, offered flowers and lit the lamp. Then suddenly turning back, he looked quizzically at me and asked, 'Wasn't the place where you lived earlier comfortable enough for you? This new palace is indeed magnificent, but the position of stars is not quite as I should have liked…you have to be careful!'

'But Guruji, this is the exact site that Reva Maiyaa had described in my dream,' I said, alarmed.

'Indeed, the Devi's blessing is as invariably beautiful as a dream. All right then, can I take your leave now?' Nayla had escorted him back to the palanquin.

I was left wondering what his parting remark had meant; I was perturbed beyond words. What did Pandijju mean? Which stars were not right, and who was I to be careful of? I had no clue at all.

VISION 58

Whether auspicious or accursed, the new palace was like a millstone around my neck. If I did not move into it, another whirlwind of rumours would certainly set in motion: 'Now that it is ready, it has become haunted. Game over for the Hindu Rani!' And if I did, my heart trembled at the thought of Pandijju's warning.

Regardless, the rumours continued to fly thick and fast. The very latest now was that Mustafa was making endless rounds of the Mughal court at Agra with his plaint. It is lucky for Baz that Akbar, an underage emperor, occupies the throne, and Bairam Khan, his regent, is busy quelling revolts in the Punjab and Sirhind as well as dealing with the palace intrigue of Maham Angaa, or else Mustafa's plea might well have been acted upon by now.

Two days after the inauguration, Nayla, with the help of Suleman, the Sultan's personal valet, had my personal effects, my clothes and jewellery, books, notebooks and musical instruments, carted to the new palace. It wasn't necessary to bring anything else. It was already furnished with beds, tables and settees, expensive curtains and carpets, candelabras and candlesticks and the like. Its broad corridors, resting on beautifully carved stone columns, and the poolside, were lined with giant brass and blue flowerpots of ferns and exotic crotons, imported from places as far as Samarkand. Huge portraits of the two of us, in gilt frames, and some beautiful landscapes of Mandav and its environs, most of them Sanwla's work, hung on the walls.

My Raniwaas in the Shaahi Mahal had not lacked for anything required for comfortable living, but even after lavish renovations, it paled into obscurity by comparison. It had at best been an apartment in an old palace complex, while my new abode was a whole new palace in its own right. With so many bedrooms, living and music rooms, suited to every hour of the day and season of the year, it was difficult to keep a count of them. My beau had indeed fulfilled his promise extraneously with this generous gift, but he himself continued to be the centre of my universe. I wanted nothing more than him to be always by my side, he gazing at me, and I at him.

As days passed without incident, my apprehensions about the new palace began to diminish gradually. After all, as Pandijju was also wont to say, not infrequently, that every creature on earth had an inescapable destiny to fulfil, so why bother living under a pall of misgivings through one's life. I told myself: *Ruupmati, go on, think of every hour as a day, every day as a year, and every year as a lifetime and you'll have lived many lifetimes, until whatever is to happen!*

Above all, age was with us. I was all of eighteen, and Baz, not more than twenty-six or twenty-seven at the time. We could do whatever we wanted, whenever we wanted—eat our fill, sleep like a log, sing all night or simply make love. And yet, we were fresh as morning dew when we woke up, looking forward to another golden day ahead.

Even before moving to the new palace, I'd had a dual image in the public eye. On the one hand, I was a wicked Hindu Rani who had tamed the Sultan, through black magic and mohini-mantra, into the proverbial 'fly on the wall'. On the other hand, I was this beautiful, accomplished and kind-hearted woman, with whom their sultan was madly in love. The latter of the two identities was now beginning to prevail, and turn into folklore. By now, many people had seen me without the hijab on my face. In any case, how long could a rani's looks and traits remain hidden, with so many maids and jaannisaars hovering around and serving her?

The lyric that Miyaan Guftar had sung in the music concert, to welcome us to Mandav, was on its way to becoming a legend:

Putting the garland around his neck
Ruupmati chose her man
And him she made her own
Forever
Our dear beloved sultan

Common folk in villages and towns near Mandav, indeed unto far corners of the sultanate, had begun to sing it as a sohar on festive occasions, weddings and betrothals, and had added their own lines to go with the mukhdaa Guftar had sung:

Like Padmini she was
Indeed so fetching, beautiful
Smitten was our sultan
With eyes like lotus
And her face as chaan
Smitten was our sultan
From whose lovely mouth
Strains of music flowed
Sweet as a cuckoo's taan
Let the other woman
Green with envy
Accuse her of magic black
Lies will be lies
And truth they'll lack
Rani's beauty had such elan
Smitten was our sultan
So smitten indeed was the sultan!

In the Jahaz Mahal complex, enclosed by high walls, we had lived away from the public eye. But here they could see, if only from a distance, Baz riding a horse alongside my palanquin up to the twin pavilions up on the hill. We often went there in the evenings, for musical sessions or to simply sit and chat. When people saw him bending down, to hold up a corner of the palanquin curtain or to whisper an endearment, they would say, 'The Rani is as beautiful as a fairy, and the Sultan so smitten with her, that he has to keep looking at her time and time again, to make sure she is still there.'

How would they know that their sultan was not half as smitten with me as I was with him! The mukhdaa of Miyaan Guftar's lyric was so pat on the spot, that I decided to add a stanza of my own to it:

From him a mere glance
Made the Rani lose at once
Her body and her soul
Sacrifice her honour and all—
Kaamdev is our sultan
Kaamdev sultan!

When I showed it to Baz, his face lit up like that of a child who had just been gifted a much longed for toy. The simile suddenly reminded me of the child we hadn't been able to produce so far, in order to stun our secret enemies into silence, with an heir to the throne. But we were so happy together, it didn't matter.

Baz immediately summoned the danseuses who had performed to Rai Chand's rendering of *Madhurashtakam*, and for several hours that evening, we rehearsed a dance-drama based on Miyaan Guftar's mukhdaa including my lines. Baz and I sat on a raised dais at one end of the music room, while the singers and their accompanists were on a mattress on the floor, behind a translucent curtain at the other end of the room. The dancing girls performed in the middle, their hand and eye gestures exuberantly portraying the ecstasy of my joyful surrender, but they did so with sober sophistication. That day Ustad Rai Chand had to sing alongside his own disciple Miyaan Guftar. By the time they reached the lines comparing the sultan with Kaamadev, the Hindu god of love, Baz himself joined them aloud, making it sound like a chorus.

He was truly a music man. I was thrilled to see him so happy. A few days later, I wrote a stanza rhyming with Jaidev Maharaj's lines as well:

Until the time
The sun and moon rise
In the sky
May Baz remain our sultan on high!
Pray we, my Lord
May Baz remain our sultan
We are your bees and you our lotus flower:
For you we pray, may you never cease to bloom.
Open your petals and we live;
Withhold your bounty and we are doomed.

After moving into the new palace, we had become more open with each other. I had acquired a new insight into his persona. Even above being a temporal ruler, Baz was a musician and thinker par excellence. Alcohol set his creative juices flowing freely, and sharpened his instincts but in the old Raniwaas, he had been cautious about drinking in my presence, whatever be his reasons. I never said anything to forbid it, but it's entirely possible that I might have looked a bit askance, when he came back tipsy after a convivial evening. Over time, my manners had perhaps become more accommodating.

It was late evening by then and he had emptied several glasses of wine. When I read my lines to him, he was thrilled.

'Bravo, Rani, those are wonderfully written, but there is one little thing out of place,' he said smiling.

'What? Tell me, I'll set it right,' I said agreeably.

'You're not the bee hovering over me, but I'm the bhaunra, enticed by your beauty.' I laughed, suddenly reminded of Bhanwar.

'By the grace of Radha-Krishna, may we forever keep competing to excel each other's love,' I said, my eyes moist with emotion.

Once again, the accompanists were sent for with their instruments.

'Meanwhile, bring me another glass of wine, Nayla bi,' he said. Turning back to me, 'Let's not bother my Ustad tonight, the two of us will practise by ourselves. What beautiful lines, Rani! I'll try and set them to a brand new tune, if I can, and then we'll present it to Ustad Rai Chand as a surprise.'

Next week we put the result of several days of practice to Rai Chandjju. On humming Baz's new composition over a few times, he said, 'Indeed, Rani Ruupmati's lyrics are excellent, but what a uniquely original score you've set it to. I'm amazed! We should honour your effort by naming it Baz-Khani dhruvpad, if it pleases Your Majesty.'

Baz bowed low and said, 'It's *your* approval we are seeking, Ustad, not mine!'

Vision 59

My dear scribe, you must surely think of me as a strange woman, who hasn't been able to be rid herself of her calf love, even after five hundred years. She goes on adorning her lover with exalted titles of musician, thinker and what have you! But believe me, he truly was all that and more.

Time, sir, is indeed all powerful. Without being aware of its true nature in the era that you live in, it is impossible for anyone to be able to rule a state. If you run too far behind, you run the risk of becoming a laughing stock like those who would refrain from taking up weapons to battle after sundown. And if you are too far ahead, you're likely to end up with a poison cup like Socrates. And those who are in sync with the mores of their time, must necessarily do all the things that their contemporaries do. My beloved also beheaded adversaries and conspirators for the sake of his kingdom. Yet, he had a heart of gold, and he was truly brave.

No, no, Rani! There's hardly any need for so defensive a preface. After all, this is your autobiography. I'm only a scribe.

You can say whatever you want, and I'll record it. It's up to the readers to decide whether or not to believe what you say of Baz.

According to the Christian era, which you prefer to follow in your day to day lives, this was 1558 AD now. Nearly three years had passed since I came to Mandavgarh.

The sun was almost gone for the day as we sat chatting on one of the pavilions, on the hillock named after me.

'One good deed is enough to cover for a hundred sins, Rani, not that you've committed any at all,' Baz was saying. 'When I come across someone doing a good deed for the needy, I am genuinely pleased. Nayla had already told me that every month or so, you have been earning punya by setting a girl free, but I had no idea those would include a Mussalman girl as well.'

This was the first time ever that I had mentioned it to Baz, but the wretched Nayla always seemed to be a step ahead!

'I don't know about earning punya. Maybe I do all this only for a good name for myself, fame probably, I have no idea,' I said a bit hotly, disappointed that he already knew of it from someone else.

'What difference does that make? A good deed is a good deed, regardless of the intention. Who doesn't like to hear their praise! But for all that, a good deed would certainly count for punya.' There was no trace of sarcasm in his tone. Reining in my annoyance, I asked, 'So, what all did Nayla tell you?'

'The very same things you've been doing without telling me. Anyhow, you did well not to ask me. If I had my way, I would shut down this whole wretched business, but that's impossible. The entire nobility would unanimously agree to have my head, if I did. So, it's good that in bits and pieces, you're doing what you can to offer succour to those in distress.'

There was a whole section in the business district of Mandav known as Baandi Bazaar, the Maids Market, where young women abducted from across the border, or even from remote areas within Malwa, or those sold by their own impoverished families, were brought to be sold into slavery. The good-looking girls were picked up to serve in the households of the rich and powerful, and the homely ones ended up in middle-class homes, for back-breaking chores in the kitchen, the scullery and such, besides, of course, servicing the lust of their masters, whenever they wanted. Most of them resigned themselves to their fate, indeed, many were even happy to have enough to eat and be safely confined within strong walls. The life of common folk in our time, dear scribe, was one long saga of dreadful destitution and insecurity.

The new palace was large, always in need of more serving hands. Every month or two, Gulrez, the best known in the trade, would bring and leave one or two maids at Nayla's disposal.

Looking at them, I would be reminded sometimes of my own kidnapping and at other times, of the lonely, subterranean existence of Rukmini and of what must have happened to Tara. I'd begin talking to them about where and how they were taken, and how they felt living in captivity. There was one terribly anguished, weeping silent tears behind her veil and by sheer chance, her name was Rukmini. She had a lover who would take her back, no matter what. 'Nayla bi, can you find a reliable jaannisaar to escort her back to her village safely, yes? Go ahead then!'

Then came along another soul, suffering similarly, and just by chance, a Hindu again: 'Nayla bi, can you do it again?' I let the bird fly back to freedom, leaving the rest to destiny. And now, this last one, Anaar, a Muslim girl. I couldn't bear her heart-wrenching weeping. She had been married barely a month when she was abducted. Will he take you back after this though, I asked. 'How will I know unless I try, and I'll die if I can't!' she said. 'Nayla bi, for Allah's sake, could you have her sent back!'

Sawaab, as the Muslims called it, and punya as we Hindus did, but I don't know what I was after. All I know is that my writ ran and I let it run whenever it took my fancy. Little did I know then, how catastrophic would be the consequence of the stories of my beauty and kindness spreading far and wide!

When I told Baz about Anaar, the first shock was that Nayla had stolen my thunder, and what put me off even more was his remark that he did not know my munificence would include Muslim girls as well, as though my kindness was blinkered by religion!

'Why does it surprise you that I helped out a Muslim girl?' I said, indignantly. 'You didn't force me to convert to your faith and you bow to my mother's idols, coming and going. So, why can't I help a Muslim woman?' My tone was veering towards acrimony.

Baz doused the flames before they had a chance!

'I bow to masjids and temples, and places of worship of all religions, but I am free of religion at heart. Religious orthodoxy has wreaked untold miseries on the progeny of Aadam and Hawwa for centuries. It is crystal clear, right there, in front of your eyes. God alone knows why you're unable to see it! Our love, this wonderful union of loving hearts, is a rebellion against all that injustice, can't you see that? If you want to quarrel with me on that, go ahead, but I know and I'm truly proud that you are above all such pettiness as well! Come, Ruup, let's go. It's time for our daily prayer to Mother Music,' he said, getting to his feet.

I was stumped, completely at a loss for words. I felt like taking him in my arms and kissing him to make him even prouder of me.

'Yes, Baz, let's go,' I said gushing with emotion, 'I'll sing *Madhurashtakam* for you through the night.' He extended his hand to help me get up.

That evening, once again, we sang late into the night in our favourite music room. On our way there, we passed through the large audience hall with vaulted double-height ceiling where Baz sometimes received dignitaries and envoys from neighbouring states. Of course, we had no idea then that a meeting that was going to take place in it within two days' time would cause a terrible upheaval in our life, leaving it in shambles! In that quiet evening before the storm, we sat making music until the wee hours, our voices entwined like creepers rising on a trellis.

My dear scribe, you must be even more amazed now, a lover all of twenty-six and a beloved barely eighteen talking to each other on such complex topics! Yes sir, they did so because they were Sultan Baz Bahadur and Rani Ruupmati. They did talk of such things. That is precisely the reason why people have not stopped talking about them even after five centuries.

She smiled and vanished, leaving me to wonder how she had divined what I was thinking!

Vision 60

The next morning it was Nayla, instead of the usual maid, who brought us our pot of kahwa and cups.

'Is something the matter, Nayla?' asked Baz in surpise.

'Jaannisaar Mohammad Khan has sent word that Aadhar Singh, an envoy of Rani Durgawati, the Chandela queen, is here. He wants a private audience to deliver her letter, addressed to Your Majesty. He says he must hand it over personally.' Baz looked at me, and then back to Nayla, 'Where is he?' he asked.

'Under Mohammad's surveillance, they have been stopped at the Laal Sarai.'

'Why was I not informed earlier, Nayla bi?' It was possibly the first time that I heard him talking sternly to Nayla.

'I had come during the night, but the Sultan was resting,' said Nayla, her eyes lowered.

'No, I mean that the envoy must have crossed over into our territories several days earlier. Never mind, we'll see later how that happened, without none of us getting any wiser. For now, tell Mohammad Khan to inform the envoy that I'll see him here day after tomorrow, three hours after daybreak. Meanwhile, he should be kept under close watch. And summon Shahabuddin; I want him here within the hour.' Shahabuddin was Baz's chief spymaster.

The news that Shahabuddin brought the next day left Baz stunned. That night, many a head rolled, one of them being that of Hayat Khan, the commander of Kadrula Fort. He was still unaware that the Chandelas had taken possession of ten or twelve of Malwa villages, on the border under his watch. Aadhar Singh and his escort had crossed over surreptitiously into Malwa, through the forests surrounding those villages.

The morning after, when Aadhar Singh left Laal Sarai for an audience with the Sultan, the severed head of Hayat Khan was hanging from a stake in front of Laal Sarai. The Chandela escort was detained at the palace gate. Only Aadhar Singh was allowed in, and seated in the audience hall.

I was watching the proceedings from across the latticework screen, on the first floor. Aadhar Singh was a tall, heavily-built man, wearing a spotless white angrakhaa and dhoti, with a mustard turban and a sandal-paste tilak adorning his broad forehead. He looked perfectly calm and self-assured. He must have seen Hayat Khan's head leaving the Sarai, for it was put up right in front of the exit only for him to see, but apparently it left him unimpressed.

An hour after the appointed time, a loud announcement was made: 'The Lord of Malwa, Chhatrapati of Ujjayini, His Excellency Sultan Bayzeed Khan is arriving.' Nayla had stopped behind the curtain of the door through which Baz presently emerged into the hall.

About fifteen arm's lengths from where Aadhar Singh sat was the sultan's golden throne, set with sapphires and rubies, obviously a masterpiece of some outstanding goldsmith. Clad in a long-coat of golden kamkhaab, blue pyjamas, a sky-blue turban, with a diamond sparkling in its front and falcon-feather sticking out on top, Baz looked as handsome as ever. He held a filigreed silver mace in his hand, and sported a dagger scabbard stuck to his cummerbund. Taking a seat on his grand throne, he smiled at the Chandela envoy, and said amiably, 'Warrior Aadhar Singh, I welcome you to Mandav. I do hope you were comfortable in the quarters arranged for you. Did they take good care of you?'

'Pranaam, Sultan,' said Aadhar Singh, rising briefly to his feet, 'but I'm not here today as a warrior but solely as an envoy of the Chandela-Gond court.'

'It's truly amazing to hear of an ambassador sneaking through the jungles! Scared for your life, you now pretend to be Durgawati's envoy?' The expression on Baz's face, as well as his tone, had suddenly changed, but there was no trace of tension on Aadhar Singh's face, as he parried with a slight shrug. 'The way politics is conducted is well known to you, sire. I had instructions from my monarch, Maharani Durgawati, to deliver her missive to you in person at the earliest. Now, if I had started seeking permission from your brass, it would have taken me months to get here. The only other option was to come clandestinely, and I'm sorry for that, but I remain an ambassador come to deliver a letter,' he said, pointing to a silver box on the table in front of him.

'Nayla bi!' Baz called out to her. She emerged from behind the curtain, walked slowly over to the table and brought the box to him.

The letter—a scroll of fine beige silk with two round wooden holders at either end—was inside a silver container, like a shorter version of the royal mace in Baz's hand. Baz rolled it open and began to read silently. As his eyes moved down from top to bottom, his face flushed a deep red and eyebrows arched high, as though he could not believe what he had just read. Then he seemed to read it all over again, and sat frozen gazing at it for a long moment. Aadhar Singh cleared his throat and said solemnly, 'The box also has a gift for Shrimant Sultan.'

Baz groped inside the box. His hand came out with a small dagger in an exquisitely carved gold sheath, the handle shaped like a falcon head, set with gleaming emerald pieces for eyes. He kept turning it over in his hands for a while, and then suddenly burst into loud laughter. He put the letter and the dagger on a side-table, and bent low clutching at his stomach as if he couldn't stop himself from laughing, 'Ha…ha…ha…' he went on for the longest time.

Nayla standing a few paces behind his throne, and I behind the latticed screen upstairs, were aghast. What is this mad behaviour? Of course, there was no one in the hall, but he was laughing so loudly that people standing outside the doors could hear him clearly. But mercifully, he stopped as abruptly as he'd started, and sitting erect again, addressed the envoy sarcastically, 'So, you brought me an ultimatum on soft silk and a dagger in a velvet-lined box from your Rani! A Maharani herself, she still needs my Rani too. You Chandelas, don't you have villages of your own to indulge in charity? Hunh?'

'What can I say—' No sooner had Aadhar Singh begun to speak, than he was cut short by Baz, his voice sharp as a whiplash, 'Absolutely! What could you, a mere slave, possibly say? But if you are done slaving here, leave immediately, and tell your Maharani that Rao Yaduveer is a fugitive, run away from Malwa law. I want him back along with my villages. If you won't cooperate, I will come and get them back myself, do you understand? And similarly, if Durgawati wants to have Rani Ruupmati, she will have to come here and take her away by force. She lives with me of her own free will. I married her without compelling her to convert, but a slave like you is not at liberty to verify these facts for your mistress. She must come here in person to do that. Now, before I forget the privilege you enjoy as an envoy, LEAVE! And scurry across the border as fast as you can.' Then turning to Nayla, he commanded, 'Tell Mohammad to let him cross over the border under close watch.'

That night, in our private living room, Baz, having polished off several decanters of wine, kept muttering endlessly, 'What if he is your father? If he needed a jagir, he should have taken it from me. As a matter of fact, there was no need to flee in the first place! Who is Durgawati to make him a grant of our villages? If it takes a war to straighten the Chandelas, so be it! And just look at the cheek of it all, that I have forced you into my harem against your will! Me? I'm myself a prisoner of your love, my darling! Have a look, read this abominable letter. Durgawati knows about your good deeds, has kept a count of the Hindu girls, but why would she keep track of the Mussalmans? Didn't I tell you Ruup, all these things—religion, caste, creed—are at the root of the problem! Come take it, go on, read Durgawati's blessed missive. Nayla, Nayla bi, where are you, bring me a little more wine!'

'I am at your sevice, Sultan,' said Nayla, looking plaintively at me.

By that time, I had gone through Rani Durgawati's letter thrice and every time I read it, my cheeks felt hot with embarrassment:

> Sultan Baz Bahadur,
>
> My greetings to you as the head of a neighbouring state as of now.
>
> Rao Yaduveer Singh Parbhar, the jagirdar of Garh Dharmapuri of your realm, is under my protection. He tells me you're suppressing and persecuting your Hindu subjects with great cruelty, and that he had to flee Malwa to save his life. I have therefore taken some ten-twelve of your villages and granted them to him in jagir for his subsistence.
>
> Rao has also told me that you sent a big contingent of your army and had his daughter abducted, and are now keeping her forcibly in your harem. I gather that she is a well-mannered, kind-hearted girl who has helped many Hindu women in captivity to return to their homes. But the question is: who will help Ruupmati herself?
>
> I, Rani Durgawati, Queen of the Chandelas and the Gonds, do hereby warn you that I shall come to her aid, and teach you a lesson, if you don't release her forthwith and send her back to Rao Yaduveer! You will be needlessly courting disaster, if you do not listen. Be forewarned.
>
> I do hope all the same that you liked the present I sent you.
>
> Seal: Rani Durgawati

Tossing and turning in bed until late into the night, I kept wondering what was going to happen now. In the thick of this political stand-off, who could I go to and declare that Baz had not had me abducted? To the contrary, I had appealed to him to save my life from a premature end, that I did not want to die, that I loved him with all my heart and had chosen him as my husband of my own free will and that he had stood by his promise and had never asked me to convert to his faith!

I kept recalling Pandijju's warning. Would Rani Durgawati really send her army over to have me rescued, merely at the say-so of Rao? O my God! Was she the one we were to be careful of? There was no one at all whom I could ask.

Baz, fast asleep on the other side of the bed, was quite unable to be of any help with my sleepless nightmare.

Vision 61

Baz was fresh as a daisy the next morning. He recalled every word of his drunken mutterings from the previous night, which I had taken for too much wine talking.

'Why are you looking so guilty? I will neither let go of my ten villages nor spare him. We will go to war, if we have to, and I will cut off his head myself,' he said.

'Who do you want to kill? Are you talking about Rao?' I asked, distressed.

'Nayla bi, have kahwa sent. Don't you worry, Rani. However wicked, Rao is after all your father. Nothing will happen to him, though he spared no effort to murder you for false pride,' he said.

Nayla stood behind us, having served our morning tea. He glanced at her, and turned to me again, 'Shahabuddin has told me that that wretched villain is the one prodding Rao into all this mischief. I won't spare him.' He looked at Nayla again, 'Rani and I would like to go out for a ride. Would you go and see to the arrangements?' Nayla bowed and left. I was gaping at Baz.

'Who won't you spare? Who is this you're talking about?'

'That wretched Revadiya! How dare he cast his lecherous eye on you!' said Baz, gnashing his teeth in fury.

I trembled, my heart racing. How on earth did he know what Revadiya did?

'Revadiya! How do you know—' He did not let me finish.

'I never told you, Rani. When Bhanwar brought your poem-letter, Rabat didn't take him to Bano, he brought him straight to me, instead. Bhanwar was full of remorse for what he had done, he kept weeping, and told me everything. He knew it all. Indeed, he made a serious mistake snitching on you, but he wasn't a bad sort. The real villain is that cad, Revadiya!'

'But surely you know that he...' I began, in a low voice, my eyes downcast.

'Of course, but what difference does it make that the bastard didn't succeed? I won't let him live. And what of Durgawati's affront? Should I gulp it down as though it was no more than our morning kahwa here? She has openly declared you a concubine kept in my harem by force. It's not a question of just ten villages, Rani. Malwa's pride is at stake. And what even if it really was a dispute over ten villages, brothers have killed one another for land measuring as little as the point of a needle here. Durgawati is not even kin to me!'

Baz was furious. I felt close to tears from a terrible feeling of guilt. So much mayhem in the offing for as little as me? And that too when I am so happy living my tranquil dream with my beloved, whom my heart craved for...

I did end up in tears; tears of fear, sadness, and curiously, of joy as well!

'Now, don't you weep, my darling, don't hurt yourself,' said Baz tenderly. 'My decision to go to war against Durgawati is no favour to you. It's necessary to redeem myself as the proud sultan of Malwa. Come, let's go out for that ride. It may be quite a while until the next time we get a chance to go out riding together.'

Vision 62

I pleaded with him until I was miserable, 'Baz, don't go, I am very afraid.'

'What do you have to fear? Half my army will remain here in Mandav, Nayla bi and Mohammad are going to be here. And in any case, I'm only going after the people who have threatened to snatch you away from me!'

'But so much bloodshed for me, I don't like...' my voice trailed off.

'Rani, I have gladly accepted being called a kafir for you. I don't care if I lose all I have, for the sake of your honour,' he said firmly.

I knew then, that he wasn't to be dissuaded.

The next day, there was a big war council in the Hindola Mahal. Imam Nuuruddin spared no effort to stoke the fire. The Sultan's decision to go to war agains the infidels is absolutely right. After all, the kafirs have challenged the might of the True Faith; this isn't war, it's jihad, that's what it is!

Baz was irritated to no end.

'This has nothing to do with kufr. If it's a jihad, it's a jihad for my love, and to teach the Chandelas good manners, that they can't get away with sending a dagger in velvet lining to the Sultan of Malwa!' he growled, looking pointedly at the Imam.

The Vizier, the courtiers and the warlords in attendance, looked on silently at his fury. The Imam's face darkened as he kept staring at the floor.

As far as I know, Nayla never said a word to stop Baz. Perhaps she had known from the very beginning that once he had made up his mind, he wouldn't listen to anyone.

The third day, Baz left with ten thousand of cavalry, five hundred each of his ace archers and the best war elephants, twenty-five cannons and gunners, and fifteen thousand foot-soldiers. Many said Baz Bahadur had gone mad, going to war leading such a large army himself, and that for a mere ten villages at stake.

After he left, I wept for days. My heart felt like a load of stones. We had been having such a fine time these last couple of years, after moving into the new palace, often riding out across verdant grasslands and woods in the mornings, and in the evenings, watching the sun go down from the pavilions, followed by delightful music sessions, devising new compositions for lyrics we had written, the enchanting dance-dramas of his danseuses. Now I sat alone, scribbling dark poems, bent over my desk all day long. If I came up with some good lines, even that instantly brought him to mind, how his face would light up—'Bravo, Rani, bravo! I'll set these to a new tune. Call the accompanists, Nayla bi!'

Baz had been gone for weeks now. That day, I wrote in my notebook:

> You took all my joys with you,
> Leaving me only care and grief:
> The days bring me no pleasure,
> The nights no relief.

'Rani, we have good news! The Sultan is doing well and he has sent this letter for you,' said Nayla, extending the scroll.

Baz had written that he had chased away the enemy from the captured villages. 'Alas! I could not have the head of that scoundrel, but I did cut off his right arm. He fled into the the jungles of Gondwana across the border, but he won't survive, the stump of his severed arm was gurgling out blood like a fount. The hand that had shot out to grab at your chastity is no more! I would be back soon, but let me first teach a lesson I had vowed I would.'

I sent a missive in reply, 'Baz, you have done what you had vowed you would. You have your villages back and wounded Revadiya so grievously that you yourself say that he won't survive. Now come back, I am so lonely here. There are a lot of new verses waiting to be set to music:

Hour after hour I turn and toss.
Forlorn, I find little sleep,
Without the opiate of your kiss
At night, or in the morning.

'Listen to me, come back now!'

A week later I was still writing, head mournfully bowed.

My paper is all too little,
And all too soon I fill it up:
Fool! Can love's ocean be contained
Within a cup?

Nayla came again to give me news of Baz. By then he had crossed over into Chandela territory, and taken a score of their villages, instead. Like the last time, I replied to his letter, 'Come back now, for heaven's sake. You have hammered enough of a lesson into their heads.'

But that expediton of his that ought to have lasted for no more than a month, or two at best, went on and on because of his childish obstinacy, finally ending in disaster, six months later.

Drunk to the gills one night, after returning from the Chandela campaign, Baz himself told me in a voice breaking with pent-up emotions, 'I lost comprehensively, Rani…it was all because of me! I was consumed by false pride and hauteur. Chasing the enemy, when we had captured a clutch of Chandela villages, everyone said enough! Khan Meerzah is almost a family elder who fought alongside Abbu for years. Even he tried to reason with me, his arm affectionately draped around my shoulders, "You're the sultan, it's your call, but if you care to have my view, don't venture too far out into the Gondwana wilderness. I've known it in the past, it's not a good place to be in." I brushed aside his counsel and called for another large reinforcement. Why him alone, I paid little heed to even your missives.'

His face crumpled in anguish, 'I was like an arrogant little boy, at least let me have a showdown with Durgawati in person,

I thought. The irony of it all was that I never once had a glimpse of her during the entire campaign. Indeed, she knows warfare better than I can claim for myself. She kept fooling me with baits, and I kept swallowing them hook, line and sinker. In the beginning, the Chandelas let us win easily, and when they had us where they wanted, they struck. One half of their army sneaked past us through the jungle paths, cutting off our supply lines, while the other half kept hammering at us in hit-and-run skirmishes, taking us by surprise like predators. We suddenly found ourselves hemmed in between a river on one side and mountains on the other, enemy in front and enemy behind. We had nowhere to go!

'In front of my eyes, three-fourths of the Malwa army was decimated, running helter-skelter to save their lives amidst brutal slaughter, and I couldn't do a thing to prevent it! No, Rani, do not commiserate with me! I, who had always preened at my ability to swoop down, swift as a falcon seizing its prey, Baz the Brave, have come back chastened, having taken rather than teaching them the lesson I had vowed I'd teach them. Here I lie unmanned, weeping in your arms.' He was actually weeping. I couldn't bear to see the deep anguish in his eyes, and began to weep myself, holding his head on my bosom like a child's.

'Yes, Rani, weep for me but please do not try to console me. It was all a result of my bull-headed stupidity. Most of all, my heart is rent by what it did to my companions. Out of the eleven gallant generals who accompanied me, eight of them lost their lives. Thousands of loyal soldiers were slain. All our expensive tents, spare weapons and equipment, cannons, war elephants had to be abandoned for future use of the Chandela army, as each one us ran blindly to save our lives every which way we could, tails between our legs. I only came back to you, because you wanted me to, otherwise I didn't deserve to show you my face again,' he moaned pitifully and lay down on the bed, the crook of his arm covering his wet eyes, and called out, 'Nayla bi, where are you? Could you please bring me some more wine?'

'I'm at your service, my sultan, but if you would be kind enough to spare my life, more wine tomorrow, sire!' Nayla said what I had in mind, though I was so full of compassion for my troubled man that had he asked me, I would have poured him my life in a cup!

Didn't I tell you, dear scribe, my Baz was truly a braveheart, honest to his core. Even after having been whipped so badly, his bravery and integrity were unimpaired, intact as ever. It takes a brave man to acknowledge a crushing defeat so candidly, and only a man of integrity can accept it without rancour or invectives for the victor. Woefully drunk as he was, Baz never once uttered a word of abuse for Rani Durgawati, not even kambakht, or kafir, or…a woman!

But who could stop others from jeering! Heartless men not only in the capital but all over the sultanate laughed their guts out. One Hindu Rani sapped him of his manliness, and the other gave him such a thrashing, the Sultan is on all fours, beaten hollow, and that too at the hands of a woman! Shame on him!

The crushing defeat did indeed leave Baz a broken man. Pandijju's warning came buzzing back into my mind. Once or twice, I felt I should go to Garh Dharmapuri and ask him whether it was Rani Durgawati we had to guard against. Or, was there another ominous cloud looming on the horizon? Would Durgawati be satisfied with her decisive victory, or was she about to send another army to have me freed and taken to the Chandela country?

Vision 63

After the fiasco of the Chandela campaign, Baz was truly transformed. The Baz of yore won't have gone to sleep like a scolded child. He would have growled at Nayla and got her to bring him another cup of wine. But the change in him was not so much on the surface as it was inside. It seemed as though the defeat was lodged somewhere deep inside him. He had become introverted, his eyes a bit lost, brooding.

He carried on with attending to matters of state the same as before, though. There was a brief jharokhaa-darshan to make sure that the peace of the realm was maintained, holding court for a while, review of troops parading once every fortnight or so, but he now abhorred the idea of sitting down with his aiyaars for akhbaaraat. For one thing, however discreet they tried to be, some public ridicule for the Sultan came through in their reports and for another, Baz's favourite spymaster, Shahabuddin, had suddenly vanished after the failed expedition. Perhaps he had fled Malwa fearing for his life. He had been the one who had brought the news of those ten villages that set off the entire chain of events.

Malwa's army had been virtually destroyed in the Chandela campaign. But the sultanate still had incalculable amounts of gold in its coffers, salted away safely in subterranean chambers under the Shaahi Mahal, and waterproof vaults at the bottom of Munj Talao. It was more than enough to rebuild and equip the army. Fresh recruitment commenced. New cannons and elephants were acquired, and in a few months' time everything was as good as new, but now Baz never even hinted at any warlike intentions, to try out the army that he had rebuilt. Indeed, at times he seemed to be gripped by a vague sense of trepidation that he would not explain. He would sometimes whisper to me in bed without preamble, 'Rani, should something happen to me, go away somewhere very far, these people will not leave you in peace here. They're very jealous of our love!' I would say, 'Nothing will happen to you and where will I go? To the Chandela Rani's protection? Will the people there let me be at peace? I'll never ever stop declaring my undying love for you, even if they kill me for it.'

He started saying these things after that terrible incident to do with Khulla Jani. I'll come to it in a moment, but let me first tell you how the most ludicrous of coincidences set off a rumour about me practising black magic.

In the past, Baz had been inclined to laugh away the rumours about us but now, every little quip, every taunt went straight to his heart like a poisoned shaft, leaving him in a sulk darker than the kohl I used.

It was peak monsoon time, the month of Saawan. Yet there wasn't a sliver of a cloud anywhere in the sky. As we sat lounging on the open terrace, at the back of our living room, Baz said quite suddenly, 'Come, Rani, sing the raga Megh-malhaar! Call the clouds to the skies.' I began to sing, and by sheer coincidence, clouds seemed to come from all over and it began to pour. Baz laughed merrily, 'You're a magician, aren't you?'

Two days later when he returned after a session of akhbaaraat with his spies, he was in a blue funk. There was a rumour doing the rounds: Rani Ruupmati practises black magic, she can make the clouds rain by her singing.

To lighten his mood, I laughed and said, 'Indeed, I sing so well that the clouds come and listen to me, and pour down applause.'

But when Khulla Jani was charred to death, I could not laugh. I trembled at heart!

Nayla got hold of the details. It was a windy night. A corner of Khulla's dupatta flew into the fire-torch burning on the terrace wall. In the blink of an eye, her kurti, made of the finest silk and embroidered with silver thread, went up in flames. The fabric was reduced to ashes but the silver thread was so deeply embedded in her charred body that she was buried with them sticking to her flesh.

One of Khulla's maids babbled to someone, 'It wasn't the fire-torch. Her kurti began to suddenly emit smoke and then burst out in flames, all on its own!'

That one spark spread like wildfire throughout Mandavgarh in a trice: Rani Ruupmati can not only summon clouds, she also knows how to burn the living down, from a distance!

The day Khulla died was the first time that Baz told me, should anything happen to me, go away somewhere far. I could not laugh it away that time. Tossing and turning in my bed late into the night, I kept thinking, 'Where, in what direction would I go, if something happened to you, my love?'

Vision 64

For some time, Baz was consumed with watching the borders of Malwa and the Chandela-Gond kingdom. Perhaps he too feared an attack from Durgawati. He appointed Mohammad, his old faithful chief of jaannisaars, as the new commander of Kadrula Fort to watch over that border. Suleman, the chief of his household, was promoted in his place as chief of jaannisaars in the royal household. Baz thought that would do.

Meanwhile, the musician inside him had begun to take real hold of him. Seldom did he even mention a morning ride or a hunting trip now. His curly brown hair grew down to his shoulders. He had begun to imbibe larger quantities of alcohol, as though to keep unpleasant memories at bay. The red wine brewed from grapes, that he used to have earlier, wasn't good enough for him any longer. He would say to Nayla, almost apologetically, 'Nayla bi, only God knows why, but I seem to have lost my taste for that red stuff, bring me some of that white one the phirangis seem to favour. Go, go on! Why do you look at me so?' Nayla would come back with a decanter of the transparent, bitter-tasting white liquor. How on earth would I know what it tasted like? Well, she was the one who tasted it, and confided in me once, 'I put a drop of it on my tongue, and it seemed to burn my gullet, right down to my gut, like a line of fire.'

Baz now drank not only in the evenings, but right through the day as though he wanted keep his blood simmering all along.

He chose to spend most of his time in the music room—singing, devising new compositions, trying out new instruments—all by himself mostly. Of course, I was there nearly all the time, but rarely anyone else. He would say to me, 'Won't you sing with me?' And I would reply, tenderly as ever, 'Why not, my dear, tell me which of the ragas you would like?' His response surprised me this once, 'That raga you were singing in Hoshang Shah's pavilion on that full moon night, before we met.' How on earth did he know that? Oh, so he was the wind rustling through the foliage that fateful night Tara was taken!

Some evenings, the dancers were summoned. They danced until they were exhausted and fell over dog-tired. Nayla was made to taste the white stuff cup after cup with him, until his eyes had gone out of focus, drooping involuntarily to shut down. Then, she would say, 'May Your Grace spare my life…' And she would say it looking at me as though to say, 'Why must I have to do things you must learn to do?'

In bed, in the small hours of morning, he would embrace me at times, and say in a voice gone groggy with too much to drink, 'Rani, you must be sulking for sure. It seems you too have turned away from me!' And despite everything, I would whisper back eagerly, 'No, my love, never, you're all I have.' It was God's own truth. Besides, whenever I was with him, when I felt his breath, when he touched me, his powerful singing voice filled my ears like a mighty waterfall descending from the heavens.

'I'm not in a sulk at all. In fact, I'm as ready as I was before for hard work to silence our critics, Ustad. Shall I sing *Madhurashtakam* for you?' I would whisper, and we would break out laughing merrily. When we were together, we hadn't a care in the world, the entire universe was just us!

But come another day, and he would return to his new-found ways! To me, it didn't really matter though. Despite his increasing addiction to the white-man's liqour, and his humiliating defeat at the hands of the Chandela Rani, we were indescribably happy in each other's company.

There were times I wished I wasn't Rani Ruupmati, but

just an ordinary nineteen-year-old and he, not Sultan Baz Bahadur—weighed down by the millstone of a sultanate around his neck—but simply my carefree lover. But eventually, I would end up telling myself: *Ruup, love is love. If you're destined to have it, you get it. Whether you're king or commoner, that does not make a difference at all. As long as Baz is by your side, you'll be happy. If not, there just isn't a way forward.*

Once again, we were so deep in our togetherness and shared passion for music and dance, that if Tara had not appeared out of the blue, I wouldn't have had the vaguest sense that there was another and a much more sinister threat in the offing.

But was she Tara? Indeed, she went on insisting until the very end that she was Zahida, not Tara. 'Maybe you dreamt it all!' What a time to recall something spoken such a long time ago. Perhaps she was neither Zahida nor Tara; the fleeting encounter did feel like a dream afterwards.

Vision 65

Gulrez, the maid-dealer, stood in the rear court with three or four girls lined up, waiting for Nayla to come and make her pick. Watching from the upper window, I had a vague feeling of having seen the one standing at the far end of the line somewhere, and looked at her intently, trying to recall. Suddenly my pulse quickened. The very same features and round eyes, and the upright stance. Of course, this is Tara, but how come she's here with Gulrez, of all people? I felt like running down to the courtyard for a closer look, but how could I do that here!

'Nayla bi, do you see the lass standing with Gulrez at the very end? Bring her upstairs. I want her as a chambermaid. As for the rest, you can decide after consulting him.'

The moment Nayla went out of the room leaving the two of us alone, I rushed to her, and lifting up her face on my index finger, peered at her. She was flustered, her eyes suddenly scared, but reflecting no recognition at all.

'You are Tara, aren't you?' It had been more than five years since I last saw Tara. She had been a teenage girl then, and the one facing me was a grown woman. I began to doubt myself. Was this really Tara or someone else with a strong resemblance to her?

'Why are you looking at me as if you don't know me? Tell me you are Tara, aren't you?' I asked again.

'Tara...who? I am Zahida,' she was dismayed.

'Liar! Trying to fool me, aren't you,' I said, insisting.

'No, Malikaa. I swear by Allah, I'm not Tara, my name's Zahida.' She did seem to be telling the truth. Perhaps it was a case of mistaken identity.

'Where are you from?'

'From a village near Mathura. I was working in the fields, that's where I was taken.'

I dropped the matter for the time being, but the more I saw her, the more I felt that she was lying. I kept at it, watching her from different angles, asking leading questions. Her deception went on for three days. By the fourth I was vexed to no end. I went to her and gave her a whispered earful, 'What is this nonsense! For three days you've been doing Zahida...Zahida! You ARE Tara!'

'I don't know who Tara is, Rani, believe you me! I am Zahi—' I didn't let her finish.

'The very same lie again! Go, get yourself with child!'

She couldn't help bursting out into an abashed giggle, hearing me bring out the old jibe of our Garh Dharmapuri days. She smiled mischievously, her eyes down on the floor. I stepped forward and took her in my arms. 'Where have you been so long, sakhi! I have missed you terribly,' I said.

'Shuhhh!' She put a finger on her lips and looked all around. We were alone.

'Let me remain Zahida, Ruup. Indeed, they sent me here for something else, but I came determined to forewarn you before leaving.'

'What is this, another falsehood now! Who sent you and to do what?' I protested indignantly.

'No, no. I'll tell you everything.'

That night when Baz was busy composing a new tune, and Nayla, tasting his drinks, Tara told me her story. After the villain who had abducted her in the Omkaareshwar fair had had his fill, he sold her to a slave trader. She ended up in the household of a landlord near Kishangarh, and spent several months with him. Then there was an armed robbery, and the robbers took her along with them. All this while, she suffered the usual fate of female slaves in our times at the hand of whoever was her master. She passed a couple of years in the bandits' den near Bharatpur and, finally, she was sold once again in the Baandi Bazaar of Agra. For the present, she was the mistress of the stable master of Prince Malik Mustafa, camping on the outskirts of Agra. Through the days, however, she worked at Mustafa's haveli, doing odd household chores.

'Mustafa hasn't given up, Ruup, and now his perseverance is beginning to bear fruit. He gets on rather well with Adham Khan Koka, the ambitious son of Maham Angaa. The mother and son are forever engaged in court intrigues and the day they gain an upper hand, take it from me, something bad will happen against your sultan. Mustafa is forever lounging around in Koka's mehfils, whispering to him lurid descriptions of your fairy-like beauty, and poisoning his ears against Baz Bahadur. Was there a spymaster called Shahabuddin here? He has also joined the coterie.'

I was alarmed.

'What? Shahabuddin...but he was Baz's favourite aiyaar!' My mouth felt dry at Tara's news.

'Favourites also have a price, Ruup. In fact, he was the one who suggested that I be sent here, to gather intelligence in the guise of a baandi. Gulrez sold his loyalties for a thousand silver crowns, too. Now someone else will come in his place to escort me back.'

I was speechless with shock at the idea of her going back to the conspirators, and almost blurted out that I had bought her already, that she wasn't free to go, but restraining my impulse to say something so offensive, I said sternly, 'You will go back to reveal our secrets? I won't let you go anywhere now, Tara.'

'If I don't go back, they'll be suspicious and start thinking of coming from a different direction.'

'What do you mean by coming from a different direction? I cannot comprehend the tiniest bit of what you're saying, Tara. If you're with them, why on earth are you telling me all this? What are you going to tell them, about us, here?' I was exasperated.

'Oh, Ruup, for heaven's sake! Don't you see that I have always been on your side and am so, even now. I haven't seen anything here that they don't already know. If I could, I would tell them that your youth is faded and your beauty has withered away, but say, who would ever believe me? Have you heard of anyone's youth fading away at all but twenty or twenty-one?' Despite all my apprehensions, I couldn't help laughing out aloud.

'So, having run with the hares, you'll go back to hunt with the hounds, and have fun both ways! But just suppose they find out who you really are and what you've told me, won't they hang you for it?' I said.

Suddenly Tara's eyes welled up with suppressed tears, and she turned serious. It wasn't like her at all.

'Can I tell you another little truth, Ruup? I'd better be dead than the way I've been living for the last five years!' she said.

Then, within a fraction of a moment, she made an about turn like the old Tara I knew, and said smiling mischievously, 'What do you mean "who I really am?" Who will tell them, you? Begone, get yourself with child!'

I said nothing in reply, thinking to myself, God bless you my friend. Amen!

'All right, so, what exactly were you trying to say about the direction from which they will come?' I said, picking up the thread.

'Yes, from whatever I've been able to gather so far, when they come at you, it will be through Saarangpur. Now, it's time for me to take leave of you. And remember, my name's Zahida, not Tara. That girl you knew is no more!'

She left the room without looking back. After that day, neither she nor Gulrez were ever seen.

After Tara was gone, I thought long and hard until my head ached. I wished I had shared her secret with Nayla, and included her in our conversation. But it was very unlikely that Tara would have opened up in the presence of a third person, and if she had, there was no telling what the outcome might have been. It was quite likely that my best friend would have been executed on the charge of spying for the enemy. Who would spare a double agent?

The next morning there was much ado over Tara's sudden disappearance. Nayla came asking questions even to me, whether I had any idea where she might have gone, but I wriggled out of it, making up some vague excuse.

Once Tara was gone and I knew that no harm could come to her, there were times when I was tempted to share with Nayla all that she had revealed about Mustafa and Koka, but a strange reluctance paralysed me. Nayla would very likely say, 'Oh Rani! Why didn't you tell me before that Mustafa had sent a spy!' And I would fall back on that fatalistic streak of mine to console myself: would anything have really changed if I had told her before? Could the inevitable be averted?

Indeed, it must have been a phantom I had dreamt of. She was neither Zahida nor Tara!

Vision 66

They say misfortune never knocks on the door before entering, but it did knock at ours. Only, Baz refused to listen to it.

Meanwhile, another year had flown by. I could never clearly

tell either Nayla or Baz all that Tara had revealed to me, but I myself began to look out. I would at times stop talking to Baz to register my protest against his excessive drinking. Sometimes I would coax him out of the music room, or point out that an inspection of the military exercises was long overdue. But alas! His instincts quickly drew him back to music and art. He would go to court, and return a while later, after desultorily hearing out Khan Meerzah's comments on the current political situation. Of spies and secret agents, he was clearly wary, and pointedly avoided them. An aiyaar named Faiyaaz Ali had replaced Shahabuddin, but his access to the Sultan was nowhere near to Shahabuddin's.

I was twenty years of age, but in the two decades of my life, I had gone through so much of good, bad and the ugly, particularly in the last five years that at times I felt I had been surrounded by intrigues and machinations for a hundred years.

It was an evening in the early spring of the year 1560 AD. Faiyaaz Ali came to the palace in a tizzy, pleading for an immediate private audience with the Sultan. He seemed to carry the burden of some alarming secret intelligence he wanted to report to him. Suleman later told me he had sent him over to Jahaz Mahal.

By that time Baz, perhaps vexed at my interfering with his lifestyle, had begun to hold his soirees, with his danseuses in attendance, more often than not in the Jahaz Mahal halls. Baz's maternal uncle, Adam Khan, and a few of his favourite warlords like Taj Khan, Salim Khan and Sufi had grown rather close to him. Maybe he felt more at at ease, sitting and drinking with them there.

Once again, Nayla was on my side this time. She would sullenly tell me everything that went on there. One day, quite clearly vexed out of her usual reticence, she told me hotly, 'Khan Meerzah has been an old family loyal since the days of the senior Khan. As a toddler, Baz used to play in his lap. Indeed, he's too elderly now for late-night bouts of wine and women, but this coterie of scoundrels has distanced even him from the Sultan, not to mention other trusted family loyals.' She stopped abruptly, as though there was more to say but she had thought better of it.

'Why, is there something special I should know?' I prompted.

'Nothing special. It is just that those sycophants keep plying the Sultan, cup upon cup, of the terrible new wine through the night. Sometimes I fear...' Her voice trailed off, and this time around I didn't need her to explain what she feared. I knew well that in our time and milieu the loyalty of even one's own offsprings couldn't be taken for granted, not to speak of uncles and warlords, however friendly or close. No one really knew who would stick a dagger in whose back, and when!

That night, when Faiyaaz reached Jahaz Mahal, begging for an urgent audience with the Sultan, Baz was in his element with a good deal of the new liquor inside him, and was polishing the wrinkles off his latest composition with Rai Chand assisting him, 'Ustad, if we repeat the "taa taa thai tat" in the vilambit at this point, how do you think it would sound?'

Handing him another cup of wine, Nayla whispered in his ears, 'I beg your pardon, Sultan, but Faiyaaz Ali is here with something very important, he says.'

'Nayla bi! Nayla bi, I've told you before, and I'll tell you again, please do not break into my rhythm when I am making music. Now, if I forget at which exact notes the raga needed to be improvised, it'll all be your fault!' he said, petulant as a child interrupted with the final piece of a jigsaw puzzle in hand, and promptly went back to his 'taa taa thai tat' consultation with Rai Chand.

The next morning when Faiyaaz Ali finally managed to see Baz in the audience hall, I sat watching them from behind the latticed screen.

'Yes, Faiyaaz, tell us where the fire has broken out.' Baz's cutting sarcasm unnerved Faiyaaz right at the outset.

'Your Majesty, I've heard—' Baz interrupted him curtly.

'You've come to report hearsay? I was told that you had an

urgent intelligence report to make. Anyhow, be quick. I have to be going out for a ride shortly.'

'Yes, sire, we have news of a very large Mughal army led by Bahadur Khan in our direction. He's no ordinary—'

'I know who Bahadur Khan is. He's the brother of the Mughal regent Bairam Khan. Proceed further. What does "in our direction" mean? How far are they?'

'They have made their first camp about twenty-five kos south of Agra.'

'So, how did you jump to the conclusion that Malwa is the target? Do you have any real intelligence, or are you just shooting in the dark?' said Baz, smiling at the other man's discomfort.

By then, the poor spymaster was clearly close to a nervous breakdown.

'May I seek the Sultan's permission to come back with more concrete intelligence as soon as possible?' Actually, he wanted to run away from his presence at the earliest possible.

'You have my permission. And miyaan, come back only after you have some real information to share.' Then, he turned to Nayla, and said, 'Ask the Rani if she's keen to go out riding with me.'

I refused. I was quite put off by the insulting manner in which Baz had treated Faiyaaz.

I thought to myself: *Tara was right. Bairam Khan must have sent his trusted brother to subjugate Malwa, and here was Baz, not willing to even give a patient hearing to his own spymaster, far less investigate what he had to say!*

I was deeply perturbed that morning. My Baz had really changed. It was the first time in the last five years that he had been away from me the whole night. For the first time ever, I feared that he might be losing interest in me, like the red wine he no longer fancied. And I could not even be very direct with him. He'd already said, 'Don't look at me so closely, Rani, you might get frightened.' Nayla had mentioned a new dancer who had come from Golconda, far to the south of Khandesh even—

Rukhsana, dark-complexioned but with sharp features and beautiful eyes. Her solo dance had outdone the six danseuses of Baz, and she hadn't taken even an hour to master his preferred vilambit 'taa taa thai tat'. Baz seemed to be quite taken with her, nodding his head and smiling in approval, 'Waah-waah! That's exactly it. Bravo!'

Could Baz have been in Rukhsana's arms last night, in his pursuit of an heir to the throne, I wondered despairingly. Who could I ask other than him and he had already declared: 'I am the sultan; I have to do many things!'

When he'd returned that morning, his eyes were red as though he had been up all night and within hours, as evening fell, he went back again to Jahaz Mahal. I could not describe the agony of it if I tried!

It was a full moon night. I called out to Zubeida, 'Get my palanquin, we'll go to the pavilions on the hill. Also, Zubeida, remember to bring my beenn along.'

Moonlight was like a gossamer sheet, spread out on the undulating grassy slopes glistening with evening dew. I could see the faint glow of fire-torches burning on the terrace of Garh Dharmapuri in the far distance below. Sitting on the south pavilion, I played raga Bhairav on my beenn for the longest time.

It was nearly midnight by the time Zubeida and I returned, no trace of Baz anywhere. Sleepless, sitting at my desk with my notebook of poems in the circle of bluish light, I poured my heart out:

> Gone is the day when you were one with me,
> And I with you:
> Now I am I and you are you again,
> Not one but two:
> What earned us your ire,
> O Destiny?

It was nearly dawn when I lay on my bed, and drifted off into a fitful sleep. When my eyes opened next, he was sleeping on the other side of the bed.

Next morning Baz smiled innocently at me. 'Would you like to see something I've prepared for you, after two days of hard labour? We finished it last night. Right now, I can only sing it myself for you. To hear it sung to music, you'll have to wait until the evening. Do you remember, it's exactly five years today since the day I snatched you from the jaws of death?' he said, looking deep into my eyes.

I was stupefied for a moment: he remembered! Then I said, pushing my notebook towards him, 'No, first you take a look at what I wrote last night.'

'Your ode to melancholy is well written but it can't beat what I have composed for you.' He took out a piece of paper from his angrakhaa pocket, and looking at it, began to actually sing:

Describe not the beauty of Ruupmati
O my heart… O my heart
Taa…taa…thai…tat—taa…taa…thai…tat
O you fool, listen you to me
O my heart… O my heart
Taa…taa…thai…tat—O my foolish heart
Describe not the beauty of my Rani
It'll set people's heart afire—
Make an enemy of the world you will
Causing infernal fire of jealousy
In every part
O my foolish heart!
Bedecked in their best finery
Beautiful maidens all come
To entice you away—O my heart
Taa…taa…thai…tat
To lure you they come
Talking glib and making eyes
But where would they find
Eyes like hers, eyes like hers
O foolish heart
Fair maidens, beautiful all
But they fail and curse

Where, O where would they
Find eyes like hers!
Describe not the beauty of Ruupmati
Do not, Oh I say, do not
O my heart

Tapping his fingers on the table in front to keep time, he went on singing for a long time. Deep into the rhythm, eyes closed, he repeated the 'taa taa thai tat' notes so many times, in so many different ways, that I kept looking at him mesmerized, marvelling at his genius. When he finally stopped, there was a long moment of silence. Then I asked in a small voice, 'Baz, did you write those lyrics yourself?'

'Who else could do it except Yours Truly, Rani? This evening, you'll see Rukhsana dance to it in your honour,' he said, preening.

My throat felt choked with a mix of relief and embarrassment. What nonsense had I been imagining these last few weeks! O my stupid, stupid heart!

I even forgot that I had resolved to ask him to call Faiyaaz Ali again and listen carefully to what he had to say. But I needn't have worried, a couple of days later, Faiyaaz came on his own, beaming brightly.

'What's new, Faiyaaz Ali?' Baz asked amiably.

'Now there's nothing to worry about, Sultan. Bairam Khan has been removed by Akbar. Bahadur Khan enjoys imperial favour no more. He has been recalled and has returned to Agra.'

Vision 67

I was reassured and my spirits soared, our love wasn't so shallow as to wear off easily. Once again, we fell into our usual pattern of giving and receiving pleasures befitting our age. For hours I would sit playing ragas on my beenn, as Baz sat listening, all ears, his eyes closed or gazing at me, enchanted.

Indeed, he organized the promised dance of Rukhsana in the music room, to mark the fifth anniversary of my great escape. Rukhsana was dark-complexioned but truly beautiful, and her dancing skills were indeed astonishing. She danced like a fairy, with Ustad Rai Chand's gorgeous singing voice paying homage to my beauty in the lyrics penned by Baz.

Sitting beside Baz on the elevated dais, I smiled with my eyes lowered, a trifle embarrassed by his tribute—'But where would they find / Eyes like hers, eyes like hers'. He was busy keeping time, vigorously patting his thighs, 'Taa taa thai tat.'

Two days later, as he returned from Hindola Palace after holding court, I pretended to be sulking. Nayla had already told me that he had not even looked towards Jahaz Mahal that day. But he was in a fine mood. Wooing me, he said, 'It's important to attend to matters of State, too, but look at the beautiful new stanza I added to the verse, even as I was listening to those awful tales the spymasters gather.' Without waiting for me to reply, he broke out singing:

Taa taa thai tat
Kanha, following you
I do lots of leela too
But beside Radha's beauty grand
Where did your gopis stand?
Taa…taa…thai…tat
Where did your gopis stand?
That my danseuses too
Need to undertand!
O foolish Baz
Do not, I say—
Do not even try
It's quite beyond your capacity
To describe the beauty of Ruupmati

The intensity of his love made me feel almost drunk with vanity!

Later that evening, I thought I must reciprocate his beautiful lines eulogizing me. In the small hours, I rose quietly and wrote:

My heart's full of cheer
My body is bubbling with joy
The night's happenings
As the sun rose
Already feel like a dream;
When my beau wakes up
Is he going to again—
Describe my beauty to me?
And make the dream real?
O my bosom-sakhis,
I feel so ashamed, I will surely die!
And still, my heart's full of cheer
My body is bubbling with joy

Baz was delighted when I showed it to him the next morning. Taking me in a tight embrace, he said, 'No Rukhsana tonight, nor the danseuses, nor even Ustad Rai Chand. Only Zubeida will play the rabab, and you, my love, will sing this for me. Bravo, Rani, I didn't know you'd entered my soul!'

But as I said, happy days have powerful wings and as winter came, they flew away to warmer climes, like geese flying south. Towards the end of 1560, Faiyaaz Ali became a frequent visitor to the palace, nearly always sombre-looking.

'Sire, let me be hanged for incompetence, but it is God's own truth, none of the agents sent north from Mandav or Saarangpur have returned in weeks. All I could manage to gather from a Mughal trader, coming down south from Agra, is that the Mughals have posted sentries and archers on every high tower and tall tree in that whole area. Not even a bird can fly southward without their say-so!'

'Didn't the fellow say anything else?' asked Baz.

'He did, sire, but only very general sorts of things already known to us—that Bairam Khan has lost out to Maham Angaa and the emperor has ordered him to go on Hajj. My agent in Gujarat has confirmed that he is already in Gujarat en route to Mecca. Meanwhile, Akbar has appointed Munim Khan as his principal vizier in Bairam's place, but in reality, Maham Angaa and her son Adham Khan Koka are the ones who rule the roost at the Mughal court.' Faiyaaz Ali fell silent, but did not leave.

'You can go ahead if you want to add anything, Faiyaaz.' Baz was in no hurry today.

'Yes, Sultan, but only if you'll pardon my insolence and spare my life…' Faiyaaz began timidly.

'Don't be afraid, never mind our conversation the other day,' Baz soothed his nerves.

'Amir, a few weeks earlier two of our informers, returning from a visit to Agra, told me that Prince Mustafa has grown quite close to Adham Khan Koka. If that's true, it could be bad news for us.'

Watching them from behind the zenana-jaali, I felt like shouting, 'Faiyaaz is absolutely right, only, he shouldn't be saying "could be". It is bad news for sure.'

But alas! It was too late for me to come clean about Tara. I did keep thinking, though, if there was anything I could do to help, but could not come up with anything.

The new year, 1561 AD, only brought bad news, one after the other.

Vision 68

The first to go was Syed Abdullah Khan Meerzah, the elderly grand vizier of the sultanate—the same who had fought for Sher Shah, alongside Shujat Khan in their younger days, and in whose lap Baz had played as a toddler. First, his hands began to tremble badly, then one day, he fell unconscious from his horse, never to get back to his feet again. When Baz returned from his funeral, he bawled like an infant in the privacy of his room. Nayla was wrong: the coterie of scoundrels might have excluded Khan Meerzah from the mehfils of nautch and wine, but they hadn't been able to take him out of Baz's affection. My beau's heart was perfectly in place, still.

A state mourning of forty days was ordered, but the world never stopped for any mortal ever—why would it stop now for Syed Abdullah Khan Meerzah!

Baz appointed his mother's brother, Adam Khan, to succeed him as the grand vizier. There was an elaborate event the night prior to the anointment ceremony—a banquet with wine flowing and courtesans performing in their best finery. The next morning Adam Khan was to be bestowed the vizier's seal and khilʿat, the ceremonial robes of honour, by the sultan in a public ceremony in the Baar-e-Aam. According to the age-old tradition, the sultan himself was to dress in ceremonial robes and grant khilʿat in open court, wearing the ancient crown of the rulers of Malwa. No one could quite recall when the crown, set with priceless diamonds and rubies, was last brought out of the secret vaults under the Shaahi Mahal.

I was watching the ceremony at court, sitting beside Badi Begum behind the zenana-jaali, Nayla standing behind us as usual. Baz, clad in a dark green kamkhaab achkan, a green turban, and cream pyjamas looked so dazzling, I couldn't possibly describe it in words. Badi Begum made hand gestures endlessly to drive away the evil eye… She was clearly overjoyed—her son was the sultan already, and her brother was now going to be anointed the principal vizier of the realm!

The bejewelled crown was to be placed on Baz's head, removing his turban, only for the duration of the ceremony. From a door to the right of Baar-e-Aam—the great hall of general audience—emerged a group of five jaannisaars, smartly dressed for a change in bottle green instead of the usual black, two in front and two in the rear, each holding his naked sword upright. The one in the middle carried a gold platter with the crown covered in green muslin. Even from under the cover, it glowed.

According to custom the senior imam of Jami Masjid—Imam Nuuruddin Khan in this instance—was designated to place the crown on the sultan's head. He stood waiting a few paces from the throne for the five jaannisaars, moving in slow motion towards him. Much as Baz detested the idea of having anything to do with Imam Nuuruddin, there was little to be done about ceremonial norms.

The great hall of audience reverberated with hundreds of duhul-taasha, jhaanjh, seeng and surnai playing in unison and the hubbub of people jam-packed in the hall. Anyone and everyone were welcome to enter and watch such ceremonies, provided they came unarmed.

The jaannisaars were only a few paces from the Imam when, all of a sudden, the foot of the soldier carrying the platter caught a corner of the thick carpet. He stumbled, and before anyone knew anything about it, he lay sprawled on the floor resting on his elbows. The platter had flown off his hands, and so had the precious crown. They both lay on the floor, a few paces away, the platter upside down and the crown sans cover, ever more radiant. With a collective gasp of a thousand onlookers, the hush of a lifetime had descended on the hall, even the musicians had suddenly gone silent. Widened eyes shifted from the Sultan to his grounded crown and back again, in muted horror.

That fraction of a moment seemed like a long time. But then the beneficiary of the day's ceremony came alive. Adam Khan, who had been waiting near the Sultan's throne, rushed like a crack of lightning to where the crown lay, picked it up and handed it over to the Imam.

The bad omen notwithstanding, the ceremony was hurriedly gone through, but the verve had evaporated. Imam Nuuruddin went through the motions, the hint of a sarcastic smile playing on his lips. Baz was red in the face. Barely able to control his fury, the moment the ceremony was over, he rose to his feet and left. The rest of the celebrations planned for the day were, of course, cancelled.

Hardly had the Sultan gone a few paces when the pin-drop silence was shattered by a buzz that sounded like a storm at sea, and yet Imam Nuuruddin was heard righteously boasting to his fellow clerics, 'It's a terrible ill-omen. You can bet there is a mighty calamity in the offing. What would you expect with a damned kafir-lover on the throne?'

That evening Baz did summon the Imam to the palace. He was seated exactly where Aadhar Singh had sat two years ago, there was the same loud heralding of the Sultan's arrival, but when he entered, the Imam did not bother to rise to his feet.

'Imam Nuuruddin! Rise to your feet!' boomed Nayla's voice from behind the curtain, so sharply that the Imam sprang to his feet with a start, looking chastened, and greeted Baz with a bow. After he had made himself comfortable on his gilded throne, Baz said, 'Have a seat, Imam Nuuruddin.' Then, he continued to stare down at the Imam for a long moment before resuming, 'I heard what you said as I was leaving the court.' He fell silent again as though giving the other man a chance to explain himself.

'What did I say that might be object—' Nuuruddin began diffidently, obviously feeling a bit hot under his collar by now. Baz held up his hand stopping him midway, 'What you said smacked of treason to me! That's why I called you here.'

'But Sultan, the Sharia is sacred—' He was cut short again.

'Enough! I don't need a lesson in Sharia from you. I am an heir to the sultans of Malwa who learnt to respect all religions equally, a long time ago. Just go and have a good bath so that you do not emit that nasty smell ever again and do not forget that you, too, happen to be one of my subjects. If your treasonous utterances cause any disturbance to the peace of the realm, you'll be dealt with like any other commoner indulging in sedition.'

'Then you have me beheaded!' the Imam burst out indignantly.

'No, fortunately, I am not yours to command whether, or when, to take such a step. May Allah keep you safe and alive, and let you see what befalls you when I am no longer around. You may leave now,' said Baz, dismissing the Imam from his presence.

O my God! I thought to myself, why did he say 'when I am no longer around'?

Is he also unnerved by that ill-omen?

For several days that followed, we avoided one another's eyes—Nayla, mine; I, Baz's; and Suleman, Nayla's—as though one of us was responsible for the mishap. Then the passing of days papered over our apprehensions.

But hardly had a couple of weeks passed when another bizarre incident made our hair stand on end all over again. In the small hours one night, someone went past the palace precincts singing aloud a lament:

> The dainty fair was laid low
> And none lifted her from the dust!

Baz woke up with a start and heard the mournful lyric distinctly. He shouted for Suleman, almost in a panic, 'Suleman, Suleman! Nayla! Wherever are you? Someone go and find out who this fellow is, singing this mournful dirge at this time of night!'

They all rushed out to search, but whether it was a gipsy, or an itinerant minstrel, or simply a beggar, no one was found. No one knew where the singer had vanished in the dark of the night.

And then the drought came, right in the middle of spring, followed by a deluge!

The last monsoon had scarcely brought any rains, and by Falgun, the sun was blazing down like the month of Jeth. The emerald grasslands wore a jaundiced look, ponds and pools shrank to their bottoms and the market yards were deserted. Then, suddenly one day, the sky was covered with black clouds, heavy with rain. The downpour that followed was so violent that the meagre crop of wheat and barley, harvested and waiting to be threshed, rotted right in front of the tearful eyes of poor peasants.

Baz looked disoriented. He would go to the Hindola listlessly, for a quick jharokhaa-darshan, or to dispose of a clutch of cases awaiting his decision. The common folk still loved him for his fair, handsome looks, his rich baritone, and generous ways. Indeed, his Hindu subjects looked up to him as a lookalike of Krishna, playing the flute beautifully as he did, and surrounded by his gopi-like danseuses, as he often was.

Unfortunately, though, he had begun to lose his grip on affairs of state, the coterie of scoundrels becoming all-powerful. Nayla said that those wretched friends of his partied through the nights at Gadaa Shah's mansion on the periphery of the old palace. Baz himself was no longer very keen on those soirees. God alone knew what evil eye had caused my beloved sultan to be so aloof and distracted, allowing evil, mean-minded warlords a free run even as he, the master of all that the eyes beheld, immersed himself more and more into his passion for musical innovations.

Brooding over it in my lonely hours, I often thought that perhaps it was entirely my fault.

People might be right, I was his nemesis and the one who had sapped his manliness. It was proved wrong, but the evidence came much later.

Vision 69

For the time being, wallowing in dark despair, I sat composing a kavita on the sad state of affairs in Mandav and the wicked men strutting around in the corridors of power:

> Oh, dear sajni, such evil has come to pass,
> My heart is heavy with pain and fear.
> The vicious eat and drink all day
> And spend their nights in debauchery.
> Honour is buried under the earth
> And each day springs forth some new wickedness.
> The Goddess sits unhonoured in her shrine,
> And has abandoned her followers.

Having finished the poem, I was shocked at what I had written in the last two lines: *O Ruup, whatever came over you to say that! Quick, strike out those lines.* But what had been already written wasn't to be undone so easily. I was about to try, though, when I found Nayla standing before me—her dark face darkened even more by an expression ever so sad!

'Rani, someone's here from your Garh. Pandijju isn't well at all,' she said.

'What? I'll have to go there, this very moment,' I said alarmed.

'But the Sultan is busy at court.'

I sent him a missive. He replied: I have to be here for some more time. If it is urgent, you can go with Nayla. Just tell her that she should take at least a hundred of my jaannisaars to escort you.

As the Garh came into sight, a thousand bittersweet memories came clawing at me. But what really hit me hard on arrival was unexpected; Pandijju was gone.

Ketki and my five guru-bhais wept inconsolably as they saw us. The fifth, who had come to fetch me, and I joined them. Ketki lamented loudly as she was wont to do, 'Hai-hai, I had absolutely no idea. For nine days he sat at his day-long Navraatra pooja, and on the tenth day, he just slumped over and was gone in a moment! Hai! The last of my brothers is gone. I have no one left!'

Pandijju had actually died two days ago. He had had the work started a fortnight before that, my guru-bhais silently carrying out his instructions. On the first day of spring Navraatra in the month of Chaitra, he had sat for his ten-day-long pooja, not inside the Devi's temple as before, but at the mouth of the staircase descending into the shrine. A few days before that, he had sworn them to secrecy and asked them to begin collecting the necessary materials—sand, lime and stone blocks from the ruins and the like. The work had begun on the first day of Navraatra. On the Dashmi, the Devi will take leave of us, he had told them as they began. They worked through the nine days of Navraatra amid Pandijju's day-long chanting of shlokas, and on the tenth day, the last stone block was put in place on the door. Within half an hour of the stairwell being sealed forever, Pandijju, still chanting from Durga Saptashati, slumped to a side and the last of the Devi's priests also departed with her. It was as though there had never been a temple there, neither a priest.

'Why wasn't I informed in time?' I almost hurled the question at Ketki through sobs, both of us were still weeping. She said nothing. One of the five guru-bhais told me the rest, 'What could we possibly do? He had sworn each one of us in the name of Devi to keep it quiet. He even said that if he were to die, no last rites except cremation would be necessary and that we were to inform you only after his ashes had been consigned to Reva Maiyaa. How could we defy our guru? Besides, he looked perfectly hale and we didn't really believe he was going to die anytime soon, but apparently, he knew better.'

Ah! I felt hurt to the core of my being, to have been excluded from my beloved guru's affections in his last days. Pandijju, why didn't you allow me a last darshan, neither your own nor of the Devi's? What offence did I cause? Did you punish me for having married a mlechchha? But no, you did come for the pooja when we invited you to the inauguration of my new palace, you even gave me the blessings of akhand saubhaagya and happiness!

Riding away from the Garh, I turned to look at it one last time. Though turning fast into abandoned ruins, it was the closest to a peehar I'd ever had. Now, even the remaining strands of that connection were about to snap. I couldn't help feeling like an outcaste. Pandijju had had the entrance to the Devi's temple sealed, and he didn't inform me. He told everyone that he was performing his own last rites, but did not send word to me. My heart felt shrivelled with suppressed tears and consternation. I was unable to understand the logic of it all, and too confused to analyse. It was Nayla who had to bear the brunt of my dejection, though I have to admit that she took it well.

For the moment, however, I felt too annoyed to keep my

cool and asked in a tone dripping with sarcasm, 'Nayla bi, you of all people, so well informed of whatever is happening everywhere down to the very depths of the netherworld, why did you not tell me that Pandijju was already dead? Why did you not let on that he had started to get the temple entrance sealed a fortnight ago?'

'What temple are you referring to, Rani?' My sarcasm turned into a rage at her pretence.

'So, you don't know anything about it, do you? So be it. Well, now that we are passing so close by the Ardhapadma Taal, shall we go and have one last look at it?' I asked, trying to restrain my rising indignation.

'No, no, Rani, let's not delay our return. It's not a good time. Let's head straight for Mandav, and persuade Baz to camp at Saarangpur for a while.'

She hadn't even finished when my sarcasm turned into rage and exploded like a volcano, 'So, you've been spying on me! Who are you to stop me from going where I like, or to join hands with me in persuading Baz, for that matter? Who do you imagine you really are, hunh?' My outburst was so vitriolic, it had brought me straight down from 'tum' to 'tu', the honorific suffixed to her name going for a toss altogether. Within the moment, though, I realized that I'd let myself go a bit too far, and looked back to see if anyone might have heard me.

Nayla rode quietly for a while, her head bowed, our horses trotting side by side.

Then she began to talk in a low voice, as though she wasn't speaking to me but simply thinking aloud, 'Rani, should you spare my life, can I say something to you today? Perhaps you have never paid much attention to what I once was for Baz and still am, in fact. His father was very kind to me. I never could understand why, unlike anyone else I knew, he had a preference for dark complexions. When I was about your age, he would mostly be in my apartment. Baz was all of ten at the time, a pretty doll of a boy! I loved him so, and never quite stopped. My own doll, black as coal with stiff black curls. Alas! The malikaas didn't let him be. No sooner had he stepped into the world than the midwife was commanded to put a big mouthful of salt into him. No one could stomach the black spot that he would have been on the Khan's fair-complexioned brood, perhaps even he himself would have been embarrassed. But even then, I could not help my feelings for Baz, after all, he was the blood of Bade Khan sahib, my loving patron. I always thought of Baz as being more precious than life. I still do, and could never allow a single hair on him harmed if it cost my own life.' Nayla raised her head and looked at me ruefully, her eyes brimming with tears. 'Rani, please excuse me, I got carried away, spilling out all this nonsense, from a long-forgotten past without quite knowing why! Let's go through the Ardhapadma Taal, by all means.'

'No, Nayla bi, you're absolutely right. There's no time to waste, we ought to go back straight to Mandav, and join forces to persuade Baz.'

My deep embarrassment had taken me right back from 'tu' to 'aap', the honorific being duly reinstated.

I never saw the Ardhapadma Taal ever again.

Vision 70

I could not go there, but I dreamt of the Ardhapadma that night. Ah! What a heart-rending sight it was: the thick growth of lotuses blighted, the emerald waters down to the last dregs, the exposed mud caked and cracked and one of the pillars of the Hoshang Shah pavilion had collapsed. Can one smell inside a dream? There was no fragrance left in Champa-aranya. When I woke up, I felt my cheeks damp. I had never known anyone weeping real tears in a dream.

Baz, once again, spent that entire night somewhere else. When he returned a couple of hours after daybreak, his eyes were red as though he had been awake most of the night.

'I was with Maamu jaan. It became so late by the time we finished with the akhbaaraat, I decided to spend the night there. The Mughals are apparently eyeing Malwa greedily. So, did you go to Dharmapuri, then? What makes you look so sad?'

I started to weep, hiccupping.

'Baz, my Pandijju is no more.'

'Oh!' he rushed to me and took me in his arms.

'I'm very sad to hear that but don't cry. If people who have to go don't, how will others who are yet to come, come? Your Bhagwan and my Allah both need good souls to return to them. Don't lament.' He kept consoling me, patting my back, and I kept weeping silently for a time. When my tears dried up, I said, 'I don't feel well here in Mandav, take me somewhere else.'

'Where should we go? You tell me.'

'They say the weather is pleasant in Saarangpur.'

'Saarangpur! Well, we'll have to go there fully prepared,' he seemed to be considering.

'So what if we have to? You said it yourself the other day, state affairs are important. If it's rumoured that the Mughals might come through there, all the more reason to be right there, fully prepared.'

'Rani is right, sire,' Nayla, clearing her throat, joined in. 'It's necessary to review the fortification at Saarangpur. I am sure the Sultan is aware.' Then she fell silent.

'Aware of what, Nayla bi?' asked Baz.

'Why, how Saarangpur acquired the name it's known by?'

'No, you tell us if you happen to know.'

'For centuries past, enemy armies intending to invade Malwa, whether from Pataliputra, Delhi, Turkistan, Uzbekistan—wherever they came from—the first warning was sounded from there, "Saavdhaan Rangpur, Beware the City of Merrymakers", and in time it came to be known as Saarangpur,' Nayla said.

Baz guffawed.

'Nayla bi is truly imaginative, isn't she, Rani? All right then, since both of you say so, we'll go there. I will begin reviewing military preparations soon. It will take a bit of time, but we'll go to Saarangpur.

He did not quite know that we'd nearly run out of time!

Vision 71

We did not have to try too hard to persuade Baz to go to Saarangpur. I don't know what exactly was going through his mind at the time. What I do know, however, is that he was neither cowardly nor a fool. By piecing together the titbits of intelligence Faiyaaz Ali and his agents had been able to gather, perhaps he knew already that Saarangpur was, as Nayla had put it, beginning to send warning signals of a gathering storm to Mandavgarh, the city of merrymakers.

That evening, I showed Baz my poem on Mandav having fallen on bad times. He gave me a long, pensive look and said, 'Ruup, how do you get to know of so many things without actually having seen them with your eyes? But I'm rather curious about the last two lines. They, er...kind of went over my head.'

I pondered over it long. How do I explain those two lines to him—that, for some inexplicable reason, they had been written even before I knew that the entrance to Devi's secret shrine at the Garh was sealed, that there was such a temple but it had ceased to exist? My late guru's voice rang in my head, 'No need to brood over it, but you have to be careful in the future.' Not that I did not trust Baz, but the story was far too complicated to begin narrating now.

'Like you sometimes say after writing extraordinary lines: '*Ye toh ilhaam huaa hai!*—it's a gift from the heavens above. Think of these as something akin to that,' I wriggled out.

'Fair enough but please do sing the poem for me this evening, and this time around, let's dispense with Zubeida even. Tonight it will be just the two of us, I shall accompany you on the tambura.'

I sang the kavita right through the evening, with Baz strumming the tambura strings in deep bass—once, twice, three times. As I came to those last two lines the third time—'The Goddess sits unhonoured in her shrine / And has abandoned her followers'—Baz jerked his head down as though to keep time with his vigorous strumming, but the curls falling over his face could not hide the teardrops that slipped out of his eyes.

In the last half hour, Nayla had come twice, peeping in through the door. The third time, she came right in. 'Sultan, Faiyaaz is here. He says we have to leave for Saarangpur without any further delay, in full force, too,' she said, her face drawn.

Baz said nothing but simply got up and followed her out of the room, leaden-footed.

It still took two days to get the troops and supply train ready for departure. There was a big crowd of people in the main square in front of the Jami Masjid. Most of them had come to bid farewell to their loved ones, but many were just bystanders, ogling idly. There were many despairing faces among them, knowing it was a big battle in the offing and not a few watched us with a cold look of disdain in their eyes. Instigated by the Imam, several malicious stanzas had been added to Baz's lyric in praise of my beauty. On arrival at Saarangpur a couple of days later, Zubeida came and told me, with tears in her eyes, that she had heard some people in the crowd mumbling them:

Black magic did the wicked Rani perform
And sapped dry
Our beloved sultan's manly form;
She summoned clouds
And made them pour at a finger's turn
Daggers she looked at sautan hers
And made her burn
Our poor, innocent Baz eventually was
Consumed by the witch's curse—

O foolish heart… O my foolish heart
We'd nothing to do with it, though
He married and brought upon himself
His mortal foe!
For sure, for sure
Poor Baz was devoured
By that wicked whore.

While leaving Mandav, I had refused to travel in a palanquin. I was on my favourite reddish-brown mare (yes, she'd turned out a female!), and Baz beside me, on his white thoroughbred. Nayla had gone through the ritual of covering my face with a triangular piece of fine silk, but people could easily make out what I looked like. The Mandav sky reverberated with the usual cacophony of mixed musical instruments and the loyal citizenry chanting victory to us. That day it could not have been orchestrated by the fawning sultanate brass to please their sultan. They had all been busy preparing to depart for what they knew would likely be a make-or-break showdown with a mighty enemy.

After we arrived at Saarangpur, Nayla also came looking for me.

'Don't be disheartened by what Zubeida seems to have heard some rogues mouthing off in the crowd. They were obviously the stooges of Imam Nuuruddin. But did you notice? Most of the subjects stood with their hands folded as though you two weren't just a pair of royals, but a couple like Radha-Krishna? I myself heard some of them singing fervently:

Baz like Krishna
Like Radha-rani, Ruupmati
Only the luckiest can find
Such fairy-like beauty, mind,
Folks, where again would you have
For all you crave
The chance again to see
So handsome a jodi
Neither is there another like Baz

Nor anyone quite like the Rani
O foolish heart mine
Dither not, nor pause
Because, where would you
Have the chance again
To behold such a jodi
Have a darshan—see!
Have a darshan… Have a darshan

I had no idea whether Nayla was speaking the truth, or if she had made it up to humour me, but I laughed. I felt like hugging her for trying to make me feel better.

'Baz is right, Nayla bi, you are truly imaginative beyond words,' I said.

'Now, now, did you say imaginative beyond words, Rani? Why, I hardly ever speak!'

She was quite right, I could hardly find fault with that.

Vision 72

Thirty thousand foot soldiers, fifteen thousand cavalrymen, a thousand elephants with their mahouts, five hundred ace archers, their attendants, minders and camp followers besides scores of warlords with their own retinue and bodyguards; Nayla and I, and our household; a large part of the Jahaz Mahal retinue and seraglio including the six danseuses, Rukhsana and their maids, all put together, a total of nearly eighty thousand of us had suddenly descended on Saarangpur. The fort could hardly accommodate so many of us. The generals, the warriors and the army camped outside the fort while the Sultan, his personal guards and the women were put up in the apartments within. Baz spent most of his time out in the camp, though, conferring with Adam Khan, the grand vizier, and his generals.

Two days after we arrived, Faiyaaz came with the intelligence that the Mughals were coming at a much greater speed, and with a much larger army than estimated. The dust that they caused to rise could be seen from several kos away. The Mughals were actually very close now. Faiyaaz reckoned they might be within striking distance in three to four days at the latest, and would then try to force a showdown.

Adham Khan Koka's stock at the Mughal court did seem to be very high. Akbar had not only given the command of an enormous army to one so young, he had also deployed so many decorated warriors of repute to assist his Koka that Faiyaaz was quite out of breath by the time he finished listing out their names: Mullah Peer Mohammad Khan, as the second-in-command, Abdullah Khan, Qiya Khan Kang, Shah Mohammad Khan Kandhari, Adil Khan, Sadiq Khan, Habib Quli Khan, Haidar Ali Khan, Mohammad Quli Toqbai, Meerak Bahadur, Payanda Mohammad Khan, Mohammad Khan Kushtigir, Meeran Arghun, Mehr Ali Silduz, Shah Fani, one more Qiya Khan—it was a daunting list indeed. My heart quivered and quaked. Was this just another military campaign or Akbar's Ashwamedh!

That night Baz regurgitated his refrain of despair, 'Rani, should something bad happen to me, promise me you'll go away somewhere far!'

'All right, I will, but you don't go anywhere. Just sit tight inside the fort, let them attack it, okay?' I said.

He jerked his head up to look at me, bewildered.

'Is that all you think of my abilities?'

'So, what are you saying, that you want to take on an army three times the size of your own in open battle. Is that what you are saying? Wouldn't that be plain suicide?'

'No, Rani, quite to the contrary, if I were to sit twiddling my thumb inside this puny fort, we all of us would soon die of thirst and starvation, and above all, of the frustrating exhaustion of doing nothing. And then, my generals and the army are all camped outside the fort. You aren't by any chance suggesting that I should keep watching Rukhsana dance, leaving them to fend for themselves, are you? No, Rani, I can't do that. I'll have to go and fight it out, win or lose.'

'Nayla bi,' I said, turning to look behind me. 'Why don't you make him see reason? We won't last long in a straight, head-on battle. Shouldn't we just go away some place else?' I myself didn't have any idea at all what my suggestion was. I was simply scared and confused.

'Rani, you don't get it, the more we run, the more we'll be chased. If I go out and make an honest fight of it, who knows I might even return the victor. Haven't you heard, a much smaller army of this very Akbar went on to win the day the moment Hemu was down with an arrow through his eye.' Baz had steel in his eyes like his armoured vest. I realized what I had been suggesting, and rather awkwardly at that. It was neither feasible nor right.

'No, Baz, I take back what I said. I don't know what came over me, perhaps it was a passing moment of weakness. Go and fight hard, without worrying for me. Nayla bi is here to look after me. May the Almighty protect you, but if something did happen to you, I would take your advice and go away somewhere far.'

Vision 73

Faiyaaz Ali's information proved accurate. Three days later the huge Mughal army set up camp three kos short of Saarangpur and began to probe how best it could breach the lines of our defensive bulwark. For the first seven days, contingents from the opposing armies kept making forays to look for weak links, like wrestlers trying to grab each other's wrist at the beginning of a bout. Though our warriors did their best, it was clear from the way Baz flopped down on the settee with a sigh, and his appearance when he returned after the day's dogfights, that things were not going very well for him; the Mughals held the upper hand.

On the eighth day, Malwa lines were severely tested as

three Mughal commanders attacked simultaneously, inflicting massive casualties and opening up a wide breach in our defences. The moment they had the whiff of a chance, two messengers galloped back at top speed to inform Adham Khan Koka. He seized the opportunity with both hands and ordered an all-out attack.

The booming of cannons in the decisive battle that followed, lasted only half a day, and could be heard as far as our apartment inside the fort. By mid-afternoon, they all fell silent.

Nayla and I, with our hearts in our mouths, were eyeing each other furtively when we heard footfalls in the corridor leading to our apartment. Then we heard them shouting, 'Nayla bi… Nayla bi…'

Suleman and Faiyaaz entered, breathing heavily, their faces dark with gunpowder-dust and dejection, streaked with lines of sweat, and perhaps tears as well. On seeing me, they bowed their heads, more to avoid meeting my eyes than in salute. Then, as though coming out of a trance, Suleman started babbling. 'It is…it's terrible news. Our Sultan has fallen,' he stammered and began to wail. Then, trying to get a hold on himself, he added hoarsely, 'Come quickly, there's no time to waste, they'll be here any moment now! We have horses ready.'

I felt as though molten lead had been poured into my ears. I lowered my face onto my palms with a keening wail and began to sob uncontrollably. A mighty spasm had seized my shoulders. I thought I was going to faint and fall to the ground. Nayla took control, issuing quick commands, 'Both of you will come with us, dressed in women's clothing.' Then, noticing Faiyaaz's hefty frame, 'You put on the guise of a eunuch, Faiyaaz!' Both hurried away inside to change.

Alas! It was too late by then.

Before we could sneak out, Mughal soldiers, dressed in all-black uniforms, had surrounded the apartment. The one in the lead started barking out orders, 'No one will move. You're all under the protection of Khan-e-Aazam Adham Khan Koka. No harm will come to you. Safdar and Ahmed, both of you will be here outside the apartment. Make sure no one comes in or goes out, is that clear?' Then he turned towards me and bowed, quickly touching his fist to his chest, and left the room.

I looked at his back in dismay, speechless, wondering what I'd done to deserve his courtly greeting. I turned to look back, intending to seek clarification, but Nayla was nowhere to be seen. A remark Baz had made long ago flashed through my mind—*Nayla will die before she betrays either of us*. My eyes filled with tears all over again. I sat down heavily on the edge of the bed, too forlorn to even cry.

Vision 74

No, Nayla had not deserted me. I kept turning my head to look back, hoping she would return. When she eventually did, it took me a few moments to realize it was she: a gaunt stooping figure covered from head to toe in a black burqa, with only two tiny meshed holes for eyes in it, and a string of prayer beads in her fingers. She bent and whispered in my ear, 'I'm Nayla Begum, your lady-in-waiting and Faarsi teacher. You can't do without me for even a moment.'

She explained to me later that her curious disguise had been imperative as she saw it.

'Who can tell what mischief might take the fancy of men, at the sight of so strange a phenomenon like me? They could have separated us,' she said, and then went on to pose the options which left me outraged, but as she said later, she did not want to take anything for granted under the circumstances.

Who could know it better than Nayla that in our time the victor instantly became the master of everything that had belonged to the vanquished? Not only his kingdom and lands and all else he owned, but also his wives, concubines and maids of the seraglio. The norm was that no one was overly embarrassed about it. Even the women in question, after a brief spell of lamenting, resigned themselves to their fate. The exceptions being those who committed jauhar, as Padmini of Chittor had done, or were slain by their own master, before departing for a battle from which they didn't expect to return alive. Who could be better aware of all this than Nayla, who had herself changed hands from Qadir Shah to Shujat Khan?

'Now there are two options, either you surrender to Adham Khan Koka, or we start looking for opportunities to take flight and go where destiny will take us. What would you wish to do, Rani?' she asked, looking squarely at me.

I felt a massive wave of indignation wash over me. I retorted, 'Nayla bi, first I was fool enough to take as many as six years to understand you, and now you seem bent upon insulting me. On the one hand, you went so far as to put Baz and me on a pedestal, comparing us to Radha-Krishna, and on the other, you are suggesting the indignity of surrendering to Adham Khan! Perhaps you forget that though Baz loved me, it was I who chose to go with him, defying the death sentence given to me by my father.' I had lapsed into a fresh bout of sobbing.

'Rani, keep your voice low. I knew you were going to say so, but it was necessary to ask you once. Now do as I say,' said Nayla.

Just then, Zubeida came in carrying a scroll-container. 'The Mughal guard brought this for you, Rani,' she said, handing it to me.

It was a missive from Adham Khan Koka.[7]

Vision 75

I was fortunate enough never to see Adham Khan in person. Even his letter reeked of evil arrogance scarcely masked by sentimentality, which too was mere lechery. I could barely stand the stench. The sinful worm wrote:

To Rani Ruupmati,

I have slain Baz. Now you are mine, and mine alone.

I have heard so much about your beauty and skills that I feel like coming straightaway and taking you in my arms. I'm dying to see you. But I understand that you must be in mourning today. I have heard it said that you truly were in love with Baz Bahadur, and used to lure him to your bed by playing on the beenn and singing taranas. It is my heart's wish that forgetting the past, you should now welcome and love me in the same way as you did him. That is the reason I am being considerate.

There are many who have been telling me, 'You are the victor. His harem is rightfully yours for the taking. If you are impatient, just go ahead and have your way with the Rani.' I can come right away if I wish, but I do not want to possess you by force. I want you to reciprocate my love with all your heart.

Eagerly awaiting your response,

Seal: Adham Khan Koka

Reading the letter, I seethed with suppressed rage, my face a dark crimson. Nayla glanced through its contents and said calmly, 'I will dictate the reply, you write it down.' I loathed the idea of responding, but there was no getting away from writing back to him.

To,

The Victor of my brave husband,

Brave warrior Adham Khan Koka.

Rani Ruupmati offers her pranaam to you.

You have rightly surmised that I am in mourning for my late husband and that I loved him passionately. It will take a long time to turn that kind of love in any other direction. Not just today, according to our custom, a mourning period of a minimum of three nights is compulsory. Allow me to inform Your Highness that my late husband did not convert me to his Faith, and allowed me to remain a rani. Hence, I still follow Hindu customs and rituals.

Then, you ask me to forget the past and reciprocate your overture. Nayla bibi has also advised me along the same lines. She says, 'Whoever the victor, he is the master and if the new master is not forcing himself upon you, but wants to have you lovingly, it is most gracious of him. Do not spurn his love!' Nayla Begum says that she is my servant, but she teaches me Faarsi, and hence, I think of her as a respected teacher and cannot do without her. I hope and pray that your people will not separate us from each other.

And yes, there is another thing. Remaining so close to the battlefield where my late husband was slain is bound to keep reminding me of him. That would make it really difficult for me to put my past behind. Should you deem it fit, allow us to accompany you to Mandavgarh. I am told that Mullah Peer Mohammad Khan is to govern Mandav but you are, after all, the chief commander of Mughal forces on this campaign. Surely, he will not disregard your advice.

While I try to turn my affections towards you, if you'd be so kind as to order me and my ladies-in-waiting to be taken to my Raniwaas in Jahaz Mahal, I'd be ever so grateful to you.

I pray for the well-being of both you and your emperor.

Seal: Rani Ruupmati

My nightmare without end had commenced, for there was little to compare between the two Ranis: the one who had risen that morning from the embrace of Baz Bahadur, the sultan of all Malwa, and the hapless widow conducting cloak-and-dagger correspondence with a crude warlord who had slain her beloved husband that very afternoon. As I sealed the letter, I was thinking, *Let us see where Nayla's carefully-worded missive takes us, and what happens.*

Vision 76

The arrow had found its mark. Two days later Nayla and I, accompanied by Zubeida and the other loyal maids, and Suleman and Faiyaaz, disguised as palace eunuchs, were back in my old Raniwaas in Jahaz Mahal. In the palanquin, all the way to Mandav, I kept breaking out in violent bouts of sobbing. Nayla kept drying my tears, holding my face close to her bosom. But as we entered Mandav, I was shocked into silence, devastated by the surreal sights that met our eyes; my tears dried up from the sheer horror of it.

The sides of roads and entrances to havelis were littered with beheaded male bodies, but there was not a single severed head anywhere. Going a little further, we discovered where they had all gone. Soon after crossing the Bhangi Darwaaza, the first Kallaa Minaar came into sight: a carefully stacked triangular heap of severed heads, eyes closed or gazing out grotesquely. Then another one, in the big square between the Jami and Asharfi Mahal, and yet another near Hoshang Shah's mausoleum, and another and yet another. The one near the Jami had Imam Nuuruddin's head at the top!

It seemed as though in the no-holds-barred brutal massacre that Mullah Peer Mohammad Khan had ordered, on taking over Mandav, all its menfolk had been put to the sword, and all the women herded like sheep, into the mansions around Jahaz Mahal and Jal Mahal, for they reverberated with a dreadful mix of women singing, shrieking, crying and laughing, all at once.

As I lay down on my mahogany lotus bed, I fell into a fitful sleep, mauled by a nightmare inside a nightmare. Every Kallaa Minaar in it had Baz Bahadur's head on top!

The memory of something that Pandijju had once said came floating into my mind across the years, 'Ruup, if you looked closely, you would see that a human life is made up of a series of dreams and nightmares, some pleasant and others dreadful. Some that we see with our eyes open and others that come to us while we sleep. But the ones that we see with our eyes shut also merge eventually into what we think we really saw in life.'

At the time, I hadn't quite grasped what he meant, but now I thought, it's exactly as he had put it. Baz's head on top of every Kallaa Minaar was a nightmare with my eyes closed, but all that had happened when my eyes were open, an unbelievably heart-warming reality for a time, also eventually ended up a nightmare!

Nayla was shaking me by the shoulder and whispering urgently, 'Rani, Rani, wake up! Oh, do wake up please and have something to eat, you need to be strong. Ah! A million thanks to Allah!'

'What happened? What's the good news that makes you thank Allah so profusely?' I asked, in a voice gone nasal from all that weeping followed by the nap.

'Suleman was confused by his ploy. He had no idea. Baz is alive, Rani, my doll is not dead!' Nayla's eyes twinkled with tears of joy. She kept looking over her shoulder, taking care no one was overhearing us. I couldn't quite believe my ears. Surely, this was only a more devious part of the nightmare, come to deceive me with false hope.

'What…are you sure?' I asked.

'Absolutely!' said Nayla with growing excitement. 'Baz had put a jaannisaar of roughly the same build as his, and in similar clothes, behind him on his elephant. When he noticed that the Mughals were getting the better of his troops, he quickly changed places with him, and got down into the thick of the battle on a horse. He fought hard alongside Maamu jaan Adam Khan, but was unfortunately incapacitated by a deep cut on his arm. By then, a score of his jaannisaars had recognized him. They took him in a cordon and led him to safety, somewhere in the direction of Khandesh but he is alive, Rani, and we must also find a way to get away!'

'Are you telling me the truth, or just consoling me, Nayla

bi? Who told you all this?' I was still sceptical, touching her hand to see if I was awake. I was.

'Faiyaaz Ali. It's true, the soldier Baz had put in his place was eventually felled by an arrow through his heart. There was no trace of Baz among the dead. The Mughals know all this, too, but are keeping it a secret for obvious reasons. Now get up, you have to take courage!' said Nayla.

Another pleasant scene added to my series of dreams. I could have jumped for joy. My beloved Baz was still alive. Nayla bi knows all the tricks, she will manage to have us reunited. But how will we ever get out of the apartment, guarded night and day, by these hawk-eyed Mughal sentries?

Vision 77

Truly, Nayla had all the tricks up her sleeve. More heady scenes kept getting added to my joyous dream in quick succession.

The next day, Nayla disappeared for a while, and returned with a plate of food. She fed me with her own hands, coaxing me gently as though I were a child, 'If you don't eat and be strong, how will you ever get to Baz? All right, now lie down and groan loud enough to be heard in the other room, as though you were in pain. I'll be right back!'

She went calling out, 'Zubeida, Zubeida! Rani is indisposed, Zubeida. She is in a lot of pain! She's like that for two-three days every month but this time around it's a bit more. Do you understand what I'm saying?' 'Yes, yes, Nayla bibi,' said Zubeida.

'If anyone comes asking for her, just say that she can't receive anyone for at least two days. Will you be able to handle it?'

'Yes, Nayla bi, you go and look after her, I'll take care of anyone that comes calling,' Zubeida said.

Two hours before sunrise, Suleman and Faiyaaz flitted

through my room stealthily, and disappeared through the door leading to the room with my mother's icons. Then, Nayla came with two baskets full of flowers. 'Where did you get these from? Did you empty all the flower vases or what?' I asked. 'No, no. Faiyaaz arranged to get these from the maalins, the flower-women, who bring flowers for the palace. Now, get up and change into these.' Nayla offered clothes that looked exactly the same as the ones worn by the maalins. She had a similar set for herself and both of us changed into them.

'Remember to draw your pallu right down to the chin, Rani, or even those who have never seen you will know at a mere glance it's you—beauty such as this! Can't be anyone but Ruupmati, they'll say,' Nayla said, smiling encouragingly.

'Wherever did you dig out these clothes from?' I asked, looking amazed. 'Why, the maalins themselves suggested it as a plausible guise!' she said. 'I didn't have to even ask them. The moment your name came up, the head maalin volunteered to help. She virtually worships you. She says Ruupmati isn't just any ordinary rani, she's the Radharani of our Sultan Kanha.' Baz's memory flashed through my mind once again, my eyes watered yet again. And it didn't escape Nayla's eye, 'All right then, we're all set. We'll make our getaway exactly an hour after daybreak. That's the time when the maalins return, having delivered flowers. Now, you lie down and rest for a while.'

I did as told, thinking I was in good hands.

I nodded off into the sweetest of real dreams: I'm in Baz's arms, craning my neck to see which of his arms had been slashed—left or right?

I woke up to Nayla shaking my shoulders again, to bring me back into the 'true' sweet dream of hope. 'It's time to go, get up!' she said.

For the very first time, I noticed that the table on which my mother's idols are kept had wooden wheels, and could be easily moved. There was a large marble piece underneath which was actually a wooden plank, painted to look like marble. Nayla lifted it without much effort. There was a steep circular stairwell descending down to a dark tunnel, that took us straight to the opening at the other end, concealed in the middle of a bed of flowering kenna. We got out into the morning sun, and right across the pathway was a group of maalins, waiting to take us in their midst, exactly at the appointed hour. Savitri, the head maalin, looked at me, smiling tearfully, as though she were about to cross the Vaitarani by helping Radha to escape humiliation. We passed through the palace gates pretending to be innocent maalins leaving the palace, unchallenged by guards!

Across the gate, there was a knoll hidden in a clump of trees. Faiyaaz was waiting for us with four horses behind the foliage. Nayla was impatient to go. 'Where is Suleman? Get him to come quickly, we might be spotted!'

'Suleman said he had a touch of diarrhoea, he just went behind the bushes to relieve himself. Should be here any moment now!' Faiyaaz said, looking a tad nervous himself. The moment passed and Nayla, growing fidgety, said, 'We can't wait endlessly. Leave a horse tethered here for him and let's go now.'

We got onto our mounts and were galloping away, towards Garh Dharmapuri.

Vision 78

The sweetest of my dreams also proved equally fragile.

Even until the time we entered the Garh, I was thinking that my five guru-bhais would protect us, until they found a way to put us safely on the road to Khandesh across the river. I would soon be reunited with Baz, the love of my life. Instead, no less than a thunderbolt awaited us in that accursed courtyard.

Nayla knew how to manage nearly everything to perfection, but clearly, she had no idea how to get inside Adham Khan Koka's devious mind!

Somewhere along the way, Suleman had been bought over.

When or for how much gold, or whether with merely a promise of his life being spared, we would never know.

The forecourt that had appeared so enormous to me in my childhood looked small and bare. Exactly at the spot where Rabat's deputy had beheaded Bhanwar, the dismembered remains of my five guru-bhais were strewn around. They had died fighting. A large posse of Mughal cavalrymen, sitting ramrod straight in their saddles awaited us, fifteen or twenty, perhaps even more. I couldn't care less how many! I had eyes only for Suleman in their midst, but he studiously avoided looking towards us.

Faiyaaz, on his horse beside ours, shook violently in sheer terror. That was the last of the poor man's body movements, as it turned out. An arrow whistling through the air at close range pierced clean through his torso. He slumped forward on his horse's mane, the arrow tip pointing skyward.

The commander of the Mughal contingent eased his mount towards us, and said, bowing with elaborate courtesy, 'Rani, we're under strict orders to not touch either of you. Please don't make us do any such thing. All we need to do is to gently bring you back to your Raniwaas in Jahaz Mahal.'

Two women, dressed up as maalins astride fine thoroughbreds, a burly cavalry commander bowing and scraping to them, I felt I was witnessing the scene perched someplace high outside of my body! It seemed like a tableau right out of a farce.

As dusk fell, Nayla and I had been escorted back to the Raniwaas. But my bittersweet nightmare, indeed more bitter than sweet, was far from over yet.

That evening I wrote in my notebook:

I take a dream to my sleep
And am dreaming as I wake—
A dream behind and a dream in front
He is outside as well as inside
My beloved is a dream, and dream my beloved
Wherever I lay my eyes

Life's a dream, and the dream my life
O my foolish heart, O foolish heart
Even as I look at the mirror now
I remember Baz

VISION 79

This time around, his missive awaited us on return, delivered in anticipation of our certain capture.

Nayla and I had forced our tears back in front of the Mughal soldiers, but as we fell into each other's arms in the privacy of the Raniwaas, we let ourselves go and wept our hearts out, so much that eventually there were no more tears to shed.

I opened the letter:

To Rani Ruupmati,

Where did you think you'd flee, leaving me so forlorn? I found you!

You cannot get away from me now. Even if you escaped to the netherworld, I would still come and get you. I haven't seen you yet, but if you are even a fraction as beautiful as the sketch that artist made, by Allah, this life is nothing, I would forsake even my devotion to Him for your sake!

Maashaallah! My compliments to Mustafa's memory of a fleeting glance of your lovely visage! He would go on describing it while the painter went on drawing and, by Allah, what a gorgeous picture he came up with! Surely, you must be even lovelier in real life.

I am, however, fast becoming the butt of jokes among my friends, fellows who risk their lives with me on the battlefield. Last night one of them, a little drunk, went too far. He said smirking, 'Khan-e-Aazam, will you go mad over a mere lass? Why not just jump and ride her!' Of course, I slapped him silent, but how long can I silence wagging tongues? After all, I'm Badshah Akbar's milk brother, no less! I shan't tolerate jibes of being impotent. Let me make it clear: I'm not willing to be fobbed off by your sweet talk any longer.

Tomorrow night there's going to be a big musical event to celebrate our conquest of Malwa. I hear Rukhsana dances like a fairy, and Rai Chand is a phenomenal singing talent. Why shouldn't it be so? After all, Baz's sole claim to fame was his being a connoisseur of song and dance!

Immediately after that concert, I shall come to your Raniwaas. Please prepare to accord me suitable welcome: do not even think of disappointing me, I won't take no for an answer. And yes, make sure that Faarsi teacher of yours is there. I have to deal with her as well. She is the root of all the trouble, isn't she?

Anyway, you must be weary after the ordeal she put you through, my dearest! God willing, you'll be refreshed tomorrow after a good night's rest.

Seal: Adham Khan Koka

I collapsed onto my bed, weeping inconsolably at my helplessness for a while. Then picking up my feathered quill, I began to write a reply. This time I decided to do it on my own.

To the Brave Warrior Adham Khan Koka,

You did right to slap that insolent companion of yours. The company of such foul-mouthed louts does not behove a mighty general like you.

But he was right in a way. I am no common country lass who will fall to lusty advances no sooner than pulled. I'm a proud rani, the widow of a sultan who bore the nickname of Baz. If someone extends a hand to grab me, I surely will struggle and try to fly away for sure.

You, sire, are a mighty warrior. You can easily get a thousand women, better looking by far than I, who will happily submit to your will. I plead with you, let me go with my honour intact. If you aren't afraid of my pagan gods, at least fear the wrath of your Allah. I'm afraid my misfortune might cast a long shadow on your life if you forced yourself upon me.

> If you are determined to have your way nonetheless, then please be prepared to allow me a lot more time. It is possible that I might turn towards you in time, but for now I'm in mourning for my five guru-bhais, who were murdered in cold blood by your ruthless men.
>
> I exhort you again with folded hands to let us go. I assure you Nayla Begum is absolutely innocent. Indeed, she was trying to persuade me on your behalf as I have already told you. It was I who forced her hands, pleading and weeping endlessly to let me out.
>
> Once again, I pray for your well-being as well as that of your mighty emperor.
>
> Seal: Rani Ruupmati

Not even an hour had passed when his reply arrived.

> Rani,
>
> You have no idea how impatient I am to take you in my arms. I pass my nights tossing and turning in bed. I'm dying to see your incomparable beauty. Believe me, you will also be consoled by my vigour and prowess. I am not going to be daunted by your threatening curses, or fooled by your platitudes of wishing me well. I cannot wait any more. Tomorrow night we will celebrate our union and no more correspondence about it now.
>
> However, if you wish to declare your love for me, or to invite me into your bed tomorrow night, you are welcome to write back. It would give me immense pleasure.
>
> Desiring you with all my heart,
>
> Seal: Adham Khan Koka
>
> Post Script: Those five men were bent on separating us. They got what they deserved. Let your foes mourn them! They were not even your blood brothers. Why should you bother to mourn for them?

I knew then, that it was the end of the road.

Nayla stood behind me, gazing sightlessly at some point in the far distance.

'Rani, don't you worry, I'll find a way. We'll escape again. The point is that Baz is alive.'

'No, Nayla bi, there is no way out now. Don't you see, that kenna bed is crawling with sentries. And even if you could find another way, I'm no longer interested in going to Baz.'

Nayla gave me a quick look of surprise.

'But why is that so?'

'He had said, "Should something happen to me, go away somewhere far." '

'But Rani, nothing has happened to him, he is alive!' Nayla exclaimed.

'That is precisely it. He is alive, and I won't let him die. My guru had given me the blessing of akhand saubhaagya. I'll not allow it to go waste.'

Nayla was stunned.

'Oh no, no Rani, do not even think along those lines! Baz cannot do without you!'

I held my hand up to stop her.

'Though I don't claim to know him as well as you do, Nayla bi, yet I too have come to know Baz a bit, in these six years. He is a tough one. He will learn to live without me but if I were to go to him now, Adham Khan will not let him live. He'll chase him down relentlessly until he's slain him. Baz had said "Should something bad happen to me." Haven't bad things happened to him already? He has been dispossessed of his kingdom, he's been slashed on the arm, he has been forced to run for his life. Isn't any of that bad enough? I just want to go away very, very far out of Adham's reach. Would you make the arrangements to send me there?' I ended up almost pleading with her. She just looked sombrely at me, without blinking.

I took off the large diamond from my turban lying on the settee, and handed it to her.

'You have to crush this into small bits, and mix it in a thick broth of opium. I'd guess opium would be easily available here, maybe in Jahaz Mahal itself. Will you be able to do it on the quiet?'

She took the diamond without a word, weeping silent tears. I went on, 'Crushing a diamond won't be easy. It's bound to make an enormous racket, but between me playing my beenn and the noise of the big music concert downstairs, I think we should manage it without being discovered.'

Vision 80

The next evening, the whole of Jahaz Mahal emptied into the big hall downstairs, inexorably drawn by the grand show organized to celebrate Mughal victory. Only Nayla, Zubeida and I were left in the apartment.

When we heard loud music playing and a number of feet, with anklets of large tinkle bells strapped to them, dancing, we knew the evening was well underway with Baz's danseuses performing the *Madhurashtakam*, which had become famous all over Malwa by now. It went on and on with the applause and clapping getting louder and still louder. And then, a performer with a single pair of anklets accompanied by musicians came on. That must have been Rukhsana dancing. Rai Chand, the star performer would come at the very end.

All this while, I kept playing my beenn as vigorously and loudly as I could, my eyes closed in concentration. The noise of the diamond being crushed was drowned between the deep bass of my beenn and the loud music from downstairs. Tung…tung…tung went the beenn and dhumm…dhumm…dhumm…the pestle in Nayla's hand, alongside the uproar of appreciation in the celebration down below.

There was no dearth of opium in the capital of Malwa. Nayla had been able to get a handful on the sly from someone within the palace. By the grace of Radha-Krishna, the pooja chest yielded a big lump of camphor to help make the broth even more potent. I was getting Nayla to make me a poison cup, far more lethal than the one that my father had told Ketki to make, in order to get rid of myself, so that my husband could live on.

After two hours of grinding, mixing and stirring, Nayla

was finally ready with the potion to send me away, somewhere very far! When I heard the rich solo vocal of Ustad Rai Chand, I called out to Nayla. By then, like me, she had also resigned herself to the inevitable. There was no weeping, no lamenting between us any more, just the last exchange of greetings and blessings.

'It's time, Nayla bi,' I said. 'Would you please bring me the red suit of clothes I wore on my first night in this Raniwaas?' She brought it without demuring. I changed into it and took one last look at myself in the mirror. To my own eyes, I looked the same as I had on that first night six years ago. It seemed like an eon ago. I asked Nayla what I looked like.

'You look even more beautiful now, Rani,' she said.

Then, taking up the feathered quill once again, I wrote my last missive addressed to that monster:

> Adham Khan,
>
> I told you—I'm the widow of Baz, the Falcon. Neither you nor your mighty army has the wherewithal to stop me from taking flight. Beware! My curse will certainly come down upon you, and indeed, prove to be your undoing. Just you wait and see!
>
> Death is a million times better than surrendering to your sinful lust.
>
> Seal: Rani Ruupmati

As I extended my hand to lift the cup, Nayla took it out of my reach, 'I will taste it first,' she said without looking at me.

'Why would you do that? It's poison for sure,' I exclaimed, amazed.

'I have to check whether it's potent enough.' She gave me no chance to say anything more. Before I could protest, she had gulped a good half of the cup's contents, and set it down on the table beside me. Then she sat down on the floor reclining on the foot side of the four-poster. Hardly had a quarter of an hour passed when her head slumped to a side, her eyes closed. She was gone.

I picked up the cup and gulped down the rest of the potion. Then I lay down on my lotus bed, mumbling drowsily, 'Here I go, Baz, somewhere far. How could I possibly break my oath, and surrender this body of mine, anointed with your love, to another man?'

My stomach had begun to hurt with a terrible stinging sensation, as though scores of sharp needlepoints were at once piercing my entrails. Thankfully, even more than the pain, I felt sleepy. A gust of wind came in through the window and scattered my curls on my face. A couplet I remembered having once read in one of Pandijju's books, flashed through my mind, about to shut down:

Gori soway sej par, munh par daare kes
Chal Khusro ghar aapne, rayn bha'i chahudes[8]

By the time Adham Khan Koka staggered into my room, swaying on his feet from the excess of wine inside him, I had been gone from the material world for over an hour. I lay dead with the red kamkhaab jodaa on. At first glance, he thought I had dressed up to receive him, and had dozed off while waiting for him. He kept shaking my corpse by the shoulder, saying, 'Ruupmati! Ruupmati, look I'm here. Oh, come on! Wake up now!'

Exasperated, he touched my forehead, and recoiled, it was cold as ice by then!

Adham Khan's face contorted into a mask of pure hatred, disfigured by fury and disbelief. Right then, he noticed my last missive to him, fluttering in my fingers. He snatched it up, glancing through it quickly, then he balled it in his fist and threw it down on the floor with an angry snort.

It was after a good while that his gaze, slowed down by alcohol, turned towards Nayla lying on the floor. The realization that she had escaped through his fingers, too, really put him in a towering rage.

'The wretched witch!' he shouted and spat on the floor, with a flurry of the foulest expletives. He turned and noticed Zubeida, trying to stifle her sobs with her dupatta. In sheer frustration, Adham pounced on her, and grabbing her by the wrist, left the room dragging her behind him.

Epilogue: The Last Vision

Madam, I am a mere scribe. I will happily write whatever you say, but I'm afraid I was unable to understand that last bit. Your readers are bound to ask how you could see Adham Khan come to your room and all those things he did, when you were dead already!

I knew you would ask this, and was about to tell you about it myself.

Having taken the poison cup and put an end to our earthly existence, Nayla and I roamed as spirits for years, protecting Baz, wherever he went.

We saw it all, how my curse hit that lout, Adham Khan. The beginning of his end had commenced shortly after the Malwa campaign. Badshah Akbar, informed of Adham stealing the most precious of plundered jewels and the prettiest women, came rushing himself, all the way down to Mandav, to investigate. Had Maham Angaa not followed him close on his heels and counselled her son, he might have been done for right then. But throwing caution to winds, Adham continued to dig his own grave with one nefarious intrigue after the other, and within a year of my suicide, we saw him being sentenced to death by Emperor Akbar, and thrown down from the upper storey of the royal apartment in the Agra Fort. The bull-necked scoundrel did not die the first time he was hurled down, and had to be thrown down a second time for his neck to be broken.

Baz wrested his capital back from Mullah Peer Mohammad Khan, who was driven out of Mandav, and so hotly pursued, that the butcher of Mandavgarh was drowned in the swirling waters of Reva Maiyaa.

We saw Baz lament us both, sitting for hours on the lotus bed in my Raniwaas, 'O Rani, I never meant for you to go away quite *so* far!'

It is another matter that he could not hold on to Mandav for long in the face of the determined counter-attack, launched by the incomparably superior imperial forces.

We, too, wandered along with him through his years of exile as he ran from pillar to post seeking refuge in Khandesh, Gujarat, Gondwana, before eventually ending up in Mewar.

Didn't I tell you? Baz was more of a musician than he was a ruler, and it was this facet of his persona that finally prevailed. His sultanate was gone, but his music hadn't deserted him. If anything, the pain of losing everything seemed to have sharpened his talent. The fame of his singing voice travelled so far and wide, that Akbar sent a special envoy all the way to Mewar to invite and escort Baz to Agra, and honoured him with a respectable mansab at his court.

I can hardly describe how filled with pride I was when Baz chose raga Bhoop Kalyan for his debut at court. I knew he was remembering me and hurting even as he sang. Such was the soulful pathos of his voice that it brought tears to the eyes of many in the audience. No sooner had he finished than the emperor leaned to his principal musician, Miyaan Tansen. 'What did you think of his singing, Miyaan?' he asked.

'Splendid. A singer par excellence without a doubt. No one can match him!' replied Tansen.

Abul Fazl, the court historian and a personal friend of the emperor, who was privy to the brief exchange, promptly summed it up in his notebook, 'Baz Bahadur of Malwa: A singer without rival'.

Baz turned out tough, as I had told Nayla. He missed me sorely, but he lived on for nearly twenty years after I was gone, and when he knew his time had come, he petitioned the emperor to have him buried by the side of my cenotaph. Akbar had grown so fond of him, he duly kept the promise he had made.

God bless Rukhsana, she served my Baz as a faithful companion through those years until the very end. She was already in Agra as part of the seraglio of Malwa. It was lucky that though she had made a mark as a skilful dancer, none of the powerful nobles at court showed any special interest in her, perhaps because of her complexion and her difficulty with the court language, leaving her free to live with Baz.

Anyhow, I have told you already and I'll repeat it for you, please do not brand my Baz a coward. If he had wanted, he could easily have fled to Khandesh, or even farther down south, at the approach of the huge Mughal army that he must have known would get the better of him. But he did nothing of the sort. Earlier on, if he had wanted, he could have asked me to convert and saved himself all the trouble he had to go through at the hands of the mullahs, but he never so much as mentioned it. He could have denied the superiority of Rani Durgawati and got his bards to eulogize him even after that terrible defeat, but he preferred to make a clean breast of things.

And please do not think, far less write, of me as a pitiable, poor young woman who did not live to be even twenty-one, and was compelled to commit suicide in dire circumstances. Look at the blessings of my brief existence: I died with my husband still alive, something that all women prayed for every morning, at least in my time. Baz never turned away from me, looking for an heir with another woman. And above all, I didn't fall prey to the lust of that evil man called Adham Khan Koka. And lest I forget, I was also spared the misfortune of having to serve as a songstress at court, like my mother, even though it would have been the imperial court in my case!

And if you ask me, it didn't matter that I had to wander for twenty years, as what you would call a ghost in common parlance. I was invisible, but I could still see my beloved while he inhabited the earth.

And what is your status now, madam? Did you dictate this whole autobiography as a ghost? I asked, totally bewildered.

She smiled brightly. A halo of light spread around her.

No, my dear scribe, we were promoted long ago. Ishwar, Allah, Devi Maa and Radha-Krishna...all of them together turned us into fairies and angels. We, all of us, live with them in the blue heavens far, far above. There is absolute peace and tranquillity there. Unlike their individual following down here on earth, led by the pandits and the mullahs, there is no disagreement or dispute at all among them. Everything they do is done unanimously, as though they were all the same, rolled into one. They hand-pick truly good souls, whatever their faith or denomination in their earthly lives, and elevate them as fairies and angels. Pandijju, Baz, Nayla bi, Bhanwar, Tara, I—we are all there together. That is where Pandijju told me one day, there is someone from my old village determined to write your story, 'Ruup. Would you be good enough to lend him a helping hand?' I couldn't possibly refuse my former guru.

But that is it. Now, I must take leave of you, my dear scribe. Keep well, won't you?

She never returned after that appearance.

Author's Note and Acknowledgements

The texts that formed the main source material for this book have been listed in the bibliography. Several, though not all, of Rani Ruupmati's poems that are part of the narrative follow closely the English versions of her compositions in L.M. Crump's translation of Ahmad ul-Umari's *The Lady of the Lotus, Rup Mati, Queen of Mandu: A Strange Tale of Faithfulness.*

I would like to place on record my debt of gratitude to a number of people who have been particularly helpful in the course of this work.

To my wife, Rekha, my elder brother Professor M.M. Thakur, and my friend Dr Ganga Prasad Vimal for being a constant source of encouragement and support.

To my sister, Sita Jha, my sister-in-law Poornima Thakur, my nephew Vinayanand Jha, and my daughter Jaya for going through the original Hindi text in a remarkably short time, and inspiring this English version.

To my nephew, Sankarshan, his gracious wife, Sona, and Rajeev Mishra of the IIC library for helping me to get hold of relevant books.

To Dr S.N. Mishra and Shankar K. Jha for valuable information on Vatsyayana's quote and musical traditions in medieval times.

To my friend, Lalit K. Joshi, Shriman Shukla, the district collector of Dhar, Ms Bhavya, SDM Dhar, and Chhotu Gower of Mandu for special courtesies during my visit to Dhar and

Mandu in August 2017, and to Abdul Quddus, my driver and companion for his assistance on that memorable road trip.

To Ankit Rakesh of the Department of History, Loughborough University for reading the manuscript and giving valuable suggestions.

And to Rukma Dev Sharma for his immense help in preparing the manuscript.

My very special thanks and blessings are due to Puja Ahuja and Anil Ahuja for designing the wonderful cover and helping with the logistics of publication.

On this occasion, how can I forget the affection and encouragement I receive from the others in my family: Dr Devanand Jha, Bhuvan, Soni, Seema, Sri Nand, Jahan, Devyani, Aayushman, Shrivatsa, Siddharth, Sanjana, Kabir, Pawan, Jayant and Banmala Jha.

Endnotes

1. The contribution of Baz Bahadur and Rani Ruupmati to the development of Hindi poetry: Prof. U.N. Day writes that Hindi poetry gained considerable popularity and influence in Baz Bahadur's time because both he and Rani Ruupmati composed poems in the Malwi variant of Hindi, and also patronized such literary activity. Ruupmati left behind a lasting legacy of her verse, which continues to be sung by the bards and minstrels of Malwa. A host of other verse-writers also copied her style and kept it alive. It is recorded in the *Akbarnama* that the emperor 'used to pour out his heart in Hindi poems descriptive of his love', and he often made a reference to Rani Ruupmati in them (U.N. Day, *Medieval Malwa*).

2. The love for music of Baz Bahadur and Rani Ruupmati: Prof. U.N. Day notes that the long tradition of maintaining large numbers of courtesans, specially trained in music, at the court reached its pinnacle during the reign of Baz Bahadur, who was himself a truly gifted music maestro, genuinely dedicated to musical innovations. In the *Akbarnama*, he is recorded as '[…] a singer without rival'. Ahmad ul-Umari also writes that Baz Bahadur was known to gather musicians and singers from the north and south and the east and west, and spend a considerable amount of his time interacting with them. The musicians he collected and nurtured at his court included a wide variety, including both men and women—vocalists and mantra-paathis as well as those who specialized in instruments such as the tambura, saarangi, beenn, surnai, rabab and nai. In this context, Rani Ruupmati deserves to be specially mentioned. According to Ahmad ul-Umari, she was a poetess of renown and also a music maestro in her own right, and 'won great benefit from the master of the art of music'. L.M. Crump says that 'Rupmati is still remembered as a poetess and musician, and is credited with the invention of the Bhup Kalyan Ragini, a subordinate mode of Hindu music'. According to legend, Baz Bahadur first composed the dhruvpad on which the Baz-Khani Khayal is based; Baz-Khani Khayal was popular in the Malwa region until recent times (U.N. Day, *Medieval Malwa*).

3. The transfer of idols of Hindu deities to safe havens: A good example of this is the idol of Krishna at Nathdwara (Udaipur, Rajasthan), which was first moved secretly from Govardhan to Agra in 1572 and kept in safe custody there for about six months, and later removed to Nathdwara—considered to be a safe haven for the deity. According to popular legend, the well-known idol of the Chaturbhuj Sri Rama temple in modern-day Mandu was also kept hidden underground by devotees for long years before the Holkars occupied the region and rehabilitated the idol in a temple located near the Jami Masjid of Mandu.

4. The doha Ruupmati remembers having once read: 'I find no peace without you / I remember you every moment, night and day.'

5. The tradition of religious tolerance in medieval Malwa: Prof. U.N. Day, the noted historian specializing in the history of medieval Malwa, writes in his book *Medieval Malwa*: 'In his devotion to cultural pursuits Baz Bahadur removed all religious bias, and the process of cultural assimilation which had started with the foundation of the independent kingdom of Malwa [around 1400 AD, approximately a hundred and fifty years before Baz Bahadur's time] reached its culmination under Baz Bahadur.' Day goes on to quote W.G. Archer, who says that in Baz Bahadur's persona 'We meet, in fact, a character in whom the twin cultures of Malwa are entangled and whose great romance, his passion for Rupmati, is itself a blending of Muslim and Hindu.'

6. Sri Vallabhacharya's *Madhurashtakam*: Referred to in 'Vision 51', this Sanskrit composition is a famous work of the saint-poet Sri Vallabhacharya (1479-1531). It comprises eight shlokas that describe the person of Krishna as Madhuraadhipati, the Lord of all that is Sweet. The shlokas go as follows: 'Everything about Krishna the Madhuraadhipati, the lord of sweetness, is sweet: his lips, his mouth, his eyes, his heart and his gait are all sweet; his speech is sweet, so is his conduct, and so, too, his attire; and his embrace, and the way he walks and strolls around—everything about the Madhuraadhipati is sweet. His flute is sweet, and so are his lotus-hands, and the dust of his feet, and his dancing, and his friendly ways—everything about the Madhuraadhipati is sweet. His songs, his drinking, his eating and the tilak on his forehead are sweet as well—everything about the Madhuraadhipati is honeyed. Madhuraadhipati's deeds, his rescuing those in distress, his leisurely wanderings, his redemption of those laid low, and the peace he bestows are all sweet; his gunjaa beads, his garland, his river, the Yamuna, and its waters and rippling waves, and the lotuses that grow in it are all so sweet—everything to do with Madhuraadhipati is sweet. His gopis, and his leela—his cavorting—with them; the union with him as well as separation from him; his gaze and his good manners, too, are all so sweet; indeed, everything about the Madhuraadhipati is sweet. His companions are sweet, and so are his cows and the stick he uses to herd them; his creation is sweet, and his crushing tribulations are as sweet as his blessing, the fruition of it all—everything about the Madhuraadhipati is sweet. O Madhuraadhipati! All that is yours, all your deeds and leelas are sweet!'

7. The exchange of correspondence between Rani Ruupmati and Adham Khan Koka: Writing on the basis of eyewitness accounts, a mere thirty-eight years after the death of Rani Ruupmati, Ahmad ul-Umari refers to an exchange of letters between the two. The possibility that they exchanged more than one letter, therefore, cannot be ruled out (L.M. Crump, *The Lady of the Lotus*).

8. A well-known couplet of Amir Khusro, the thirteenth-century nobleman of the Delhi sultanate. It says: 'The fair maiden lies on her bed, her hair covering her face / Khusro, let's head back home, the night falls over all four quarters!'

Bibliography

Banarasidas. *Ardhakathanak*. Translated from the Hindi by Rohini Chowdhury. Penguin, 2007.

Day, Upendra Nath. *Medieval Malwa: A Political and Cultural History, 1401-1562*. Munshi Ram Manohar Lal Oriental Publishers, 1965.

Dwivedi, Acharya Hazari Prasad. *Charu Chandralekh*. Rajkamal Prakashan, 1993.

Eraly, Abraham. *The Age of Wrath: A History of the Delhi Sultanate*. Penguin, 2014.

______. *The Mughal World: Life in India's Last Golden Age*. Penguin, 2007.

Fazl, Abul. *The Akbarnama*, Vol. II. Translated by H. Beveridge, FASB. Rare Books, 1972.

______. *The Ain i Akbari*, Vol. I. Translated by H. Blochmann, revised and edited by Col. D.C. Phillott. Asiatic Society, Calcutta, 1927.

Gupt 'Kumud', Ayodhya Prasad. *Madhya Pradesh ke Mele aur Teej-Tyauhar*. Department of Public Relations, Madhya Pradesh Government, 2005.

Keay, John. *India: A History*. HarperCollins, 2001.

Luard, C.E. *Dhar and Mandu*. Reprinted by erstwhile Dhar State, 1912.

Malcolm, Sir John. *A Memoir of Central India including Malwa and Adjoining Provinces*, Vol. II. Parbury & Aleen, 1824.

Mohammad, Malik, ed. *Amir Khusro: Bhaavaatmak Ektaa ke Maseeha*. Pitambar Publishing Company, 1987.

Patil, D.R. *Mandu*. Archaeological Survey of India, 2004.

Rutherford, Alex. *Empire of the Moghal: Ruler of the World*. Headline Review, 2011.

Umari, Ahmad ul. *The Lady of the Lotus, Rup Mati, Queen of Mandu: A Strange Tale of Faithfulness*. Translated from the Persian with editorial comments by L.M. Crump. Oxford University Press, 1926.

Weiss, Brian. *Many Lives, Many Masters*. Piatkus Books; repr., Manipal Technologies, 1994.

Yazdani, Ghulam. *Mandu: The City of Joy*. Reprinted by erstwhile Dhar State, 1929.

Zaman, Shazi. *Akbar*. Rajkamal Prakashan, 2016.